LOVE SONG

Also by Ethan Mordden

LOVE SONG

The Lives of Kurt Weill and Lotte Lenya

Ethan Mordden

St. Martin's Press

New York

B
WEILL

Frontispiece: For two generations, Mary Martin's singing of "That's Him" in *One Touch of Venus* on a chair set downstage overlooking the orchestra pit was one of Broadway's Official Memories. Having just come off writing musicals for Walter Huston and Gertrude Lawrence, Kurt Weill was in his heyday as Composer To the Stars.

All illustrations courtesy of the Billy Rose Theatre Collection; The New York Public Library for the Performing Arts, Astor, Lenox and Tilden Foundations; and private collections.

LOVE SONG. Copyright © 2012 by Ethan Mordden. All rights reserved. Printed in the United States of America. For information, address St. Martin's Press, 175 Fifth Avenue, New York, N.Y. 10010.

www.stmartins.com

Design by Phil Mazzone

Library of Congress Cataloging-in-Publication Data

Mordden, Ethan.
   Love song : the lives of Kurt Weill and Lotte Lenya / Ethan Mordden. — 1st ed.
      p. cm.
   Includes index.
   ISBN 978-0-312-67657-5 (hardcover)
   ISBN 978-1-250-01757-4 (e-book)
  1. Weill, Kurt, 1900–1950.   2. Lenya, Lotte.   3. Composers—Biography.
4. Singers—Biography.   I. Title.
   ML410.W395M67 2012
   782.1092'2—dc23

                                   2012028287

First Edition: October 2012

10   9   8   7   6   5   4   3   2   1

To Jon Cronwell

Contents

Acknowledgments

To my agent and actor friend Joe Spieler; Vicki Lame; Kevin Sweeney; Clint Bocock; my excellent Johnny-on-the-spot copyeditor John McGhee; my wise musical-theatre historian friend Ken Mandelbaum; and my wonderful Golden Age editor Michael Flamini.

LOVE SONG

Introduction

When she was little, Lotte Lenya asked her mother, as little girls will, if she was pretty.

"No," her mother replied. "But all your life, men will be crazy about you."

The tale changed a bit over the years, for Lenya was a keen story-teller, quick to adapt to her audience: a performer, but a warm and giving one, quickly intimate with anyone she liked, adding her sardonic commentary to every narration with her patented "You know?" tacked on at the end. She was short and slim with a one-in-a-million roguish smile and she could play everything from the merrily heartless Jenny of *The Threepenny Opera* to the helplessly coquettish Frau Schneider of *Cabaret*, versatile but formidable.

Even as a teenager, she was a gossip's delight, often seen being met by men, walking with men, dancing with men, laughing with men—and, her fellow actress Elisabeth Bergner recalled, "always different ones." You've seen actors whispering to other actors in Ernst Lubitsch's films; Lenya was what they whisper about. She had more sheer mystique than Mata Hari and Lola Montez put together—"an air about her," said Bergner, "of something taboo."

There are plenty of Lotte Lenya stories, and, in all of them, she seems to be having a grand time on the planet Earth. Unlike a lot of theatre people, she didn't let little things dismay her. On the verge of her fame in 1928, just before the first night of *The Threepenny Opera*, it was discovered that her name had inadvertently been left off the program. Many another actress would have gone into Implacable Tantrum Mode, but Lenya shrugged it off. "They'll know who I am tomorrow," she said.

Much later, in the 1970s, she was taking the Sayville ferry to Fire Island, and on the boat with her were Christopher and David Alden, identical twins who were themselves on the verge of fame, as opera directors. Just now they were kids fresh out of college, amused to be on board with the empress of Brechtian mischief. When the ferry docked, they approached Lenya and asked if they could help her with her bag. "Don't worry," she told them, a musical-comedy Mother Courage. "It's only a toothbrush."

She had a mischievous side, which is why she loved playing tough customers in her Hollywood films—the baleful procuress in *The Roman Spring of Mrs. Stone*, the masseuse in *Semi-Tough* who demolishes football player Burt Reynolds, and especially the lesbian double agent in *From Russia With Love* who tries to kill James Bond with a poison-dipped blade in her shoe. She's a persuasive villain, yet still a hoot. As Spectre's nameless operative Number Three, she visits a bad-guys' training camp to inspect recruit Robert Shaw. "Homicidal paranoiac," she is told, of Shaw. "Superb material."

Number Three will see for herself. Fresh from a loll in the sun, Shaw presents himself wearing only a towel around his middle. Silently circling him, Lenya slips on a row of brass knuckles, then smashes him in the stomach as hard as she can. The movie audience jumps ten feet in the air to a man, but there's no reaction from Shaw.

"He seems fit enough," says Lenya. "Have him report to me in Istanbul in twenty-four hours."

The blend of the character's deadpan evil with the actress' wicked humor is pure escapade. Spoofing the situation while remaining true to the story, she produces something rare in pop moviemaking, the kind of super-irony that only Europeans seem to understand.

So Lotte Lenya not only played Characters: she was one, a bank of anecdotes. But there are almost no Kurt Weill stories. Studious, quietly smiling at some private joke, wrapped up in music, he said little except when working. Here's a Kurt Weill story: in the fall of 1939, he and Moss Hart had lunch at an upscale New York restaurant called the Hapsburg, talking over theatrical plans and ending up somewhat later with the idea for *Lady in the Dark*. Ten months along, they learned that the show's elaborate dream sequences with their rapid set changes would force the show's capitalization into the upper reaches of Broadway budgets.

"All this," Hart muses, "from that little lunch at the Hapsburg."

And Weill, referencing a popular chain of pancake houses, replies, "We should have eaten at Child's."

Here's the other Kurt Weill story: his next Broadway show, *One Touch of Venus*, was originally to have starred Marlene Dietrich. However, after reading the script, Dietrich decided to pull out. Her excuse was that the idea for the piece, in which the Goddess of Love visits modern-day New York, had seemed witty and graceful but the script turned out earthy and coarse. Dietrich and Weill were speaking on the telephone, she in California and he in New York. Also present was *Venus'* producer, Cheryl Crawford, who must have been amused to hear two Germans conversing in English—this, no doubt, at Weill's insistence, for once he became comfortable in his adopted culture and language, he never spoke German again unless absolutely necessary.

Now, Weill's experience on Broadway taught him that it was much easier to sell a musical with a star at its center, so he was determined to keep Dietrich on board. She was just as determined to jump ship.

"It is too sexy and pwofane," she explained, in her famously rhotacistic English.

Weill argued, noting what a boost a Broadway hit could give to a movie star's career—especially Dietrich's, which had been undergoing an up-and-down phase.

"No, I cannot do it," Dietrich insisted. "It is too sexy and pwofane."

Weill pointed out that she *must* do it. She had agreed to do it. She had signed the contract.

Dietrich maintained that she was a mother with a daughter of tender age (actually eighteen-and-a-half at the time). It would not be fitting to appear in a piece filled with raucous burlesque jokes and erotic carnival doings. "It is too sexy and pwofane."

Weill almost never lost his temper, so he kept his cool as he persisted. It seems likely that in fact Dietrich had simply caught the disease common to theatre people who spend years exclusively in the movies: stage fright. Habilitated now to the safety net of retakes and microphones, Dietrich was insecure about live, viva voce performance. Still, Weill felt he could walk Dietrich back to the concept of Broadway stardom. After all, what professional femme fatale could turn down the role of Venus?

Dietrich could turn it down. "It is too sexy and pwofane," she said again, and Weill snapped. It was now absolutely necessary to speak German.

"*Du dummes Stück!*" he cried. You stupid thing!

Two stories: because Weill was too obsessed with work to figure in anecdote, even as the Lotte Lenya tales tumble over each other in profusion. So Dietrich's consenting and then refusing to play Venus inspires another Lenya story, told by Hal Prince. He of course knew Lenya through having produced and directed *Cabaret*, and one evening he and his wife dropped in to see Lenya in her dressing room before the show, which had moved from the Broadhurst Theatre to the Imperial. The Princes were dolled up, he in a tuxedo, and Lenya asked, "Where are you off to, kids?" Prince replied that they were first-nighting Marlene Dietrich's solo show at the Lunt-Fontanne, around the corner.

At the mention of Dietrich's name, Lenya flashed on how the movie star had toyed with *Venus*, betrayed her husband as he tried to build a new career in a new country—"conceited," Weill told Lenya, "like all those Germans." So far had he entered into his second life, as an American: Germans, to him, now, were someone else.

Lenya did not make nice to those who thwarted her husband's program. Without skipping a beat, looking into her mirror as she applied her makeup, she told Prince, "Say hello for me to Miss No Talent."

So Weill and Lenya were unalike personalities that formed a tight unit. They also came from very unalike backgrounds. Hers was working-class and poor. His was middle-class—and note that he was named Curt* Julian Weill, the middle name, at Frau Weill's behest, after the protagonist of Stendahl's novel *The Red and the Black*, Julien Sorel. This suggests a cultured family, not only because of the literary allusion but because the Germany that Weill grew up in regarded France as its mortal enemy. Only very well-read Germans ventured into the French canon—especially to this title, often denigrated because of Stendahl's carefully plain-spoken narrative, so offbeat amid the fanciful voices of early-nineteenth-century fiction. Further, Julien Sorel is an unlikely hero for a mother to invoke when naming her son, for Sorel is a manipulative social climber who rises from peasant to the fiancé of an important nobleman's daughter. He starts by seducing the wife of his first employer, Madame de Rênal, asking himself, as he creeps back to his room after their first assignation, "Did I play my part well?" Worse, he ends by attempting to murder Madame de Rênal—shooting her in church, no less!—and atones, as French law then demanded, on the scaffold.

On the other hand, Julien Sorel is magnetic and intelligent. Not yet twenty at the novel's start, he already knows the New Testament by heart in Latin. He is as well fiercely self-willing, a world-beater who refuses to accept his class destiny. And although Weill's mother could not have foreseen this, her son, too, proved powerful in his refusal to accept what we might call his *Zeitschicksal*, the destiny assigned to him by his historical epoch. The Nazis identified Weill as the most dangerous of the music world's "cultural Bolshevists" because of the

---

* For unknown reasons, Weill changed the spelling of his first name to "Kurt" while still a teenager.

leftward tilt of his work with Bertolt Brecht and the subversively "un-German" sounds he made in their jazzband cabaret. And Weill was Jewish to begin with. After the Nazi seizure of power, on January 30, 1933, Weill had to flee his native land like so many other artists. Few prospered elsewhere. Weill, however, sought to take charge of his future, pursuing his artistic ideals without compromise—on the contrary, he regarded his new home, the United States of America, as uniquely welcoming to his experimental art, a blend of the elite with the popular. And only in America—the very size of whose culture made room alongside the commonplace for the exceptional, the curio, the invention—could Weill have executed his program. Like Julien Sorel, Weill resisted social control, to map his idiosyncratic route through life.

Lotte Lenya, too, had a destiny, wrapped up in Weill's: as they loved and married, as she won professional notice in his work, as they fled a hate-filled Europe to become Americans together. The two were bound even more after his death, as she was heard by an ever-growing public as not only the voice but the *meaning* of Kurt Weill, of the unique way his music defined their lives. Strange to tell, at one point they separated, even divorced. But he knew she must return to him, because they were virtually living inside the art they made: as if it were his music that gave them their liberty.

It's almost a political romance, a parable about two extraordinary people running for their lives through Western Civilization. Long before story's end, they realize how much their mutual affection depends on the right to express themselves artistically, a characteristic of democracies that sets them apart from the rest of the world. Weill and Lenya's is an absolutely twentieth-century story, from the time when Western Civilization suffered its great civil war over exactly what *civilization* means. And tucked into this grand saga is the diaspora of émigré Europeans who enriched American arts culture, from opera to the movies.

America enriched Weill and Lenya in its turn, offering a more expansive platform in their milieu, the theatre, than any available in Europe. The very year in which the pair arrived in New York, 1935, saw the production of a tragic-romantic all-black opera on Broadway that remains one of the most influential works in the American theatrical calendar—a work, I emphasize, that had and could have had no European counterpart in even the loosest sense, because its mixture of elite and popular derives from America's mixture of ethnicities and races, of traditions and idiosyncrasies, of sure things and gambles.

It was as though Weill and Lenya had to come to America not because they were on an enemies list at home but because they could not achieve fulfillment in Europe. Their love and their individualism became as fused as their destinies. And their art—or, rather, their ability to create art in the way they wished to—became part of the democracies' war against the barbarians. It made them so strong that, along with statesmen like Winston Churchill, scientists like Albert Einstein, sociopolitical Jeremiahs like Alyeksandr Solzhenitsyn, and a few other artists such as Greta Garbo and Andy Warhol, Kurt Weill and Lotte Lenya stand among the defining people of their century.

1

Kurt And Linnerl

S he was born first, about a year and a half before him, in Vienna, on October 18, 1898. Karoline Wilhelmine Charlotte Blamauer was the daughter of a coachman, Franz Blamauer, and a laundress, the former Johanna Teuschl. If young Linnerl—a standard nickname for Karoline—was to captivate men, as her mother predicted, it may have been one of those traits acquired by imitation, for her mother was a pet of the local lads. "Frau Blamauer sees pants on a clothesline," the neighbors would carol, "and she's pregnant." But of her many gestations only five children were born alive, three girls and two boys.

The firstborn, Karoline, died at the age of four, and the future Lotte Lenya was named after her. There were as well her older brother, Franz; her younger brother, Max; and her younger sister, Maria. It was Linnerl who attracted their father's particular attention, for he had loved his dead Karoline and hated the one who replaced her. Young Linnerl lived in terror in the Blamauers' small apartment, in a five-storey block of masonry way out to the southwest of Vienna's "inner city," on the southern edge of the district of Penzing, where it borders Hietzing. The area was so distant from Vienna's core area around St. Stephen's Cathedral that from the window of the Blamauers' kitchen one could see Schönbrunn, the summer palace of Austria's royal house, the Hapsburgs.

It is an odd trick of the abusive parent to select one child in particular to destroy. The others are ignored or even favored, and Franz singled out the surviving Linnerl for intimidation with the constant and very real threat of violence. If he wanted a stein of beer from the corner tavern, it was always Linnerl who was sent to collect it and slapped if he suspected that she had spilled any of it. When he barged into the apartment after a night of carousing and demanded a song, it was Linnerl who was pulled out of bed—a wooden box with a removable cover for use as an ironing board or in preparing dough for noodles—and forced to sing for him.

It was a hard life for the family in general, for despite the impressive look of the apartment building, at 38 Ameisgasse, the Blamauers were poor. One of the souvenirs that Linnerl took with her on her global journey from Vienna to dwellings in Switzerland, Germany, France, and finally America is her photograph with neighborhood children and their mothers when she was three or four. Some forty-five souls pose, from infants in arms to a few grandmothers, the little girls in pinafores or Sunday dresses and the boys dolled up in jacket, high collar, and flowing tie. Scarcely anyone smiles; most look worried, Linnerl especially. Her mother seems to have been unwilling to protect her daughter (or herself) from her husband's rages, but Lotte never blamed her mother as an enabler. On the contrary, many years later, when, as Lotte Lenya, she received her mother and sister on a visit to the Weill place in Rockland County, north of Manhattan, Lenya seemed genuinely touched—and amused—by her mother's absolute lack of character growth. She had remained the same withdrawn, incurious, and blunt being she had been when raising her children, taking life's jests and jostles with a kind of Penzing fatalism. She was even living in the same old two-room flat.

Franz Blamauer, for all his paternal cruelty, was a neighborhood celebrity, as coachmen often were. A fixture of Viennese life, the cabmen drove horse-drawn vehicles ranging from bumpy, roofless one-seaters to carriages fit for a regal suite, and like the taxidrivers of

New York in the 1950s and 1960s they were official City Characters. No other European town seems to have celebrated its hackney drivers the way Vienna did, although their vehicle, the Fiaker, was of Parisian derivation, introduced by the Hôtel St. Fiacre and nicknamed after it.

Vienna's coachmen were truculent but helpful, eccentric yet bound to custom and the old ways of doing things. They would invoke a bygone age as if intimately connected to its day-to-day life and speak of the great Metternich as if they had driven him to Mass at St. Stephen's just the other day. Blamauer was not a freelance driver for hire, however. He held a steady post in the household of a well-off industrialist. For a working-class fellow of unsteady habits with a drinking problem, this was what Penzing called—to use modern lingo—a "good job."

One of the most famous of Viennese songs of old, Gustav Pick's "*Wiener Fiakerlied*," in the softened German of Viennese dialect, tenderizes the coachman figure with "*I hab' zwa harpe Rappen . . .*" (I drive two strong black horses . . .). The verse, in $\frac{4}{4}$, catalogues his doings, which includes the exercise of utmost discretion when taking a certain Count Lamezan, a pair of lovers, and even Grandpa to dodgy rendezvous. And the chorus, in a melting waltz, assures us with poetry fit for his gravestone: "My blood is easy and light on the wind, for I am a true *Wienerkind*" (Vienna boy).

The reality of the Viennese coachman was a good deal less demure; it was said that when police work did not involve surveillance of political adventurers, it almost always involved a coachman. Yet the *Fiakermann* stands for the thing Vienna most loved: tradition. The city's attitudes were frankly ultra-conservative—as befits the cultural capital of Prince Klemens von Metternich. This is the name that historians—and, indeed, every intellectual of the early-middle nineteenth century, Metternich's own era—have pasted onto political absolutism and reaction. Perhaps the most reviled figure of his century, Metternich inspired a book's worth of false tales delineating a fatuous popinjay. This was the most powerful figure short of warlord or monarch? When the Russian ambassador suddenly dies just before a diplomatic conference, Metternich becomes entranced with suspicion, his favorite mode. "I wonder why he did that," Metternich exclaims.

And yet Metternich, as Austria's Foreign Minister and then Chancellor, was the diplomat with the tact—at least, the cunning—to lay out a blueprint for the power structures of post-Napoleonic Europe even while Napoleon was still in business. After all, Napoleon was France: and France was contagious. "When Paris sneezes," Metternich observed, "Europe catches cold." Metternich's sway outlasted that of Napoleon by more than thirty years, till it was ended in the cascade of continental revolutions in 1848. Still, Metternich left his repressive sociopolitical system as an example to governments throughout the continent—especially in Central Europe, dominated in the north by the Kingdom of Prussia and, in the south, what in 1867 became the Dual Monarchy of Austria-Hungary.

This was the nation, or agglomeration of nations, that Karoline Blamauer grew up in. Besides Austria and Hungary themselves it included Bohemia, Moravia, Slovakia, and Sudetenland of later Czechoslovakia; sections of Poland, Romania, and Ukrainia; Bosnia and Croatia; and the Italian Tyrol. Because the dual monarchy recognized two thrones but was governed from Vienna, representatives of the empire's constituent peoples flooded Vienna, making it the most cosmopolitan city in Europe. Adolf Hitler, who spent his youth there trying to launch a career as an artist, hated its lack of nationalist values. Vienna was not a melting pot, exactly. It laced a multi-ethnic stew with exotic chunks of music and costume and language from afar: a chowder of Babel. Other great cities were filled with tourists; Vienna was filled with foreigners, and they were staying.

Ironically, it was a smallish place that had only recently expanded to absorb suburbs and outlying villages into a *Grosstadt*, a metropolis. The inner city, its narrow streets spreading out radially from St. Stephen's, was crammed, albeit with Beethoven, Schubert, the playwrights Grillparzer and Nestroy, the waltzing Strausses. It counted a population of only half a million in 1858, when the city's outer defensive walls were pulled down—literally detonated, with high explosives, as they proved too thick to respond to conventional demolition. The work lasted well into the 1860s, and when it was over the vast open space left encircling the inner city became the boulevards known as the Ringstrasse, giving spectators room to marvel at a crescent of public buildings in neo-style, from Greek through Gothic to Baroque: the Opera, the Parliament, City Hall, the Memorial Church, the University, the Burgtheater, the Academy of Fine Arts, the Stock Exchange. It seems characteristic of Vienna to be the last great European city to lose its outlying armor—as though, unlike revolutionary Paris, businesslike London, and eternal Rome, it viewed its battlements as protection from such modern ideas as democracy, a free press, and liberalization of lifestyle. But then, Vienna was also the easternmost of continental Europe's metropolises. The armies of Islam twice besieged it as they swept through southeastern Europe, in 1529 and 1683, both times unsuccessfully, though the second try nearly came off. The invader had breached the walls and was just smashing into the city when a Christian relief force arrived and turned history around. The Turks retreated so precipitously that they left everything behind, including hundreds of bags of coffee beans. These were immediately put to use—or so the legend runs—in initiating another feature of Viennese life, the coffeehouse.

Vienna's most identifying feature, however, might be its related worlds of music and the stage. The Viennese are born theatregoers—opera, the classics, low comedy, and operetta all have their publics, and it is worth noting that, aside from a few nomadic excursions, Karoline Blamauer was to live her entire life exclusively in theatre capitals or their environs, even when she was not actively working as a thespian. After Vienna there was Zurich (a modest arts capital, to be sure, but the only Swiss town with something like a theatre community), Berlin, Paris (briefly), and New York. One could argue that the future Lotte Lenya's wish to take a big bite out of life naturally led her to cosmopolitan places, with their bohemian subcultures. But it is also true that Vienna nurtured the theatrical personality, addicting it to the flamboyant "all the world's a stage" living style common to cultural capitals.

The Blamauers were too poor to take part in theatregoing, but all the city, regardless of class, followed the news of the arts world. Stage-and-concert gossip was the next topic after the weather for much of the population, and when Gustav Mahler took over as director of the Opera, the announcement that he was converting from Judaism to the state religion, Roman Catholicism, did nothing to soothe a controversy that raged citywide throughout his ten-year reign. Then, too, music was available everywhere, especially from the typically Viennese Schrammel band, after the late-nineteenth-century composer Johann Schrammel, who left his name on a quartet of two violins, clarinet, and guitar.* Thus, Linnerl Blamauer grew up in an atmosphere rich in the playacting and music-making that would stimulate the longings of a girl of high-concept imagination.

And, indeed, the palace of Schönbrunn was not all that Linnerl could see from the kitchen window. Also in view was a small mom-and-pop circus in which the parents and their kids did everything from tear the tickets to play the clown. It was as close to The Theatre as five-year-old Linnerl had ever got, and somehow or other she conveyed her intense interest to the circus manager and won her first job in show business, dancing in Hungarian folk garb while smashing a tambourine.

Years later, as she recounted the tale, friends would ask what she danced to.

"Oh . . . Brahms, you know?" she would reply. "Not that it made any difference as they Schrammeled their way through it."

Tiny circuses offer humble attractions, and in due course little Linnerl walked a tightrope a mere four feet above ground, with an exotic paper umbrella for balance. No crowned heads were scheduling command performances, but to a stage-struck five-year-old it must have seemed a lovely dream. Nor did the senior Blamauers hinder their

---

* By Linnerl's youth, the violins were usually playing with an accordion and either a zither or cimbalom, a kind of shortened piano using wires instead of keys and played with hammers, found throughout Eastern Europe but especially associated with the culture of Austria-Hungary.

daughter's ambitions. Frau Blamauer could see how happy it made her, and, said Lenya, "My father could not have cared less."

This is how it always begins: the so very young and unhappy child learning to substitute the appreciation of an audience for the affection she cannot get at home. Performing becomes one's support system—and surely the next stop is a trip to the theatre that impassions self-belief. The actors control a wild magic, and the public needs to share the enchantment. Yet when the Blamauers did take Linnerl to a show, she could scarcely follow the event from the inexpensive seats they held, and the trip was a waste.

Anyway, Linnerl's parents had no fancy plans for her; she was not even to finish school. At fourteen, she was apprenticed in a millinery shop. The work was monotonous—but delivering the finished hats to a middle-class clientele gave Linnerl tiny access to a world she had known nothing of, wherein people had the money with which to pleasure their lives. Some of her errands took her into the inner city, the old Vienna town of history and fable, the Beethoven-Stadt that, by Linnerl's youth in the 1910s, had become the radical place of the playwrights Arthur Schnitzler and Frank Wedekind, of Sigmund Freud, of the dangerous inventor of the music that only other inventors liked, Arnold Schönberg. Vienna was stirring, and Linnerl Blamauer needed to slip out of Penzing and its animal-biscuit circus into the pleasurable life. So she followed the example of other girls in the shop and took to selling herself on the streets.

Years later, Lenya enjoyed sharing the secret with virtually anyone—wives of producers and playwrights, fellow actors, strangers at parties. She presented it as another piece of the Lenya Legend, simply what happens to penniless young women who need *Extrataschengeld* (pocket money) to keep up with Dorothea and Mausi. "And," she would add, "no one was forcing us, you know?" Lenya's biographer Jens Rosteck even sees Lenya-as-prostitute as another preparation for her career as a performer: "She smoothed out her future in those early sexual dealings with men, calculating how to interest them in various ways—a skill she would find very useful in the tough world of the theatre." And yet, Rosteck adds, it helps explain Lenya's femme fatale side as that of a hobbyist in gender relations: "Like an insatiable collector, she was ever starting off on the hunt once again."

Kurt Weill had one thing in common with Karoline Blamauer: he, too, grew up with two brothers and a sister. Each was born a year apart. Nathan was the eldest, then Hans,★ then Kurt (who arrived on March 2, 1900), and at last Ruth.

Beyond that, the difference between what Linnerl and Kurt heard in the word "family" were wide. The Blamauers were Catholic but not technically observant, although Johanna made church visits in times of stress or thanksgiving. The Weills were Jewish and pious; Kurt's father, Albert Weill, was a synagogue cantor, singing the musical sections of the liturgy, and Kurt's mother, Emma Ackermann Weill, was the sister of a rabbi. We have already noted a cultured background in the Weill home, and as a cantor Albert naturally exposed his children to music. It was a close family, too—and a young one, for Albert and Emma were married in 1897, when he was thirty and she twenty-five. All four children were born in the following four years.

By contrast, the Blamauers had their children over the course of twelve years. Franz and Johanna Blamauer, too, were young at the time of their marriage, both in their late twenties, but there was no music in the home, and Franz, after the death of his beloved first Linnerl, showed no interest in his other offspring besides that eerie hatred of the second Linnerl. Further, his work driving his employer's coach and his habit of topping off the workday with a drinking binge made him something of an absentee father.

Albert Weill, by contrast, was strictly a family man, and he worked literally next door, for the Weills lived one address over from the synagogue. Where Franz Blamauer could lord about Penzing as both

---

★ This name is often rendered as Hanns, but Kurt always referred to his brother as "Hans" in his letters. Further, the score that Kurt regarded as the center of his legacy, *Street Scene*, was dedicated "To the Memory of My Brother Hans Weill."

coachman and village bon vivant, Albert Weill was brand new in town. A year after he married, he moved from his ancestral territory in the neighboring states of Württemberg and Baden in southwest Germany to his cantorial job in Dessau, in the province of Anhalt, halfway across the country to the northeast, on the road to Berlin.

This was the old Germany, united into an entity as recently as 1871 but composed nonetheless of a mass of kingdoms, grand duchies, duchies, principalities, and free cities: the Holy Roman Empire, now nationalized as the Second Reich. That first Reich, as Voltaire famously joked, was "neither holy, nor Roman, nor an empire," but this is wordplay. It was indeed holy Roman (meaning "Christian"), and if it was less an empire than an agglomeration of states, it comprised a vast domain—roughly Central Europe from the North Sea to the Alps and from the Frankish west to the Slavic east. It was loosely unified by its German dialects and its emperor, the Holy Roman one, from Charlemagne on to the last, Francis II, at the start of the nineteenth century. Now it had become a nation with something it had never had before: a capital, Berlin. Even so, the land retained its separate ruling houses, its court traditions, its provincial identity politics. And if Prussia was huge, Bavaria culturally distinguished, and some of the duchies incidental yet somehow imposing, a few of the puzzle pieces of this German Empire were so small you could scarcely fit an operetta inside them.

The duchy of Anhalt, when Albert Weill reported there to take up his post at the Dessau synagogue, was not the least significant of its kind, though rules of title inheritance and the bickering of sons led to constant partitioning, reuniting, and repartitioning over the centuries. Anhalt was separate from yet very much a part of the much larger state of Saxony, and Saxony was what one might call Basic Germany, with such major cities as Dresden, Leipzig, and Wittenberg and important history as the cradle of the Reformation and a central battle area in the Thirty Years' War.

When Cantor Weill took up his post, in 1899, Dessau was a prince's capital, with an old-fashioned and strictly observed hierarchy, from the court of Duke Friedrich II of Anhalt down through the professions and skilled service industries to the workforce, the whole taking tone from the noble family and a social life centered around Dessau's one theatre, subsidized by courtly indulgence. It employed a permanent ensemble of musicians, singers, dancers, and actors putting on everything from Shakespeare to Wagner. The programming was conservative, with the occasional prim novelty, for instance allowing Beethoven's inheritor Brahms but disdaining the overstating Bruckner.

Dessau was not a forge on which a Julien Sorel hammers out his destiny. Still, if everyone starts somewhere, it is worth noting that at least German-speaking Europe offered an abundance of cultural advantages. Kurt Weill ended as an American, not only in citizenship but in attitude; he was marinating in Americanism from the moment he stepped off the boat. But if he had started as an American in the equivalent of Dessau, a backwater of modest accomplishments—something like Harrisburg, say—Weill would not likely have had access to the world of theatre and music that Dessau's Hoftheater offered. *Court Theatre:* a home of talents of the lesser divisions, but a prideful place all the same, making the best art of second-rate materials. Here, young Kurt formed his first association with a mentor, the new *Kapellmeister* (music director) of the Hoftheater, Albert Bing. Kurt was already skilled enough as a pianist to take part in recitals,* and now Bing gave the teenager his first lessons in harmony—the building blocks of composition. And Bing told Kurt that Europe was filled with pianists but always ran short of good composers.

---

* Some who heard Weill at the keyboard in later years claim he was only fairly capable—better than, say, Cole Porter, whose technique was rudimentary (though his sense of rhythm was keen), but less than professional. However, this observation fails to consider Weill's priorities as a musician. He tended to focus on the driveline of any situation, letting subsidiary factors take care of thmselves. When playing Chopin or Liszt in public, Kurt the student would naturally be at his best; he wouldn't have been permitted to play if he couldn't justify the scores. Later on, Kurt Weill the composer would be intent on the work at hand and not on exhibition. Further, he was not a piano-based creator, composing at his desk rather than at the keyboard.

As it was, Kurt had already been composing for as long as anyone could recall: songs, an intermezzo for piano (Brahms had written a set of intermezzi that every senior piano student in Central Europe was bound to master), a four-part chorus, even a short opera, now lost. Thirteen years later, Kurt told an interviewer, "I composed for the school orchestra and—astonishingly, given who I am today—war choruses."

The war—the Great one, now termed World War I—had started when Kurt was fourteen, and over the course of its four years it affected the Weills ever more intensely. Kurt's two brothers were drafted when he was sixteen and seventeen, and soon enough it would be Kurt's turn. As he approached eighteen, his classes at school became smaller as boys a few months older than he were, one by one, pulled from their books. Not all were drafted; many joined up under pressure. "Even one's parents," Erich Maria Remarque tells us in *Im Westen Nichts Neues* (All Quiet on the Western Front), "were ready with the word 'coward.'" Typically, Kurt found a musical solution to the problem, taking up the trumpet so he might be spared fighting at the front to serve in a band unit.

He was as well giving piano lessons to youngsters in Duke Friedrich's family, and studying orchestration with Albert Bing, and interning at the Hoftheater as a coach and accompanist. Most important, at the age of sixteen Kurt composed the first piece that he himself regarded as a kind of "Opus 1," the initiating work of an oeuvre: a setting of five poems translated into German from the ancient Hebrew of Judah Halevi, entitled *Ofrahs Lieder*.

Music was his only interest, in total immersion—particularly in attending operas at the theatre. One that left an indelible mark on him, as we'll see, was a newish piece, introduced as recently as 1903, Eugen D'Albert's *Tiefland* (Lowlands). A German of French descent, D'Albert was at first primarily known as a virtuoso pianist. However, opera was music's booming industry, with a demand for new works so intense that a flash success could count dozens of productions, from St. Petersburg to New Orleans, within two years of its premiere—and flash successes were the rage. Every musician who could do so got into the opera business, and music publishers took to signing up hopefuls fresh from the conservatory in hopes of securing the next Puccini.

Tiefland was typical of the day in its peasant characters and violent action, in the hint of the popular in some of the tunes, and in the composer's reputation eventually coming to rest on the survival of this one work. Nineteenth-century opera generally favored the doings of the leadership class, whether a Druid priestess or an Egyptian army officer, not to mention the gods and heroes of Wagner's *Ring* cycle. These characters tended to converse politically when not making love, and their music was what Western listeners regarded as high art. Suddenly, near the century's end, a realist vogue took over, introducing characters of obscure social background who conversed about day-to-day matters and sang, at times, the kind of melodies that some thought more suitable to arena events than to an opera house.

The Italians copyrighted the form as *verismo* (realism), in such founding works as *Cavalleria Rusticana* (1890), *Pagliacci* (1892), and *Andrea Chenier* (1896): Sicilian villagers, adultery and murder in a strolling-players troupe, the French Revolution, complete with bloodthirsty proletarians. And, in standout tenor solos, *Cavalleria*'s Siciliana and *Pagliacci*'s "Vesti la Giubba" (the one that climaxes with the sob-strewn "*Ridi, Pagliaccio!*"), the border between the melodic contour and discipline—the high art—of Bellini and Verdi on one hand and the sensual corruption of folk song or the salon trifle on the other appeared to dissolve. *Chenier*, even worse, is a kind of highlights in search of a score: bustle music, anguished *recitativo*, then a Big Tune, then clatter leading into screamy crowd noises, then subdued *recitativo* capped by another Big Tune, and so on.

With its punchy dramatics and—some said—cheap musical thrills, *verismo* put a *whack!* into opera, and it conquered Europe just when the first days of the gramophone provided infrastructure for those Big Tunes. *Tiefland*, a sort of German *verismo*, told of a mountain-dwelling shepherd lured to the lowlands to wed the local landowner's mistress. It's a front marriage, for the landowner intends to maintain his liaison.

Tiefland never quite breaks out into one of those pop melodies that *verismo* loved, but it always feels as if it's just about to, and it has an arresting musical "image," in a four-note theme representing a wolf that the shepherd takes on in mortal combat. It's something the young Kurt Weill especially would have noticed—a musical tic that unifies the work in its many appearances while explaining its central concept. These four notes dominate the shepherd's *Wolfserzählung* (Wolf Narration), recounting in detail how fiercely he defended his flock and how close he came to death; thus revealing his vulnerability but also his passion, the shepherd draws his humiliated and resentful bride to himself. At *Tiefland*'s end, the shepherd must again defend what is his when the landowner tries to claim "his" woman. The two men fight to the death, and, to the four notes of the Wolfkill, the shepherd fells his foe once more. And as the airy leaps and curves of the opera's opening "mountain" music peal out *fortissimo*, the shepherd and his wife depart for the freedom of the highlands as the curtain falls.

Tiefland is a heady piece—romantic, raucous, sentimental, cruel— a work to mesmerize a young man besotted with the classics from Mozart to Wagner but now discovering in this new style the possibilities in opera. As we'll see later on, *verismo*'s popular tang was to figure importantly in Weill's growth as a theatre composer—and the four notes of the Wolfkill will be heard again, in an hommage in one of Weill's last great works, when another husband needs to protect his homestead.

Kurt's interning at the Court Theatre had made him a useful contact in the local prima donna, Emilie Feuge, and she invited him to become her official accompanist. When he was still seventeen, he traveled with her to Köthen, ten miles southwest of Dessau, to play for her recital for a remuneration of forty marks and a set of Grieg solos for himself. In the coming few years, Kurt would continue to play for Feuge and for her daughter Elisabeth; the Feuges would appear to be the first singers to present Kurt's vocal work in public on the professional level.

Meanwhile, Kurt had achieved his *Abitur* (graduation) from the Herzogliche Friedrichs-Oberrealschule (roughly, Duke Friedrich High School), and for a young man so imbued with the making of music, there could be but one immediate goal, the Hochschule für Musik in Berlin, perhaps the outstanding conservatory in all Europe. Kurt was now subject to the draft, yet somehow or other he managed to stay out of the war even as the American Expeditionary Force threatened to break the stalemate of trench fighting and pour over no-man's-land into Germany itself. Desperate, the war machine recognized no educational deferments, least of all for the study of music. Nevertheless, at the end of April, 1918, Kurt Weill—eighteen years and two months old—arrived in Berlin to matriculate at the Hochschule, the Prussian State College of Music.

Karoline Blamauer didn't wait till she was eighteen to set her life in motion; nor did she take an *Abitur.* But where Kurt always sought to direct his life, establishing long-range goals and diagramming points of approach, Linnerl let destiny fly her about. Granted, she was not without resources, especially in taking advantage of her natural charisma in captivating others. But she applied her gifts for purely social (or sexual) purposes. She wasn't a user. She simply liked people and wanted to be liked in turn.

No wonder Aunt Sophie took a shine to her. One of those little-known older relations who, one day, bustles in, takes over, and changes your life, Sophie was Frau Blamauer's older sister. She visited Vienna back in the summer of 1913, when Linnerl was nearly fifteen and desperately hoping for something picturesque to happen to her, especially if it took her away from the millinery business. Aunt Sophie was that something. Thrice married and thrice a widow, Aunt Sophie (as Lenya puts it in her autobiography, in her characteristically deadpan way) "mysteriously landed up in Zurich." And now Aunt Sophie proposed to pack Linnerl off to live with her in the artistic capital of Switzerland. This is mysterious, too, because Aunt Sophie had no room for Linnerl: she was living as the housekeeper of a retired doctor who was extremely protective of his privacy.

Still, a break is a break. Linnerl's mother certainly saw it as one. As they said goodbye in the train station, Linnerl holding her humiliat-

ing little tramp's bundle—there was no money for a proper suitcase—
Frau Blamauer told her, "Be smart, Linnerl, and, if you can manage it,
don't come back."

Perhaps Aunt Sophie had entertained a secret plan after all, for soon
enough Linnerl was moved out of the doctor's flat to stay with the Eh-
renzweigs. An older, childless couple, they took to Linnerl and she to
them. Better, Herr Ehrenzweig was a photographer with a practice
favoring the bohemian world of the theatre, and he offered Linnerl as a
student to Steffi Herzeg, the ballet mistress of the opera company at
the Stadttheater (Municipal Theatre). If Linnerl proved capable, she
could count on taking part as a supernumerary in the operas and perhaps in small speaking roles at the Schauspielhaus (Playhouse), home
of spoken drama.

Zurich ran its main stages in an orderly separation of skills. The
Corso Theatre produced operetta and other light fare. The two big
houses, the Stadttheater and the Schauspielhaus, were independent
companies under a single management. Still, the pair followed distinct
programs. The Municipal Theatre was conservative. The Playhouse
was innovative, becoming especially so during the years of the Third
Reich, when many German and then Austrian actors and directors fled
to Switzerland.

As it happened, Linnerl was not cut out to be a ballerina in any real
sense. But she moved well enough and was fascinating to look at, unlike
the usual ballet girl with her face in a kind of pretty mask. At the Stadttheater, Linnerl played so many pages, squires, and Nibelungs that she
could sing her way through whole chunks of opera scores, startling
Kurt in later years, because she couldn't read music. Meanwhile, at the
Schauspielhaus, Linnerl learned her Shakespeare, Molière, and plays by
Tolstoy, plays based on novels by Tolstoy, and plays in the gritty, realistic style of Tolstoy's plays. It was a life beyond the expectations of
Penzing, and an education as well.

Years later, as always recounting the episodes of her life to all who
would listen, Lenya had little to say about Zurich except that it was so
rich even the streetwalkers looked prosperous. "Every second house,"
she observed, "was a bank." It must have been a strange adventure for

her, thrust into a land that most German speakers find incomprehensible and irritating. For one thing, the various Swiss dialects are all but impenetrable beyond Switzerland's borders, and the obsessive use of diminutives—half the nouns end in -*li* (as in *Müesli*, oatmeal)—makes everything sound like a grandparent cooing over an infant.

Then there is the Swiss personality, best described as "unexcitable to a fault." A story: the conductor Karl Böhm is trying to get soprano Lisa della Casa to put a little more oomph into Richard Strauss' *Arabella*. Della Casa was known for her creamy vocalizing in Strauss and as Arabella in particular, in an arrestingly nuanced portrayal. But Böhm, it seems, liked his Arabellas broad enough to see from the moon. "More surprise!" Böhm called out during a run-through with the orchestra. Then: "Here she is dejected." And "Nein, nein, you must seem to explode with defiance!"

Never getting what he wanted, Böhm stopped the orchestra and laid down his baton.

"Where are you from, Fräulein?" he asked.

"Burgdorf, Herr Professor. Bei Bern."

"Switzerland," he replied, nodding. "I thought so."

Still, Karoline Blamauer—her working name, at the time—was thrilled to be far from her evil father and her irksome day job. And she was on the stage!: only fifteen when her first season of performances commenced. It was all the more devastating when, at the season's end, Aunt Sophie announced that it was time for her niece to return to Vienna. But why? Wasn't she supporting herself, and at work in the arts? As Lenya later told it, one noticed the holes she always left in certain stories, especially about her family. If asked for details, she would simply shrug, you know?

For instance, did Aunt Sophie worry that, with the theatres closed for the summer, Linnerl would be gallivanting about and getting into mischief? Was Aunt Sophie subject to the old prejudice about ballet girls—that they were prostitutes in tutus? Had she repented of interfering in the life of a self-willing girl, heedless of control?

Back in Vienna, Linnerl's mother was not glad to see her. ("If you can manage it, don't come back.") But hadn't she missed her daughter?

Frau Blamauer's life, too, had changed: Franz had walked out on her and she had taken in a boarder who was now her temporary boy friend. One tenant and the other children in that same one-bedroom-one-kitchen flat?

Worse, this was the fatal summer of 1914, which began on June 28 with the assassination in Sarajevo, Serbia, of the heir to the Austro-Hungarian throne. On July 23, encouraged by Berlin, the Dual Monarchy hurled the threat of the power of Central Europe upon little Serbia with a humiliating ultimatum and then, responding to aggressive noises from Russia, declared war on Serbia on July 28. Other nations began to mobilize and make their own declarations, and by the second week of August Europe was almost wholly at war.

Except for Switzerland. Not only was Linnerl eager to return to pursue her wonderful livelihood: Zurich would be a much happier place than a belligerent nation, as the sanctions of a war economy lean most heavily on the poor like the Blamauers. For starters, both Linnerl's brothers, aged seventeen and fourteen, were recruited for war work. And, just to make things interesting, the Blamauers' boarder died of tuberculosis and his successor, Ernst Hainisch, proved every bit as unpleasant as Franz Blamauer had been. Linnerl was now desperate to get back to the theatre and away from home altogether.

Civilian travel was already severely restricted, and Linnerl had to get into order paperwork fit for an adult; she wrote to the intendant of the two city theatres in Zurich, Alfred Reucker, for confirmation of her labor contract so she could proceed. Reucker had to break the house rules to grant her the necessary permission—another reminder of how most people took to Lenya all her life—and by the middle of September, two weeks late for the first day of rehearsals for the new theatre season, Linnerl was on a train bound for Zurich.

It was a terrible trip, though of course the high point of her narrative much later on, when she would tell of the atmosphere on the train: stuffed with men in uniform, slowly chugging along the slowest possible route to the Swiss border and constantly stopping for interminable waits while some soldiers disembarked and others took their place. Finally, the train neared Switzerland, as Linnerl's heart pounded. Would authorities suddenly appear to commandeer the train for the war effort? Would she be taken off and spirited away somewhere?

She was not quite sixteen, barely a dancer, and not remotely important as the governors of the world saw things. Many, many others were to make comparable and genuinely dangerous journeys over the next generation or so, but as Lotte Lenya was to tell the tale in the safety of her later life, at Broadway revels or backstage gossipfests, it was simply a thriller. There was no historical long view of the émigré in flight from an attempt to eradicate his personality, nothing about the war, and the ugly peace, and the friend with connections warning you to run. Don't worry, it's just a toothbrush: the border, now . . . "Ihre Pässe, bitte!" . . . the train continues . . . a silent sigh of tremendous relief. But still not home yet. Not till Linnerl looked out of the window on her left to glimpse the long, narrow curve of Lake Zurich did she feel she must be safe. The stations: Männedorf, Heilen, Erlenbach, Küsnacht. Yes, she was surely safe now. "Zurich!" the conductor called. And Linnerl stepped down from the car, a free young woman with all her life before her.

At this point in their story, Karoline Blamauer had traveled much farther—in every sense—than Kurt Weill, who was then a schoolboy of fourteen. Let us jump ahead, then, to April, 1918, when Kurt matriculated at the Berlin Hochschule für Musik as a full-time student in harmony, composition, counterpoint, and conducting. Indeed, for a brief time Kurt considered making the baton his primary instrument. After all, it was traditional in German music that composers conduct and conductors compose. Richard Strauss was once almost as famous for leading orchestras as writing for them, and Gustav Mahler, in his lifetime, was thought the greatest conductor alive but hardly a composer at all.

However, the infrastructure of a music conservatory gives a budding composer the tremendous advantage of the school's instrumental students, eager to play his compositions. It's tempting. Of course, the wise young composer pleases his tutors with a conservative output;

this is an educational process, not a revolution, and one learns by doing what the Masters have done before you. Kurt yields up his String
Quartet in b minor (1918) and Suite in E Major for orchestra (1919) in
six movements—Introduction and Allegro Vivace, a slow movement,
a scherzo, minuet, and intermezzo, and then a finale. This is the bed-
rock of tradition, Classical structuring as known to Haydn and Mozart.
Then, for something Romantic, more up-to-date: a tone poem drawn
from Rainer Maria Rilke, *Die Weise von Liebe und Tod* (The Melody of
Love and Death, 1919).

Though lost, the score might well constitute Kurt Weill's first major
work—not a student's exercise but an outpouring of passion. Rilke's
narrative, now in prose and now in verse, tells how his namesake the
young Cornet (cavalier) Christoph Rilke rides with his companions to
fight the invading Turks in 1663. The cadre puts up overnight in a castle, where Rilke romances a countess. But the Turks fire the place, and
Rilke leaps up half-dressed, escapes the blaze, and storms by horse into
the center of the battle, where he falls, beautiful and reckless, lover and
fighter. First published in 1906, the poem was a cult favorite in Germany for its love of that national icon the suicidal hero, and for its rousing look at a life short on time and long on valor:

> Yet his proud banner cannot be found.
> Call out: Cornet!
> The desperate horses, the prayers and the sound
> Of curses: Cornet!
> Swordplay to swordplay, command and respond,
> Yet there's silence: Cornet!
> And once more: Cornet!
> Down with the foeman and ride him to ground!*

In a letter to his brother Hans, Kurt outlined his plans for the
piece, designed to stand on its own as absolute music yet stormy with

---

* Unless otherwise noted, substantial translations from the German are the present
author's.

youthful bravura, ardent with desire, resounding with the shouting and fighting. Kurt wrote such letters to Hans all their lives, telling his brother what he would make of his music: the only way to be close to Kurt was to be close to his work.

After Albert Bing, back at the Dessau Court Theatre, Kurt's next mentor was his composition teacher at the Hochschule, Engelbert Humperdinck. The man who wrote the music to *Hänsel und Gretel* (1893) and the then popular but now near-forgot *Königskinder* (Royal Children, 1897; heavily revised 1910) enjoyed a major reputation and was the first genuinely prominent composer Kurt had met—as much so, almost, as a Strauss or Puccini. When Kurt visited Humperdinck at his home, the composer's son, Wolfram, then twenty-five and still contemplating his professional future, told Kurt that if he, Wolfram, had Kurt's gifts, he would follow his father's route: because, again, there was nothing in the European arts world like being the author of a smash-hit opera. We've seen this with *Tiefland*, and it was true as well of *Madama Butterfly* (1904), *Der Rosenkavalier* (1911), or, for that matter, Franz Lehár's *Die Lustige Witwe* (The Merry Widow, 1905), an unprecedented blend of opera's lyricism with sex farce, and an international sensation. In the end, Wolfram Humperdinck became a stage director. But he left young Kurt with a potent piece of advice: "Write an opera and you are a made man!"

Indeed, much later, Weill—who never tired of stating his artistic beliefs in print—said, "I made up my mind, at the age of nineteen, that my special field of activity would be the theatre." First, however, Kurt had to stabilize his income, for while the war ended in the middle of his first term at the Hochschule, the term's end, in the spring of 1919, found Germany racked with famine, foreign occupation, and the on-and-off hot war between factions of far left and far right. The nation was in a state of near-collapse and, on the personal level, so was the Weill family. Albert Weill's synagogue, financially pressed, would not likely be able to keep him on. (He was in fact dismissed in the summer of 1919, though the family was allowed to stay in the parish house till Albert found other employment.) Kurt himself had been living in Berlin on earnings as a choir director at a synagogue in Friedenau, southwest of

Berlin proper and not far from the Tempelhof parade ground and air-craft landing field that in 1923 became Berlin's first official airport. Pupil by day, teacher by night: "Interesting evening, after two com-position lessons I had a choir rehearsal," Kurt wrote Hans, "in which I had to simultaneously direct, sing tenor, play the organ, and yell at the women." Worse yet, the organ motor wasn't working smoothly and the synagogue's cantor was out moonlighting, "singing in a cin-ema." But the Friedenau job paid 250 marks a month, a sizable salary for the time.

Nevertheless, Kurt was now to leave the Hochschule. Besides fi-nancial considerations, he had it in mind to take Wolfram Hump-erdinck's advice and find some project in music theatre. And yet didn't he need seasoning as a composer, barely nineteen as he was? A new idea: intimate study with a composer Kurt admired. And that com-poser, who lived in Vienna, was Arnold Schönberg.

It was the Schönberg of the tone poem *Pelleas und Melisande* (1905) and the gigantic dramatic cantata *Gurre-Lieder* (1913) that attracted Kurt. This was the early Schönberg, intoxicated with the Wagnerian brew of myth and *Leitmotiv*. Interestingly, our one impression of the lost music of Kurt's Rilke tone poem, through a report by the critic Heinrich Strobel, suggests that it compares to Schönberg's *Pelleas*. If this is a fair assessment, it reveals *Weillmusik* we know nothing of, en-thralled by the big sound and drunken pastels of the *Spätromantik*, the last burst of the Romantic Era, which had started with Beethoven and peaked in the tone poems of Richard Strauss: *Don Juan* (1889), the hero as sensualist; *Also Sprach Zarathustra* (1896), the hero as superman; *Till Eulenspiegels Lustige Streiche* (1895), the hero as scamp; *Don Quixote* (1898), the hero as dreamer.

The very notion of the hero (preferably with a poetically eerie yet sacrificially redeemable flaw) is a Romantic narcotic, and the nine-teenth century was mesmerized by the doings of Manfreds, Kings Ar-thur, and above all Siegfried, dragon-slayer and tamer of wild Brunhild of Iceland. Siegfried is betrayed, as all the best heroes are; because they cannot be conquered, they must be scammed. Thus they remain the two favorite things that German heroes can be: superhuman and dead.

The Nazis were careful to pack that concept into their baggage—and there it is in Kurt's Rilke piece, his *Melody of Love and Death*. We can't access the lost music, of course. Still, in its subject matter it is unquestionably a tour through Romanticism's clamorous mythopoeia—or, to put it another way, society's wish to glorify massacres with the propaganda of youth and beauty. "Swordplay to swordplay, command and respond": the words sound bizarrely fierce on Weill, even if he was using them only as a trot for an orchestral reading. In fact, some pages hence, Weill becomes the symbol of the *Kulturbolschewismus* that the Nazis loved to hate: the "cultural Bolshevism" made of equal parts—they claimed—of defeatism, satire of the sacred, and America's mongrel jazz. That is the Kurt Weill we all know, leading his band of musical cutthroats in spoof operas that laugh about sex and tear down your heroes, Public Composer Number One on the Nazis' enemies list.

So it is astonishing that here, in 1919, Kurt was entranced by what was left of the Romantics and planning to move to Vienna to study with Schönberg. And Schönberg said yes.

So far, so good—except, by this time, Schönberg had renounced Romantic music for jagged, discordant expressionism, the art that explains reality by distorting it. Further, Schönberg was now developing his unique field of dodecaphony, or, more commonly, "twelve-tone" music, in which an arbitrary placement of the twelve notes of the Western scale is reused in infinite variation to create an entire piece, whether a short piano solo or a full-length opera.

Was Kurt aware that Schönberg had, so to say, tuned himself out of the Wagnerian style? True, not till 1925, in Schönberg's Piano Suite, op. 25, did he finally make a public statement of the twelve-tone method. The piece is presented in strict neo-Classical shape, with Prelude, Gavotte, Musette, Intermezzo, Minuet, and Gigue all baffling the ear in the seductively creepy twelve-tone manner. Still, throughout the 1910s, Schönberg was clearly turning himself into the inventor of what detractors used to call Modern Music: the kind nobody likes. Indeed, by the late 1920s Weill was to disparage—in print—composers so intellectualized they created "as if behind closed doors." Weill wanted music "one can comprehend without special explanations."

Is that why Kurt never made it to Vienna? He was himself to embark on an enfant terrible phase in the mid-1920s, getting into atonality, which is also Modern but not as radical as Schönberg's twelve-tone rows. Yet for a talent as rooted in tradition as Kurt's was, Schönberg would have made a direly incorrect mentor. On the contrary, it was when Kurt Weill discovered his own twist on traditional composition that he became, in a very different way, as influential as Schönberg.

Kurt's next move could be seen as a return to basics in every way: he moved back to Dessau to take the position of *répétiteur* at the city theatre, now called the Friedrich-Theater because the collapse of the Kaiser's Reich when Germany lost the war did away with the nation's courts and their court theatres. Kurt was living with his parents and sister, playing the family wageworker but spending all his time in the world of the musical stage. Third in line below the music director and his chief conductor, the *répétiteur* is literally the "rehearser." Just as when he was interning at the same theatre, Kurt's duties included accompanying rehearsals, coaching singers, drilling the chorus, and being present at all performances in various supplementary functions, such as keeping offstage singers in synch with the conductor in the pit.

Unfortunately, the house had hired a new music director, Hans Knappertsbusch. Eventually to be known as one of Germany's greatest musicians, celebrated for Wagner and above all for his management of the battling soundscapes of the earthy and the holy that permeate *Parsifal*, Knappertsbusch was the typical tyrant at the controls of the power grid. We will see this in operation throughout Kurt's German career: the rule of those with Position over those without. This gives way to the merry democratic chaos of Broadway when Kurt gets to America.

Knappertsbursch was not simply one of those arts despots: he really knew opera and conducting. At the slightest cue of his baton, the orchestra *played*. The critic John Rockwell tells a story: he was in Germany at a performance of Wagner's *Der Fliegende Holländer* (The

Flying Dutchman). Knappertsbusch was conducting. As always in opera, the show really begins when the conductor enters the pit, as the audience greets him with applause, as he gains the podium to take his bow, as he then collects his thoughts, raises his baton, and launches the music. *The Flying Dutchman* begins with choice music indeed, a Nordic storm over the sea on which sails the Dutchman's ghost ship with his ghost crew. It is one of the most exciting initiations in the repertory. This night, however, Knappertsbusch had no intention of submitting to the Conducting 101 puppet show. As he stepped among the players, still thirty feet from the podium, he suddenly gave them all a look, raised his baton, and signaled the downbeat—and, instantly, the overture to *The Flying Dutchman*, storm, sea, ghosts, and all, raged into life. It's not nice to fool Mother Nature.

The problem from Kurt's view of things was Knappertsbusch's habitual scorn for assistants. Worse, Kurt's quiet nature lacked the sycophantic bustle that tyrants such as Knappertsbusch like to see in their shop. Knappertsbusch was an anti-Semite as well, and very vocal in his contempt for Kurt's short stature—just five feet, three-and-a-half inches. This is the kind of thing Kurt was exposed to: one night, when Knappertsbusch was conducting, Kurt, who was backstage to prompt a tenor on his entrance, somehow or other fell through a trap door. The tenor failed to appear on cue, and at intermission Knappertsbusch came roaring into view to find out why. Knocked unconscious, Kurt wasn't even available for a scolding. "Always he was so small!" cried Knappertsbusch, as Kurt later recalled it. "Now he's gone completely!"

Luckily, opportunity called halfway through that season, when the town of Lüdenscheid, on the other side of central Germany in Westphalia, hired Kurt as its theatre's *Kapellmeister*. The good news is that now Kurt was his own Knappertsbusch: the *Kapellmeister* (literally "chapel master," from long-ago days when serious music was church music) is the music director. The sad news was that Lüdenscheid's theatre was strictly fourth division, the kind that must simplify even the thinnest operetta for a helter-skelter company and an insecure orchestra. When Kurt arrived to take up his post, he was told he would be conducting Friedrich von Flotow's *Martha* that very night. (For the first time in his life—and *Martha* has some tricky ensembles.) Looking through the orchestra score, Kurt found it rendered impenetrable by cuts marked in various colors, coded to indicate the "Dresden cuts," "Hamburg cuts," and so on.

"Which are the Lüdenscheid cuts?" Kurt asked the orchestra leader.

"I'm not sure," came the reply.

And yet: what better way to steep oneself in the mysteries of music theatre than to be hurled into the thick of a repertory's worth of it, night after night? Some of what Kurt put on was, he thought, lame musical comedy. Some of it was *Die Fledermaus*—a great musical comedy—and some was Verdi and Wagner. Perhaps Kurt remade the acquaintance of *Tiefland*, with its mild-mannered young protagonist who turns savage when defending his marriage—a tale to remember.

And the calendar would surely have included the smash-hit operetta *Das Dreimäderlhaus* (The Home of the Three Girls), adapting the melodies of Franz Schubert to narrate a more or less romantic episode from Schubert's life.* This work stands out because its routine libretto (Schubert loves beauty, sends handsome buddy to woo for him by singing "*Ungeduld*," loses beauty to buddy, dies) is redeemed by the superb music. But then, German operetta usually mated superb music to routine librettos. Rehearsing and conducting day after day, Kurt must have wondered why the librettos couldn't be superb as well, and what sort of theatre might be thus created—not just better operettas but new forms of singing drama. At Lüdenscheid, Kurt later said, "I learned everything I know about the theatre." The main thing he learned was to seek out for his own works writers who *weren't* librettists: to avoid routine and create uniquely in each new piece.

---

* The American version, in a heavy revision, is *Blossom Time* (1921), a cornerstone of the American operetta foundation and a national touring attraction for over a generation. In a Broadway cognoscente's joke, the last tour is still roaming the hinterland, recalling the legends of Japanese soldiers on remote Pacific islands in the 1950s who didn't know the war was over.

Karoline Blamauer's second year at Zurich, a few years before this, was in one important way equivalent to Kurt's immersion in the day-to-day of stage production: because she, too, found a mentor, to graduate her from supernumerary to potential leading lady. But hers was far more influential than Kurt's mentors had been. Linnerl's mentor was acting coach, Pygmalion, and best friend in one: Richard Révy, the head stage director at the Schauspielhaus. Révy was the first to discern what used to be called "star quality" in Karoline; he thought she was put on earth for far more challenging work than pirouettes and walk-ons. Révy deconstructed the girl to put her back together with a smoother accent in pure *Theaterdeutsch*, better breath control and projection of dialogue, and a mind stimulated by reading.

This ranged from the classics to the latest playwrights—not the chic ones, but the ones making history, from Ibsen to Chekhof. In accordance with the German theatre's passion for Russians, Révy assigned his pupil Dostoyefsky, and she dubbed him Vanya, presumably after Ivan Karamazof, the intellectual of the three brothers. Révy called her Grushenka, after the playfully amoral girl involved with the hot-headed sensualist brother, Dmitri, who then falls for the pious brother, Alyosha. "All your life, men will be crazy about you"—the prediction of Linnerl's mother, we recall—could have been said of Grushenka as well, and in adaptation for stage or film it would have given Lotte Lenya a major opportunity.★

From a kid in the chorus, Linnerl was turning into a cultured young would-be actress. What Révy gave her, it seems, was not only an education but confidence. Other men liked her; Révy admired her. "Need-

---

★ When the famous Hollywood *Karamazof* adaptation (1958) was made, with the hotheaded sensualist Yul Brynner, the intellectual Richard Basehart, and the pious William Shatner, Lenya was too old for consideration; the role went to Maria Schell. However, one glimpses in Schell's toothy insouciance a picture of what Lenya was like in her youth. Ironically, a German version, *Der Mörder Dimitri Karamasoff* (1931), might well have cast Lenya, as she was by then prominent in Berlin theatre circles and made her film debut that same year. Anna Sten, soon to try Hollywood as the Goldwyn Garbo, played Grushenka.

less to say," she recalled, "we slept together, too, but that was my way of paying him, you know?" He gave her something else, a little thing, but long-lasting: her name. To accompany his Vanya, he turned Linnerl into a Russian *Linja* that somehow or other edged sideways into *Lenja*. This eventually came to be the name by which everyone called her, including her husband—just "Lenja," neat, later to be revised phonetically for Americans as "Lenya."

For now, though, she was still billed as Karoline (or sometimes Caroline, but also Lotte, short for her second middle name) Blamauer, and still a dancer and stage extra, though she did take small parts at Zurich's operetta house, the Corso Theater, during the summer when the municipal stages were closed. Then, too, Linnerl was getting around Zurich more, enjoying its nightlife when not on call at the theatres. Swiss cities don't favor the drinks-and-a-show boutiques we call "cabarets"; they make the police nervous. But Zurich had a few, including a noteworthy piece of art history in the Cabaret Voltaire, where dada was born. Tom Stoppard's comedy *Travesties* (1974), set in Zurich in 1917, plays with that bemusing moment in the course of Western Civilization when James Joyce, Lenin, and dada's godfather, Tristan Tzara, were all in Zurich at the same time. Stoppard might have included the young Lotte Lenja as well.

But then, she was not hobnobbing with the intelligentsia then. She took a rich old Czech as a lover for the material comfort, only to throw him over because it just wasn't her way, you know? A chauffeured car and sables make life easier but not more fun. Linnerl preferred the company of a gal pal, Greta Edelmann, with whose family Linnerl was boarding. The Edelmanns' was a colorful household, starting with breakfast, when the chowbell consisted of Frau Edelmann's running a finger down the piano keyboard, *glissando*, and when she would then reprimand Herr Edelmann for his various failings with such stunning report that he would be silent for the rest of the day.

Greta was one of Linnerl's fellow dancers at the theatres and, like Linnerl, a sensualist. Another of the later Lenya's recollections: Greta was "pregnant practically every month," but for cover she kept a boy friend, a proudly nationalistic Serb whom Linnerl didn't think much of. In her memoirs, she mentions that Serbia was where the Archduke Ferdinand was assassinated, but says nothing more about it. This is odd, for the assassination produced the European cataclysm that was then in its third year and the first fact in the daily life of everyone from Glasgow to Moscow. Even in peaceful Zurich, war profiteers conducted business in shady corners of see-no-evil cafés or escorted their trophy *Mädchen* to the opera with the flamboyance of the parvenu who thinks that money is character. "It was like Shanghai," she told an interviewer many years later, "and what was going on was nobody's business."

Indeed, on another visit home late in the war, Linnerl was startled by how exhausted everyone looked. Zurich really was a paradise; despite sending her people care packages and money, Linnerl had not realized quite how bad things were, how abnormal normal life had become. More bad news: Linnerl's mother had married the aforementioned Ernst Hainisch, though how she could have divorced the still-living Franz Blamauer in Catholic Austria in 1916 Linnerl does not explain.

Back in Zurich, Linnerl was graduated to lead roles in straight plays under Richard Révy's guidance. Did she intend to settle in Zurich and make her career there? She must have known of the world of theatre, music, and dance that prospered on the main stages of the great European capitals, for many of the most interesting productions traveled from city to city and Zurich was a major stopping point. Any night that she was free, Linnerl attended: a company put together by Max Reinhardt, the outstanding director of the age; or the dance troupe formed by Michel Fokine after he broke with Diaghilev and the Ballets Russes. Zurich was an anomaly in Switzerland for its expansive arts scene, but perhaps it was less a cultural capital than simply a center for artists on the move, whether touring their work or sitting out the war. Zurich was Linnerl's school; absorbing the lessons of the gifted was how she developed her matchless technique. Watch her forty-five years later in *The Roman Spring of Mrs. Stone*: her derisive smile, her crisply tentative gestures, the way she gets two thousand years of hand-to-mouth hunger into the sight of a lobster buffet.

Even when still filling out the scene as an extra, Linnerl took each performance as an education. Elisabeth Bergner, later one of the stage's greatest classical actors (till she fled the Nazis and found her accent hobbling her in Britain and the United States), came to Zurich in some play with a party scene. Karoline Blamauer was on site as Guest Number Three or something, and, to suggest the joie de vivre of the high life, Guest Number Three held her champagne glass with her pinky extended. Bergner discerned a teaching moment and a crowd-pleaser at the same time, crossed over to Karoline, pushed her finger back, and announced, *"Das macht man nicht in feiner Gesellschaft"* (That isn't done in the best company). The audience laughed, the ad lib went into the script, and Linnerl never made that mistake again.

So Zurich was working out well for her. And then Richard Révy said he was going to try his luck in Berlin.

Kurt had lasted half a season in Dessau, and it was the same at Lüdenscheid. His parents had moved to nearby Leipzig, where Kurt's father finally found a position, running an orphanage. There Kurt joined them, finding more work directing choruses while considering his next move. Like so many others drawn to Berlin, Kurt wondered if he ought to try it again, not as a student in a conservatory but on the rarified level, in a master class taught by Ferruccio Busoni. One of the most prominent men of the day, Busoni was a piano virtuoso; an editor of so much keyboard Bach that he created a new byline as "Bach-Busoni"; and a composer who was as much an intellectual as a musician, the "thinking man's" minstrel.

Kurt was making another of his Decisions—not just to study with Busoni but to resign any thought of doing so with Schönberg. For Busoni was Schönberg's opposite, a conservative to Schönberg's revolutionary. However, Busoni was not easy to approach, and master classes as a rule are small and exclusive. It was apparently the critic Oskar Bie who gave Kurt the necessary introduction, for Bie was a Busoni enthusiast. In his monumental history *Die Oper* (1920), Bie expressed a reservation about Busoni's brainy approach to music yet called him "one of the most idealistic, pure, and sincere of artists living today—stimulating in every sound he plays or writes, bold and spiritual in all his theories about the future of music."

Each in his way, Busoni and Schönberg had an agenda for Western music. Schönberg wanted to demolish and rebuild it from the ground up; Busoni wanted to innovate by redeploying its past. And that was the road Kurt chose when Busoni accepted him, the course of study to begin in January of 1921. Later that year, Karoline "Lenja" Blamauer and Greta Edelmann took the train from Zurich to Berlin with a new dance act they had worked up.

So Kurt and Linnerl finally reach the same place at the same time, as if in a screwball comedy of the 1930s: and when they meet they will meet cute.

2

Artist's Life

Weimar Berlin is a romance as locked into history as Renaissance Florence or Dickensian London: as a capitalist Babylon high on jazz cocaine where a coterie of artists, musicians, and writers invented the twentieth century. It was Neverland for grownups, though it started its modern saga as a warriors' city, a garrison town of the Prussian military caste. Officers' whim was law; intellectuals avoided the place. There wasn't even a university until 1810. But the consolidation of German states into the Second Reich, in 1871, forced the creation of Imperial Berlin, hastily erecting a pride of public buildings to headquarter the trappings of state. Then, in 1920, Greater Berlin absorbed its suburbs into a metropolis of nearly four million, after New York and London the third biggest address in the world.

Weltstadt is the German term for a town this grand: a topmost cultural capital, "city of the world." Yet unlike others such—Paris or Rome, say—Berlin became a capital before it had a culture. Even New York, with little sheer time behind it, coordinated the social and artistic traditions that mark the *Weltstadt* by the mid-nineteenth century. Berlin in effect created its traditions overnight.

Other Germans made a policy of loathing Berlin. It was ugly, they said. It was rude, immoral, criminal, its people always hurrying to some slimy assignation, its business life a black market. "*Alles schwindel!*" (Everything's a cheat!) was the gleeful cry of a popular song of late Weimar, in 1931: Papa cheats, Mama cheats, Aunt Otilie cheats . . . the whole family cheats, right down to "*der kleine Hund*" (Fido). Buyers, sellers, burghers, politicians, "*Jedes Girl und jeder Boy.*" Even in children's literature, in Erich Kästner's phenomenally popular *Emil und die Detectiven*, the plot centers on theft—by an adult of a sleeping child, no less—and a horde of the kids of Berlin unite to unmask the thief.

Mark Twain called Berlin "the German Chicago," because the whole place was in a hurry. "A favorite word of the time was 'Tempo,'" wrote Brian Ladd in *The Ghosts of Berlin*. "When the Jewish-owned Ullstein press syndicate launched a tabloid newspaper of that name, in 1928, it immediately acquired the nickname '*die jüdische Hast*'—'Jewish haste,'" a colloquial German phrase that recalls the linkage of Jews, commerce, and perpetual motion.

There were other comparisons. Bertolt Brecht saw Berlin as his personal atelier, filled with his workshop elves helping him sort out newspaper stories, political observations, and trendy sayings, all to swell a scenario as Brecht executed his revolution in the writing, staging, and acting of plays. That was Brecht's Berlin; Hitler's was a raw city to be rebuilt as the Nazi capital of the world, renamed Germania—right after the place was purged of its artists, musicians, and writers, especially Brecht. More than anywhere else in Europe, Berlin was the location of the future.

Another of those cabaret numbers caroled, "*Es Liegt in der Luft!*" (It's in the Air!). Whatever "it" was—the song doesn't quite specify—it felt "idotic" but also "hypnotic." And there *was* something in the Berlin air. Something bracing; everybody noticed it. It lay in the city's geography, overlooking the junction of two rushing watercourses—the Spree, which flows up from the southeast through what was once the twin villages of Berlin and Cölln, and the Havel, into which the Spree pours at Greater Berlin's western edge. The two run on together to join the Elbe at Havelberg, thence to the port city of Hamburg and the North Sea. Berlin counts as well much park- and farmland, cutting the typical metropolitan industrial effusions with a sort of organic central air-conditioning.

But "Berlin means boys" was Christopher Isherwood's cry of eureka when he arrived, in early 1929. Actually, Berlin meant Everyone for Hire. This was partly because of the economic tantrums of the Weimar period, from the Inflation to unemployment, but it was also because of the racy, experimental nature of life in Berlin. There was a legend that the stone lions on the Boulevard Unter den Linden would roar if a virgin walked past them; the lions never roared.

"What did you expect, a virgin in this place?" comes the reply from the Berliner *Schnauze*. The word means "snout," but it stands for a particular brand of knowing sarcasm, native to Berliners of all classes, roughly comparable to New York's "Fuggedaboudit." It wasn't simply that sex-for-hire permeated Berlin: it was the specialist nature of the work. Berlin's gay scene was internationally celebrated, not for concepts of dignity and equality but for its flamboyant role-playing, with schoolboys dressed as sailors dancing in after-hours dives with stockbrokers or government ministers made up as brides. Prostitute culture was so evolved that it spoke its own language—"grasshoppers" were homeless women who met clients outdoors somewhere; "boot girls" advertised their sexual forte according to the color of their footgear.

All this was a sign, to some, that postwar Germany—mainly Berlin but the Weimar Republic generally—had gone out of control. Another sign was the sudden cluster of *Lustmorde* (thrill killings) in both art and life. All at once, in the early 1920s, reading about demented serial homicides became, almost, the rage. Carl Grossmann sexually assaulted and stabbed fourteen young women to death, then hacked their corpses into bits, some of which he kept and others of which he sold to butcher shops or threw into one of Berlin's many canals. Karl Denke, a deacon of his Lutheran congregation in Münsterberg, killed and cannibalized thirty victims for more than twenty years before he was exposed. Like Grossmann, Denke hanged himself while in custody, but unlike Grossmann Denke kept meticulous records of his activities, noting the dates of each murder and his victims' physical characteristics. (His jottings were exact enough to exculpate another man who had been jailed for one of Denke's killings.) Fritz Haarmann, of Hanover, was the homosexual in this set, with a tally of more than two dozen, memorialized in children's doggerel popular in the 1920s in variant versions. Here's one:

> Warte, warte nur ein Weilchen,
> Bald kommt Haarmann auch zu dir.
> Mit dem Hacke-Hacke Beilchen
> Macht er Rindsgulasch aus dir.*

The best known of this group was Peter Kürten, the "Düsseldorf Killer," convicted in 1931 of nine murders, though he probably slayed many more, mostly women and very young children. Fritz Lang is said to have modeled the childkiller played by Peter Lorre in *M* (1931) after Kürten, because the arts were keen to explore this new aspect of life in uproarious Weimar, the land of Here You May. The artists Otto Dix and George Grosz especially seemed to people their view of daily life with homicidal ghouls. Grosz's *When It Was All Over, They Played Cards* is a black-and-white drawing of three men gaming at a kitchen table in a run-down apartment, one of them perched on a crate into which a murdered woman's corpse has been carelessly stuffed.

Lang's *M* is regularly singled out as somewhat sympathetic to the killer, because of an episode near the film's end. The police have pressured the underworld on the theory that all crime—even *Lustmord*—lies in their purview and power, and the criminals identify Lorre in a chalked M (for *Mörder*, meaning "Murderer") on the back of his coat. Hunted, caught, and tried by his fellow outlaws, Lorre cries out hysterically that he is helpless in his addiction to killing little girls, that no one understands what hell he lives in.

---

* Which is, roughly: *Wait a bit and you'll go pop!*
      Haarmann's coming just for you.
      With his axeblade, chop and chop.
      Then he'll cook you into stew.

Virtually every film historian sees this as a welcome humanizing of the demon. They eagerly feel his pain. However, it is the victims and their mothers that Lang humanizes—in the first murder, relayed to us in the increasingly desperate actions of the victim's mother, cooking dinner and constantly looking down the apartment-building stairway; or when Lorre sidles up to a girl in front of an eye-filling shop window. "*Bücher, Bilder, Plastik*" reads the shop sign—Books, Pictures, Dolls—but it's really a gadget store, a fairyland to attract the young. As we worry, the girl's mother suddenly appears to take her away, unmistakably placing Lang and us on one side and the murderer on the other. For a final Langian touch, Lorre's nemesis, the leader of Berlin's outlaw community—a subculture but also an organization—is ruthless yet intelligent and determined. Heroic, even: and he is disguised (ironically or perhaps not ironically) in a police uniform.

This was the radical art of Weimar, and, clearly, Karoline and Kurt were now headed for a sort of test, a crucible: the place in which rich talent undergoes development and fulfillment while the limited talent fails. Karoline was simply obeying the laws of the entertainment industry prevailing in Europe at the time: one can make a hit in the provinces, but one makes a reputation in the capital— Paris, London, Budapest . . . Berlin. Kurt, however, was once again creating his future, using the Busoni master class as an ontological process: to sample the kinds of music to discover which one seemed the most promising. This is Berlin as a laboratory. However, the city was more than Germany's cultural capital. It was where World War I had moved on to.

The war had brought about an almost civilization-wide revulsion at the Old Order and its values. The most obvious example was the overthrowing of the Russian autocracy; a less obvious revolution is that of the New York theatre world, which saw the rise of a generation of writers headed by Eugene O'Neill and animated by expansive social critique; the flowering of the musical; and the adoption of wisecrack humor as the voice of a no-longer submissive working class that, moved to the Hollywood talkie, became the voice of the Depression generation. But the place where the insurgence of art, social innovation, and fury at the war's outcome were all most strongly felt was Berlin in the Weimar period.

Some writers find the roots of Weimar Berlin in earlier years; this ignores the massive upheaval in postwar attitudes in the West generally and Germany in particular. Essentially, intellectual Germans felt that the war had revealed the incompetence of monarchist politics and the corruption of social hierarchies and the Rule of Fathers. Meanwhile, nationalist Germans held that the war had ended but hadn't been lost and thus needed to be started up again till the Enemy—both at home and across the borders—was defeated.

Yet it was a war about nothing. The Sarajevo assassinations were bound to lead to a strictly local fight, as Austria crushes Serbia. No other nation had a place in the quarrel; and Europe had not seen continent-wide eruptions since Napoleon. On the contrary, the Congress of Vienna hoped to limit conflict to brief excursions (like the Franco-Prussian War) or neighborhood rumbles (like the Balkan Wars of 1912–1913). This new war in 1914 was to have been, in effect, a Third Balkan War. But the Prussian military caste running Berlin feared that hostilities with Russia were inevitable and that Germany had to take on the sluggish eastern colossus before it industrialized its military response time. Historians generally blame Germany for the disaster that overtook the mixture of finesse and brinkmanship in the weeks that followed Sarajevo. Even that professional contrarian A. J. P. Taylor specified three villains, all German or Austrian.* The notion that partial mobilization led to total mobilization in a kind of diplomatic hysteria has been set aside as shallow and romantic. As Robert Conquest put it, "The long-held ideas that World War I came about through accidental concatenations, or that it was due to commercial

---

* They were the former German Chief of Staff Alfred von Schlieffen, Reich Chancellor Theobold von Bethmann Hollweg, and the Austrian Foreign Minister, Leopold Berchtold. Schlieffen, who died in 1913, gave his name to the famous Plan that became an obsession of the German High Command, by which their right flank on the Western Front would drive through the Low Countries, thence west and south in France to encircle Paris and cut into the French Army at its rear. It was supposed to win the war in the west in six weeks.

rivalries, has been abandoned by most historians, and it is now clear enough that the Kaiser's regime was inherently headed for war."

To the rest of Europe, that was the central issue—Germany's responsibility. To Germans, the issue was: How did we lose without being invaded or laying down our arms? For four years, a controlled press told of nothing but success, and, after all, Germany had beaten Russia. Who had surrendered? Not Germany: a band of traitors snatching defeat, so to say, from the jaws of victory.

This was the infamous conspiracy theory of the *Dolchstoss,* the "stab in the back": liberals, Bolsheviks, and Jews threw the war away when Germany was about to win it. On the contrary, Germany was dissolving in revolution, famine, and bankruptcy. The British blockade of German ports was starving the civilian population; the American Expeditionary Force was overrunning German positions in the trenches. An invasion of the homeland was mere days away. The presiding generals, Paul von Hindenburg and Erich Ludendorff, refused to besmirch their reputations with surrender, leaving the leaders of the Social Democratic Party to sue for peace to save their country. It was a fatal mistake for democracy. The war had been the work of the old regime; losing it had been the work of Hindenburg and Ludendorff. By ending the war *themselves,* the Social Democrats took the blame for a monumental failure they did not cause while making the incipient republic the apparent instrument of humiliation and weakness.

Worse, the first German democracy had to start by signing a blank check for reparations to be totted up later. Historians blame the Allies for "punitive" retribution—but "The hour has struck for the weighty settlement of our accounts," said the French Prime Minister, Georges Clemenceau. In sheer numbers, operating the war had cost the French over 140 billion gold francs and would now cost them nearly 135 billion in repairing material damage to land and property—some 275 billion francs in a nation whose annual budget before the war began was no more than five billion. "While Germany was quite intact," writes the historian Alistair Horne, "the shattered skeletons of broken towns across the northern countryside of France glared reproachfully." And as Margaret MacMillan records in *Paris 1919,* "A quarter of French men between eighteen and thirty had died . . . Twice as many again of its soldiers had been wounded . . . Six thousand square miles of France, which before the war had produced 20 percent of its crops, 90 percent of its iron ore and 65 percent of its steel, were utterly ruined."

Much of this devastation occurred when the German Army retreated at the war's end, blowing up or burning virtually everything it passed. Clemenceau personally remembered the Franco-Prussian War—and the punitive reparations Germany exacted when it was the winner. "My life hatred," Clemenceau said, "has been for Germany because of what she has done to France." Is it simply a legend that he asked to be buried standing up and facing east?

Further, Germany itself had exacted a punitive settlement from Russia when it dropped out of the war after the Bolshevik takeover— and the Allies knew that the Kaiser planned to bill them for the war if they lost. And more: if reparations were *not* punitive—crippling, to be exact—Germany would be able to mount another war, with the love of atrocity that it apparently regarded as correct military style. To pick one instance, the Belgian university town of Louvain, a gem of medieval architecture with a priceless library of books antedating Gutenberg, was destroyed by the German Army even though it was of no strategic value. Its surviving population was mercilessly driven out, and, at the sight of the library, the Germans reacted as barbarians instinctively do and burned it all away to ash. Was this one of European civilization's essential nations, the land of Goethe and Beethoven? In *Faust*, Goethe's hero cries out, *"Zwei Seelen wohnen, ach, in meiner Brust"* (Two souls dwell within me), and one soul was culture but the other was war, beyond ruthless into a very immolation of culture.

"The real problem with the peace," says the historian Niall Ferguson, "was not that it was too harsh, but that the Allies failed to enforce it. . . . Rather than using occupation as an incentive to encourage reparation-payment, the Allies—or rather the French— sought to use the threat of a larger occupation as a sanction to discourage default. . . . It encouraged the Germans to gamble that . . . the French were bluffing."

In literal terms, the Weimar Republic lasted fifteen years; in effect, it didn't last a day, because from its inception much of its power structure anticipated the Nazi state: in the army's tolerance of right-wing aggression and the law courts' coddling of right-wing terrorists. No wonder the arts world was radical. It was obsessed with monsters and their victims, as if daily life were a horror film; and with the glory and despair of the Western Front, because the war about nothing *hadn't* ended; and with the deconstruction of theatre realism into fantastical epics, to reflect the disorder that democracy begot.

The republic failed also because it tried to instill middle-class values on the federal level amid a storm of hatred—from both right and left—for middle-class behavior. Extremists loathed the debate, planning, compromise, and above all respect for others' opinions that characterizes what Germans call *der Mittelstand*. The struggle for the control of Germany's two souls was the Weimar Republic's fault line, for extremists were determined to dominate the world or destroy it.

And right into the middle of all this, Karoline Blamauer and Greta Edelmann stepped off the train from Zurich in the fall of 1921 with trunks of costumes for their ballerina duo act. Karoline's mentor Richard Révy met them and deposited Linnerl in a room in his boarding house while Greta went off to stay with a relative. Interestingly, the memoirs of Lotte Lenya give no indication of how she viewed the political war then breaking into constant street battles and even assassinations. Perhaps, like many others, she saw it as just another symptom of the Republic's neurosis. "The really important thing during any crisis"—so said a veteran of Berlin's 1920s to the writer Otto Friedrich—"is whether the streetcars are running. If the streetcars keep running, then life is bearable."

Sadly, Linnerl and Greta found no bookings for their act; and Berlin was dingy and hungry and penniless after Zurich. Although the Inflation had not reached ruination level, it was proceding apace, and Linnerl was bemused to learn that the only bargain left in town was little potted cactuses. So she made a collection of them, on a typical Lenyan theory of survival in bad times: if you can't afford what you enjoy, enjoy what you can afford.

Her passion was theatregoing. Révy had instilled in her that love of the lively arts that would be one of the binding forces in her and Kurt's relationship. She attended almost indiscriminately, from Shakespeare to music hall—and not excluding professional wrestling. This was very popular in Germany and rather theatrically presented, with the contenders more or less invincibly parading into the arena to the tune of Julius Fučik's "Entry of the Gladiators."* Greta Edelmann, however, wasn't captivated by cactuses and wrestling, and when she was offered a choreographer's job in Elberfeld, way off to the west near Düsseldorf, Greta quit Berlin. Karoline Blamauer was now on her own.

But "I was glad when [Greta] left," she wrote later. "Now I didn't have to run daily from one stupid agent to another." Then Révy told her they were seeing dancers for a children's pantomime; he hoped to attach himself to the production as overall director. The work was entitled *Zaubernacht* (Magic Night), the author of the scenario was Wladimir Boritsch, and the composer was Kurt Weill.

Meanwhile, Weill himself had begun his master class in January of the same year, 1921, encountering in Master Ferruccio Busoni the first Weill mentor who was a figure of world-class importance. By coincidence, Busoni, too, had been given a birth name of cultural significance—several, in fact. Ferruccio Dante Michelangiolo Benvenuto Busoni bore tokens of one poet and two artists, and his family heritage was famously half Italian and half German. Thus he was congenitally linked to two primary music cultures of Central Europe, the song of one merged with the symphony of the other.

However, Busoni's social ancestry was entirely Italian, because his German "half," on his mother's side, was actually only a quarter, and

---

* My readers may know the piece without recognizing the title, for its descending chromatic melody has long been used on Hollywood soundtracks to accompany circus footage.

in any case his mother was born and raised in Trieste, an Italian colony in the middle of Slav territory.

All the same, Busoni spanned two worlds: musical ones. He was part Romantic, part neo-Classical, imbued with the nineteenth-century cult of the piano virtuoso and the excitement of display yet attracted to the eighteenth-century love of the tidy miniature. The Romantic sought fulfillment in the vast thematic goulashes and dense orchestral textures introduced by Richard Wagner and enlarged by Richard Strauss; the Classicist reveled in chamber orchestras and a discrete separation of parts. The Romantic was haunted by a fear of engulfment by the spirit world and hid himself in myth; the Classicist tamed heroic romance and, with measured step, entered the sunlight to revive the figures of the *commedia dell'arte* and the transparent counterpoint of Bach.

Bridging these two worlds makes Busoni's output complex. His Piano Concerto (1904), one of the greatest technical challenges in the repertory and, at some seventy-five minutes, physically exhausting, combines Classical stability with Romantic fervor. The five movements culminate in a five-part men's chorus—a hallmark of Romantic style ever since Beethoven added a (mixed) chorus to the finale of the sacred Ninth. Yet Busoni's second-movement scherzo toys with an undulating Italian folk song (marked *"in modo napolitano"*), an intrusion upon solemn Romantic unity much favored by Classicists.

Why was Kurt drawn to Busoni in the first place? It might be because, unlike virtually every established composer of the time, Busoni was uncategorizable—and so was Kurt Weill. No wonder he never went to Vienna and Schönberg. That would have meant immersing himself in the most "difficult" style available. Busoni was "easy" yet a rich mix—"the last Renaissance man," Kurt wrote in 1925, a year after Busoni's death.

Busoni was the ideal chief for a master-class group, because the art of composition—in effect, the imagination that drives creativity—is too abstract to "teach" in the first place. The master class really functions well only for performers. Singers and instrumentalists are the software of music, easily instructed: they perform and the master critiques their technique, stylistics, *espressivo*. It's a skills set; skills can be improved. But composers are the hardware: once they have absorbed the crafts, from harmony to fugue, they work in the bizarre alternate universe of creation, an unteachable state beyond "skill."

So Busoni's class would be less a seminar than a relationship with a genius. Kurt and his four fellow pupils, none of whom became even temporarily famous, met more or less every weekday in Busoni's home for a sort of intellectuals' tea. Over time, the students composed and the master commented, so it was pedagogical but also dialectical: as if Socrates played a piano concerto as big as Europe. Busoni didn't think of his group as students; he called them "disciples."

They were virtually working musicians, because they got to hear their music performed in public. On December 7, 1922 the Berlin Philharmonic gave a concert devoted entirely to the "*Schüler aus der Meisterklasse*" of "Prof. Dr. Ferruccio Busoni." Wladimir Vogel, the oldest of the quintet at twenty-six, offered his Symphonic Prelude; Robert Blum an Overture, Intermezzo, and Rondo; Walther Geiser Overture To a Comedy; and Luc Balmer the ambitious last movement of a symphony in the form of Theme, Countertheme, Recitative, Reprise, and Finale. Kurt's contribution was the Chorale-Fantasy from his Divertimento, for small orchestra and men's chorus, with the choir of the Kaiser Wilhelm Memorial Church.

Clearly, Busoni's pupils were composers-in-training on the elite level. Even so, the pianist Artur Schnabel, later to be the first to record a complete cycle of Beethoven's thirty-two sonatas, thought Busoni as much a kibitzer as an inspirer. Schnabel revered the man, but in his memoirs he wrote that Busoni "had a great affection for freakish people . . . With a devilish glee he would tell them the most absurd things about music, which he simply invented. They accepted blindly all these fantasies and would afterwards spread them as the last word on music."

It isn't clear whether Schnabel was referring thus to the master class per se, but we do know that Kurt found exposure to Busoni ideal for his development as a composer, for he stayed with the class from

January of 1921 to December of 1923—three years, a very long stay by master-class standards. Among Kurt's compositions were the usual string quartet (his second, after a student piece for Humperdinck at the Hochschule) and a shortish seven-piece song cycle for soprano and five instrumentalists on medieval texts, *Frauentanz* (Dance For Women). There was a symphony as well, but Busoni thought it technically deficient, and he assigned Kurt to Philipp Jarnach, Busoni's primary disciple, for remedial study. In deference to the master, Kurt set the symphony aside, and in due course it simply vanished. At his death, Kurt thought it gone forever—but we will hear of this work again, much later on.

Frauentanz is one of Kurt's very best early pieces, in which the interaction among the soprano soloist and the flute, clarinet, horn, bassoon, and viola creates a bizarre intimacy. In the fifth number, accompanied by viola alone, a male surprises three girls in an orchard and seizes one for a kiss. Each tiny verse ends with a *"harbalorifa"* nonsense refrain, and, as the maid tries to resist, Kurt unveils her secret delight as the *harbalorifas* become more and more tentative, a marvelous touch.

Chamber works like *Frauentanz* are practical, because even amateur outfits can take them up. Better, Germany was in the middle of a chamber-music fad, and prestigious festivals were always scouting for the next sensation. One's reputation could spike overnight if the public cheered one's piece—and it's going to happen to Kurt Weill a few pages hence, at the premiere of the first version of *Mahagonny*, as a staged song cycle. For now, Kurt's great career breakthrough lay in his getting a publisher—in fact, Europe's outstanding publisher of young classical talent, Universal-Edition. Busoni wrote to Universal's chief, Emil Hertzka, with a personal recommendation, citing Kurt's second string quartet as "'modern' through and through without any unpleasant features." We hear the reticence of the conservative in this, for Busoni was paradoxically new-fangled in an old-fashioned way, suspicious of "too much" innovation.

Hertzka, however, was entirely new-fangled. Though in appearance an old codger in a Santa Claus beard, he specialized in new-wave talent—including Schönberg, unpleasant features and all. The typical pale-green cover of a Universal printing of your music was the mark of your arrival in the great world, and Kurt soon saw his own Universal edition, number 7700—that same Busoni-approved string quartet, numbered "One" as if Kurt's first (and thus suppressing the earlier Hochschule quartet). He also got a monthly stipend from Hertzka as an advance against future royalties, a very welcome sign that Universal expected to sell enough Kurt Weill to have to pay them.

As it happened, when Kurt made his approaches to Universal, in mid-1923, the Inflation was in full rage and moving implacably into the liquidation of the German economy. In 1914, before the war began, one American dollar was worth 4.20 German marks. In 1922, one dollar was worth 3,000 marks, then yet more marks through 1923, when the government, avidly pumping ever more worthless paper currency into the crisis, produced its masterpiece, the 100-trillion-mark note. By then the dollar was worth 4,200,000,000,000 marks: exactly one trillion times the dollar's exchange rate in 1914.

Foreign money and objects for barter—especially food and shoes— were all that held value in the land, and the population survived by conning and finagling. The social hierarchies by which Germans lived dissolved into the miserable hating the "speculators." Hating farm folk, sitting on their food stores like Fafner on his hoard. Hating industrialists. Workers. Outsiders. Jews. It was at the Inflation's evil height, when a stein of beer cost a billion marks, that Hitler executed the failed Beer Hall Putsch in Munich, on November 9, 1923. One week later, as if in self-defense, the government finally came up with a solution to the Inflation in the Rentenmark. It was a rabbit-out-of-a-hat fix, with ruthless budgetary cutbacks, and it was instantaneously successful. The Inflation, along with the social dislocation that encourages revolutionary outbreaks from both left and right, was over.

So when Kurt finally signed his Universal contract, not only had he gained position professionally: all Germany was now to move into a period of social stability and economic growth. It is tempting to romanticize the coincidence and see a little more destiny at work, for Kurt, barely twenty-four, now looked forward to one of those golden ages with which Western Civilization periodically honeymoons with a new generation of creators. The very month Kurt signed his Universal contract, April of 1924, was also when the American banker Charles G. Dawes presented a plan to ease the schedule of Germany's reparations premiums (though not the amount, set by Versailles at 226 billion marks).* Adapted in August and put into execution on September 1, 1924, the Dawes Plan greatly eased tensions throughout Europe; it was succeeded by the Young Plan (after a second American banker, Owen D. Young), which reduced the reparations bill to 34.5 billion marks, spread out over payments to be completed by 1988.

And Kurt Weill and Lotte Lenja finally met—or finally didn't meet, depending on how one views it. It was at the auditions for *Zaubernacht*, the aforementioned children's piece that Richard Révy had looked to for career advancement, with a Berlin credit as *Regisseur* (director). Révy did not get an offer—Franz-Ludwig Hörth directed, to Mary Zimmerman's choreography—but Karoline Blamauer did, as a dancer. Out of loyalty to her mentor, she turned it down. In fact, with the insouciant "So what?" that Lotte Lenja was to maintain as her signature mood (saluted in the song of that title that Kander and Ebb wrote for her in *Cabaret*), she didn't bother to decline the part. When Révy told her he didn't get the job, she simply didn't show up for rehearsals.

This is our first look at (to borrow a title from Thomas Mann)

---

* Some might wonder why the government didn't pay off its reparations bill during the Inflation. It wasn't possible: the terms called for payment in gold marks, not paper bills. However, Arthur R. G. Solmssen's novel *A Princess in Berlin* (1980) includes a stunning scene, set during the Inflation, wherein the last surviving scion of an impoverished noble family walks into the bank that owns the mortgage on his land and pays the entire amount off in worthless paper. The bill totals nearly four million marks—now worth, we are told, "about one hundred and thirty dollars." The very appearance of this *Junker* prince—"very young, very blond, with gloves, riding boots, sword handle protruding through a vent in the long greatcoat"—accompanied by a corporal bearing black leather briefcases "packed so full that they were almost round"—in the Jewish counting house is a tell. So is the fact that the bankers had compassionately carried the mortgage in default rather than foreclose to sell the family's ancient estate "to some Ukrainian stock market operator." This was Germany after the war about nothing: a dog-eat-dog chaos that all but begged artists to turn it into art. Solmssen gives us, albeit decades after it happened, a *Threepenny Opera* of the aristocracy.

Lotte in Weimar: Karoline as a theatre animal in Berlin, ready to make her history. Of course we want to know how she presented herself. The auditions. They call her name: "Fräulein Lotte Lenja!" Her new stage name, the paint still wet on it; she didn't realize at first that they meant her. Barefoot and ready to go through her routine, she asked the unseen pianist in the pit if he could play Strauss' "On the Beautiful Blue Danube."

"*Ja*," he replied, with mild amusement, "I think I could get through that."

He was Kurt Weill, and they didn't see each other—didn't *meet*, really—because he was below her sight line under the overhang in the orchestra pit.

And that was the whole of their first encounter. But they'll cross paths again quite soon.

3

They All Look Alike

Zaubernacht brings us back to 1922, when Kurt was still in Busoni's master class. A one-act about nighttime doings in the nursery, it brought the name of Kurt Weill into the commercial theatre for the first time, in a Christmas booking for a few matinees at the Theater am Kurfürstendamm, a major house. There was further distinction in the participation of Elfriede Marherr-Wagner, singing the work's sole vocal bit, as the Fairy.* More interesting yet, *Zaubernacht* was to give Kurt Weill his first Broadway credit, again as a Christmas children's show, at the Garrick Theatre, in 1925. True, this was an obscure credit, not only for the usual limited holiday run but because the Garrick was by that time a house in its dotage. Standing on Thirty-fifth Street just east of Herald Square, it was out of the way, a place for bare-budget

---

* Elfriede Marherr, as she was more usually billed, was a Staatsoper soprano of the second division, not a genuine star but all the same a company member at Berlin's most prestigious (of three) opera house. She is known to opera buffs by accident, because she sings the supporting role of Brangäne in one of the most reissued of 78s, Frida Leider's recording of the Narration and Curse from *Tristan und Isolde*. Marherr also sang one of the Three Ladies in another 78 evergreen, Thomas Beecham's reading of *The Magic Flute*.

companies like the fledgling Theatre Guild; or for the *Garrick Gaieties*, an informal Guild revue featuring Rodgers and Hart's first complete Broadway score.

Still, we note that twenty-two-year-old Kurt has made it onto one of Berlin's main stages, in his first work of theatrical narrative: the music of his future. In the 1940s, during his réclame as composer of a couple of smash hits, he still recalled *Zaubernacht* as "a stepping stone to success." Indeed, the music does suggest a storyteller at work, as two children undergo a toys-come-to-life adventure harried by Hansel and Gretel's Witch. Always an ingenious orchestrator, capable of making a pit of nine or ten sound like two dozen, Kurt relaxed his "modern" edge in a musical kindergarten, scored for string quintet, flute (and piccolo), bassoon, piano, and percussion. *Zaubernacht*'s impresario, Wladimir Boritsch, took the parts with him to America for that New York stand. The orchestration then vanished for eighty-one years.

The piano score survived, at least, and Kurt had extracted about half of his instrumentation in a suite he entitled, misleadingly, *Quodlibet* (1923).* But the complete *Zaubernacht* could not be performed, either on stage or in concert. A Welsh musician, Meirion Bowen, undertook a restoration and rescoring, adding in a clarinet part to the original nine players; this was premiered at Cologne in 2008.

No one knew at that time that the original parts had remained with Boritsch, who had Americanized his name to Boritch, and that his widow had passed the parts on to the Sterling Memorial Library at Yale University, in 1959. For some reason, the Boritch bequest was not catalogued but simply locked in a safe and forgot. In 2005, a locksmith was called, the safe was opened, and along with business notes, a set of silver flatware, and odds and ends, the librarians found the lost *Zaubernacht* orchestra score.

---

* The true quodlibet (Latin for, roughly, "Perform it as you please to") is a piece incorporating different melodies, either in succession or simultaneously. The latter is the more typical, as in many choruses in Gilbert and Sullivan or duets fashioned by Irving Berlin to partner a "smooth" melody with a "rough" one. Berlin's "Play a Simple Melody" virtually defines the quodlibet, with its lyrical strain, its ragtime response, then the two sung at the same time.

This coup of rediscovery will become almost routine in the Kurt Weill saga: the loss and reclamation of music from the German half of his career. It reminds us of the difficulty, during forced emigration, of keeping one's work intact, and it tells us why, after he got to Broadway, Kurt Weill painstakingly retained personal ownership of his compositions. Such bookkeeping was all but unknown among the writers of Broadway musicals, which is why so many shows of the 1930s and 1940s (and even later) have to be "restored" to be heard again. Orchestral charts, scripts, lyrics, music . . . any element of a musical produced on Broadway may be missing. Even onetime hits turn out to be Humpty-Dumpty titles, never to be put back together. Mindful of how the Nazis not only wanted to kill him but kill his work as well—even to hunting down prints of the film made of *The Threepenny Opera*— Kurt oversaw publication of his music to the last detail, including intricate indications of his orchestration in the piano-vocal scores. Further, after the New York production and post-Broadway tour, the performing materials for his shows would be returned to him for safekeeping and potential revival in their original form.

So, again, we find in Kurt Weill one of the most doggedly ungovernable of creators—like Julien Sorel the resolute author of his life. Or like—to light upon brand names of Western Civilization's stock in free will—Socrates, Cervantes, Voltaire. To put it another way, Kurt was born into a Jewish family scarcely a century after the ghettoes of Europe had been liberated—a religious family, at that. Yet Kurt chose to live areligiously, with a spouse who was Roman Catholic yet similarly areligious, and to answer his professional vocation in the theatre, historically a very revel of unbelievers. In many European countries as late as the eighteenth century, actors could not be buried in churchyards, or in any public cemeteries.

The freedom unique to Western society lies in the making of such choices, and Kurt as well had to choose a "music" from the broadest range of styles ever available in the history of the art. First Beethoven, then Berlioz and Liszt, then Wagner expanded the very sound of music. By the mid-1920s, the menu was vast. *Kolossal Spätromantik*. Neo-Classicism. Schönbergian tone row. Stravinsky's dry styles-within-styles. Soon enough, Prokofyef and Shostakovich would add to this their grotesque tragic-satiric voice, as if mocking the very devastation of the wartorn twentieth century.

Kurt must have known that he was invented to be a nonconformist of some kind. He certainly didn't want to write what other composers could write. From *Frauentanz* on if not before, Kurt Weill never sounds like anyone else, which is why he is so easy to imitate. Ironically, his teacher Busoni is inimitable in the worst way: inconclusive, almost a theorist more than a composer. His music wasn't just music but a statement on the ontology of music. Of course he would have made an opera on *Faust* as his masterpiece—Faust the magician-scientist and lover-psychopath of Western art, as beautiful as a youth sculpted by the devil. Busoni called it *Doktor Faust* (1925), and Busoni was Doktor Faust. His untimely and painful death of kidney disease in 1924 all but shattered Kurt, as so often happens in the passing of one who is not only dear but has helped you to discover a better version of yourself.

How is any student to emulate a Busoni? The most apparent link between master and pupil lies in the quirky commentative aspect of neo-Classical music, its love of referencing. Romanticism immerses the listener in sensuality: Be one with me! Neo-Classicism jokes around: Look what I'm doing! Thus, Stravinsky builds a ballet, *Pulcinella* (1920), out of melodies from the eighteenth century, rescored for a modernist's tour of the archives, and the plot treats *commedia dell'arte* figures. The entire piece is a pastiche.

Comparably, though with as much innovation as restoration, Busoni created a double-bill of one-act operas, billing them as "*La Nuova Commedia dell'Arte*": *Arlecchino* (Harlequin) and *Turandot*, premiered together at the Zurich Stadttheater during Busoni's wartime exile in neutral Switzerland. The Romantic theatre beckoned one into a civilization-wide sharing of myth: as in Wagner's *Ring* in Wagner's drama palace at Bayreuth. There Wagner did away with the ceremonial aspects of opera-going, with the boxes where notables lorded over the public downstairs and with the house lights burning so the audience could read the libretto or glance about. Wagner submerged one in the dream.

In revolt, Busoni (and others) brought back the *commedia dell'arte* because it broke the dream up as one pins a balloon. Wake-up nudges abound: in *Arlecchino*, there is a little quotation of *Don Giovanni*'s Champagne Aria, "*Finch' Han dal Vino*," and the title role is a speaking one amid singers, which allows directors to cast comics or acrobats. (Arlecchino does have a bit to sing at one point, but he's offstage, so another cast member can fill in for him.) In *Turandot*, the Chinese setting allows Busoni to flood the action with Eastern "bustle" music and even, for unknown reasons, "Greensleeves."

The use of pastiche is essentially humorous, jesting with the public through its store of knowledge, as when, in Gilbert and Sullivan's *The Mikado*, at the line "By Bach interwoven with Spohr and Beethoven," Sullivan relishes the pairing of an also-ran with a thoroughbred by giving the clarinet and bassoon a quotation of Bach's Fantasia and Fugue in g minor. Or: in Saint-Saëns' *Le Carnival des Animaux*, the movement dedicated to "L'Éléphant," in an *Allegretto Pomposo*, derives its weight from a double-bass playing the Sylph Dance from Berlioz's *La Damnation de Faust*. The joke, of course, is that Berlioz's gossamer sprites have turned pachyderm simply through a switch in the scoring.

Alternatively, composers can invent their own quotations, so to say, creating new music in an old style, as in Offenbach's interpolation of Spanish rhythms or yodelling into his scores. Kurt made this sort of parody a feature of his work throughout his life, experimenting with the "voice" of his music like a new celebrity trying out different penmanship flourishes when handing out autographs. The raucous dance-hall two-step in *Happy End*; the absurdly maudlin piano solo in *Mahagonny*, to which an unsophisticated listener purrs, in philistine appreciation that Brecht must have relished, "*Das ist die ewige Kunst*" (That is eternal art); the cowboy song and French nurse's chanson in *Johnny Johnson* all suggest a composer traveling the world in search of fresh melody. One of Busoni's most potent pieces of advice warned Kurt not to fear letting pure song—even of the most elemental sort—beguile his scores. Referring to this much later, Kurt told a colleague that the fear of melody was "why 'modern music' got more and more removed from reality, from life, from . . . real emotions."

It was to become Kurt's credo—but not yet. He was still in a modernist mood when he met the librettist of his first opera. This was the distinguished playwright Georg Kaiser, who was looking for a composer to collaborate on a dance-pantomime. Kaiser had seen *Zaubernacht*, and he must have liked it, because he asked Fritz Stiedry, conductor of the premiere of Kurt's *Frauentanz* songs and a Kaiser intimate, to bring him and Kurt together.

For a twenty-four-year-old composer still in the Getting Mentioned phase yet short of a breakout success, an invitation from a prominent literary man was more than a honor: a sign that important work was expected of him. Early on, the plan to create a pantomime re-adjusted itself into a plan to turn one of Kaiser's recent plays, a one-acter called *Der Protagonist* (1921), into an opera. At some point in 1924, Kurt was asked to spend time with the Kaiser family at their villa, in Grünheide. "Greenheath" lay to the southeast of Berlin on one of the many lakes that dot the area, the lentil-shaped Petzsee. Kurt was told to take the suburban train out, to be met at the station by Kaiser's *au pair*. The two could then walk to Kaiser's house around the lake's circular edge—pleasant enough, but longish. And there was Kurt's bag to carry. Why not take the house rowboat to ferry Herr Weill straight across the water? Kaiser was an aficionado of ships great and tiny, and he commanded a flotilla at Grünheide, from paddle-boat to canoe. If watercraft could somehow be finagled into any event, it would be. So the trusty *au pair* would pick up the visitor in the rowboat.

"How will I know Herr Weill?" she asked Kaiser.

"All composers look alike," Kaiser replied, brushing this aside. *Himmel*, the questions they ask!

Do you believe in fate? The *au pair* was Lotte Lenja, whose stage career had not prospered. She had taken a position with the Kaisers that was halfway between employee and guest, because like everyone else the Kaisers—Georg and Margarethe and their children, Anselm, Sybille, and Laurenz—wanted to adopt her.

She loved telling this story, with the usual Lenja variations. In one version, Kurt recognizes her from her *Zaubernacht* audition, though he presumably couldn't have seen her from down in the orchestra pit. In another version, he impulsively asks her to marry him. Whatever happened in the rowboat, Lenja does seem to have got one detail wrong. When Kaiser said, "All composers look alike," she thought he was referring to a particular hat supposedly favored by composers, with a band around the crown and a broad brim. Weill did affect this model at this time, perhaps because it gave him a slightly exotic air—but in fact German composers did not sport a club hat. Kaiser was a wag, making another of his jokes. Maybe he was thinking of Kurt's hat; maybe he was being silly. What he could have said was: "He's about twenty-four years old, five foot three, balding, and he wears thick eyeglasses. His mouth is usually curved in an ironic smile that seems condescending, but you'll get used to it."

So Weill and Lenja have finally met, as she rows him across the lake to Georg Kaiser and to Weill's realization that he is a theatre animal and must make his home with theatre people. He has two realizations to come after that: one, that he must cut his "modern" style with the melody that Busoni had urged upon him, and, two, that he will be happiest doing this with Lenja singing his music. Just now, however, she is no more than an arresting young woman rowing him across the lake to his next mentor, the brilliant, bizarre, and extremely successful Georg Kaiser.

4

"But, Lenja, You Know You Come Right After My Music!"

Gerhart Hauptmann was the pre-eminent German playwright at the turn of the century. Most particularly, he was the leader of the realist movement in Central European theatre, akin to Ibsen and Strindberg in Scandinavia and admired above all for *Die Weber* (The Weavers, 1893), on the oppression of and resistance by Silesian textile workers. Hauptmann even won the Nobel Prize; few playwrights do.

But Hauptmann was overtopped by Georg Kaiser, the leader of the expressionst theatre movement, though Kaiser worked in many forms, roaming through mythology and history when not inventing odd blends of naturalism and fantasy. He wrote a Tristan und Isolde play as *König Hahnrei* (King Cuckold, 1913); a Socrates play as *Der Gerettete Alkibiades* (Alcibiades Saved, 1920); a St. Joan play as *Gilles und Jeanne* (1923), giving the sinister Gilles de Rais a major part. However, unlike Hauptmann—or Ibsen or Strindberg, for that matter—Kaiser lacked international importance. Even his most famous plays, the so-called *Gas* trilogy of *Die Koralle* (The Coral, 1917), *Gas I* (1918), and *Gas II* (1920), did not travel much.

Perhaps it's because Kaiser's expressionism turned the form inside out, soothing the distortions and excess that made it so theatrical, so shocking and adventurous, in its day. In Kaiser's hands, expressionism gets a makeover as nutty parables in which archetypal characters switch roles with each other, usually for no apparent reason. In *The Coral*, a figure called simply The Billionaire shoots The Secretary and then pretends to be The Secretary Who Shot the Billionaire. In the early plays of Eugene O'Neill, America's great expressionist, events proceed inexorably from one central problem, as in ancient Greece. In Kaiser, any character can at any time change the problem, virtually changing the play as well.

The best playwrights are like their characters. O'Neill not only wrote of doom but lived in it; and Kaiser was as unpredictable and whimsical as the people he wrote about. And the opera that Kaiser wrote with Kurt, *Der Protagonist*, concerns an actor in Elizabethan England who so confuses living with performing that he murders his beloved sister during a rehearsal because, lost in his role, he thinks it's part of the play. Company horrified, fast curtain.

Der Protagonist gave Kurt his first collaboration. He wasn't setting pre-existing words in a song cycle but engaging in debate with a part- ner on how the piece should sing, and he enjoyed himself immensely. Part of the fun lay in the way the Kaiser family welcomed him into their personal lives. Cut off from contact with his family, Kurt kept love alive through the mail, especially with his siblings Hans and Ruth. Kurt told his sister that the Kaisers "have become dear friends and perhaps the only ones who could replace part of what I lost when Busoni died."

Finished in early 1925, *Der Protagonist* would not reach the stage for a year, yet Kurt had made it onto the short list of the Young Turk composers of Weimar Germany. The *Frauentanz* songs, after a distin- guished Berlin premiere, would be heard at the Salzburg Festival and on the air. Another piece derived from Rilke, *Stundenbuch* (Book of Hours), a song cycle for baritone and orchestra that is now mostly lost, was given by the Berlin Philharmonic with Manfred Lewandowsky as soloist in January of 1925. An important work, the Concerto for Violin and Wind Orchestra (dedicated to Joseph Szigeti, though he never played it), was first performed in Paris in June of 1925 and quickly became Kurt's most popular concert work.

Further, Kurt undertook a recurring column in the magazine *Der Deutsche Rundfunk* (German Radio), lasting from January of 1925 to 1929 (when a heavy workload made it troublesome), reviewing new work and generally considering the impact of this new tool of the music world. With the Inflation over, people were buying again, and city dwellers—in Berlin and Hamburg especially—found a home radio connection indispensable in enriching their lives with music. Then, too, German radio was fragmented in a network of stations, each able to share programs with others or sponsor its own. Thus, a mini-culture of pieces written on radio commission sprang up, with everything from plays with incidental scores to song cycles using odd chamber groupings. This open market of new music made the most offbeat composers into something approaching household names. Thus, when there was a theft in the bed-and-breakfast in which Kurt was living, and when the culprit accused Kurt of the robbery, the prosecutor asked if this was *the* Kurt Weill. When Kurt—presumably with some amusement—said he was indeed *the* Kurt Weill, the prosecutor turned on the accuser and he got six months.

Kurt's music at this time was generally atonal—a technical term, purely categorical, that has come into popular usage incorrectly as a term of personal judgment meaning "music I don't like." Written outside of the orderly harmonic structure of traditional Western music, atonality is simply a free use of musical materials. It is what Busoni meant by the "unpleasant features" of modern music. As we know, Busoni warned Kurt not to disdain melody—yet, in another part of the forest, Busoni also questioned Kurt's intention, then still inchoate, to write melodically. "What do you want to be," Busoni asks, in a famous quotation, "a Verdi of the poor?" This suggests the prestige blackmail that kept many composers avant-garde rather than traditional: the commentariat would scorn them if they, so to say, went Puccini. In Weimar's mid-1920s especially, modern was in the air; one couldn't rival that headline-catching Hindemith if one wasn't an *enfant terrible*—and

Alban Berg's *Wozzeck*, largely atonal, extremely expressionistic, and the classic in this line, was first performed at exactly this time, in 1925. Admirers of the *Threepenny Opera* Kurt Weill who encounter, say, the Violin Concerto, are nonplussed by the apparent lack of tunes. After all, the Weill they know is the composer who virtually invented "crossover" composition, fusing elite craftsmanship with melody that would colonize the globe.

We hear virtually nothing of that Kurt Weill at this point. His music for *Der Protagonist*, for example, suits the action without any melodic distinction, though it does enjoy two set pieces played as actors' pantomimes, the first comic and built around a goofy four-part madrigal and the second serious, punctuated by drastic eruptions from all over the orchestra.

However, an influence now steals into Kurt's life that is at once musical and not musical; and Kurt's life and music will change. Because Lotte Lenja may not be exaggerating when she tells us that Kurt proposed marriage to her when they crossed the Petzsee in that rowboat. Maybe he didn't utter the words "Will you marry me?" But she sensed his attraction to her; she was used to it by now, from men and women both. However, this man was no mere potential fancy. She didn't follow the classical music world at this time, but Kaiser must have warned her that Kurt Weill was of the leadership class, born to culture, young and free. Too short, yes. But gentle, and perhaps a piquant sort of dish in his bow tie and that broad-brimmed hat.

Just as German-literature students must learn the names of Goethe's mistresses with the start and end dates of their liaisons, Weill scholars will supply the name of Nelly Frank, Weill's only known love before Lenja. Married to another, Nelly was also, oddly, a distant member of the Weill family (Weill was in fact her maiden name) and, as well, related through her husband to the woman who married Kurt's brother Hans. Kurt and Nelly met at some event related to the nuptials, and, much as Goethe's work owes something to the passion sparked by his flames, Kurt dedicated the *Frauentanz* cycle to Nelly.

It makes a quaint introduction to Kurt's wooing of Lotte Lenja, because his letters to her in the beginning of their intimacy, from

December of 1924, suggest the amazed rhapsody of a young man in first bliss. "The most beautiful wish of my life," we read. There is fear in her displeasure, yet a twinge of satisfaction: only those who care really get mad at us. He is inexperienced in these matters, he explains, but he will learn. He will be her "*Lustknabe*" (roughly, "joyboy"). He is not merely enamored but poeticized; he does everything but break into "Younger Than Springtime." Then they quarrel and she hurts him with an attack word—in Swiss, no less ("*Tschumpel*," meaning "dope"). But they quickly make up, and he is back to sounding a merry note in the correspondence with a succession of gag signatures—from pet names ("Weillili," "Pünktchen," "Frosch," "Schnube") to sobriquets ("Buster," a bow to Hollywood's comic auteur Buster Keaton, whose films were a sensation in Berlin). As always in his letters to those who matter to him, Kurt writes of his music, as when he travels to his hometown of Dessau for the German premiere of his Violin Concerto. It was a mess, he tells Linnerl, with a conductor, Franz von Hoesslin, who doesn't correct the players' many klinkers. Perhaps he doesn't even hear them—yet von Hoesslin was a noted Wagnerian!

Music, music. We wonder to what extent Linnerl wants to follow the details of Kurt's career. But then one couldn't know Kurt Weill without hearing about his work: he was always either composing his music or thinking about his music or talking about his music.

Then Kurt and Linnerl moved in together. And *then*—on January 28, 1926—they were married, in a civil ceremony with just two witnesses. They then became, to all who knew them, Weill and Lenja. His religious parents were not overjoyed to have to embrace a Roman Catholic daughter-in-law, and upright folk of that day were also nervous at the thought of An Actress in the Family. As for the Blamauers, it is not clear when Lenja told her mother that her last name had been changed to Weill, or even when Weill, on his several trips to Vienna, actually met his mother-in-law. But Lenja did not share Weill's strong family feeling. "It'd be best," she once said, "if we could come into the world as orphans."

Neither Weill nor Lenja maintained traditional scruples about their marriage vows, either. Lenja was too sexually adventurous to "settle down," as our wistful phrase has it. Lenja wasn't the settling type. She married, she said, simply to still the tongues of gossips—but even in the libertarian world of artists she was known for her lavish appetite. Weill lived with it because he had no choice; anyway, it showed spirit, and a love of life. There was an excitement about her. Lys Symonette, the rehearsal pianist for many of Weill's New York shows, told Lenja's biographer Donald Spoto that Lenja was "ideal" for Weill: "She was bright without being educated or an intellectual. She was naturally musical without being a trained musician. And she was a highly erotic personality." Spoto himself adds, "She drew out the playfulness in [Weill], and the latent sensuousness. She could be impulsive and whimsical, and she loved to relax and enjoy herself—something he never did easily."

Then, too, Lenja had only just become a citizen of the Berlin theatre world, the most keyed-up and intense venue in what may have been the freest city on Europe. Through Georg Kaiser, Lenja had at last made some contacts that brought her work, understudying the lead in Shakespeare's *Romeo und Juliet* and then taking over the role when the star left. Performing was Lenja's delight, then and always—but it was invigorating, too, to enter the confraternity of the merry outlaws whose religion was art, frolic, and shattering bourgeois commandments. The two witnesses that Lenja had brought to her marriage ceremony were lesbians—keepsakes, perhaps, of her guiltless tour through the Berlin of "Here you may." Christopher Isherwood's "Berlin means boys" was incorrect: Berlin meant everything. Vienna was old-fashioned and Zurich efficiently placid, but Berlin was the Wild West without a sheriff.

And, after all, Weill was a part-time husband, because even when he wasn't working he was working. He carried the music in his head, so he didn't need a piano. At any moment, even if you were telling him something important (important, at any rate, to you), his eyes would get glassy and he'd take out a piece of paper—anything, from an envelope to the back of an old bill—and scribble a staff and some notes on it: his next theme. Lenja was learning about the hardship of being a music widow. True, it was fascinating to see a man so enlightened by his own creativity. Yet Weill could never quite share himself with you. There was always something else in the room with him, something hypnotic and mystical: his music. As the day began, Weill was at his desk, working. Lenja made him breakfast, and, as he ate, he talked of his work. Then it was back to his desk till lunch, during which he talked of his work. And so on. "What kind of life is this for a married couple?" she complained. "I see you only at mealtime!"

And Weill, in a tone of surprised innocence, would reply, "But, Lenja, you know you come right after my music!"

5

It's In The Air

Weill may not have known it, but by the late middle 1920s he was at a crossroads, as was German arts culture generally. The term that "explains" this new wave in fact explains nothing: *Die Neue Sachlichkeit*. Translated literally as "The New Objectivity," it actually means something like "The New Calmed-Down Post-Expressionist Creativity," but the concept is even more slippery. It would appear to mean "The New Rationality," but maybe "The New Truthiness" would be more appropriate, because the phrase was applied omniverously till it meant everything and nothing. Our cabaret number "*Es Liegt in der Luft*" cited it as one of the things that was "in the air" precisely because no one knew what the thing was, except a punchline for satiric revues.

The phrase was coined by G. F. Hartlaub for an art exhibition he curated in Mannheim, in 1925. "The New Realism," perhaps? Still, as the words were punted about from field to field, they meant whatever a writer needed them to mean. In music: less of the screechy solo violin and more of the "cool" woodwinds. In movies: fewer vampires and lots of young lovers. In architecture: the Bauhaus, which moved in 1925 from Weimar to Weill's birthplace, Dessau, and brought forth buildings making use of geometrical shapes, as if the Old Woman had moved into a supersonic Shoe.

In lit, the classic work of this type is Erich Maria Remarque's aforementioned 1928 novel *All Quiet on the Western Front*. The saga of four schoolboys who fall victim to jingoistic propaganda, enlist, and, one by one, die, the novel is all the more touching because of the stoic reportorial tone of the first-person narrative. (Remarque himself has to conclude the story in a kind of voiceover, explaining how the narrator died.)

Remarque troubles to warn us that his version of the war is (in A. W. Wheen's translation) "neither an accusation nor a confession, and least of all an adventure." Instead, "it will try simply to tell of a generation of men who, even though they may have escaped its shells, were destroyed by the war." Throughout, Remarque observes and comments but seldom laments: it just happens. Very rarely, something unbearable breaks in, as if raving:

A little soldier and a clear voice, and if anyone were to caress him he would hardly understand . . . There are sights there that he has not forgotten, because he never possessed them—perplexing, yet lost to him. Are not his twenty summers there?

Compare that to the also stoic yet bloodthirsty "other" German book on the war, Ernst Jünger's *In Stahlgewittern* (Storm of Steel, 1920), a work as much hated as admired. A Nationalist, to counter Remarque's liberal politics, and an ardent lover of war, Jünger never varies his tone and certainly never gets dreamy about his experience. Remarque's war derives from the Devil's nihilism, a Goethean concept. Jünger's war is a series of learning moments and calculated sadism. Of an English lieutenant killed by Jünger's unit, he says (in Michael Hofmann's translation), "In his notebook, I came upon a lot of addresses of girls in London, and was rather moved." Just a few pages later, Jünger tells of the sabotage the retreating Germans left behind them: "Every village was reduced to rubble, every tree chopped, every road undermined, every well poisoned . . . everything burnable burned." He tells of "spiteful time bombs," one of which "blew up the town hall of Bapaume just as the authorities had assembled to celebrate victory." In all, Jünger speaks of "some truly malicious inventions" in a voice that reads to some as distilled evil, Caligari in white gloves.

German cinema especially appeared relieved to throw away its early-twenties monsters. A typical film of the New Whatever It Was would be Walter Ruttmann's *Berlin: Die Symphonie einer Grosstadt* (1927), in which the "metropolis" is composed as a visual symphony, in an introduction and four movements. Earlier in the decade, such a film would have had to riot in debauchery. Instead, Ruttmann gives us one full day of a strangely tidy place, from the opening shots of a train hurtling through the suburbs into town to the night life of lit-up shop windows, a revue filled with ballerinas, cyclists, and the like, sporting events, a dance hall with charlestoning feet, the streetcar home, and, at last, fireworks and a crashing *tutti* on the soundtrack. Some complain that Ruttmann objectified Berlin by eliminating all the people. Actually, they are part of the visual program, but as little more than stick figures. Ruttmann's machines are more interesting.

Maybe the New Realism was the New Suave. In *Cafe Elektric* (1927), an Austrian silent film directed by Gustav Ucicky and released in Germany as *Die Liebesbörse* (The Stock Exchange of Love), con man Willi Forst spots a Fräulein of interest in a café at "five o'clock tea." (This is always the place and time, in Weimar art, for erotic highjinks.) At the bandstand, Forst, rapt in studying his prey, waves his right arm across his chest to signal the players. Title card: ". . . Black Bottom!" An admiring camera follows his confident takeover of his next love victim, and she is utterly conquered.

She is also Marlene Dietrich, plump and ordinary, ahead of the extreme makeover she would undergo with the director Josef von Sternberg in *The Blue Angel* (1930). Here she just looks German; in *The Blue Angel* she looks interplanetary. *Cafe Elektric* even gives Dietrich a nice-guy boy friend (Igo Sym) with a good job, a romantic accessory that Dietrich would abandon as she became one of Weimar Germany's very few top-class international stars.* The film historian Siegfried Krakauer, looking back on the years leading up to Hitler, concluded that fantasy golems anticipated a real-life golem as the head of a state run by psychopaths. Maybe there never really was a *Neue Sachlichkeit*—or maybe the term was simply another way of saying the Inflation was over.

Of course, many artists continued to work in at least a variant of expressionism. Weill's opera with Georg Kaiser, *Der Protagonist*, had its premiere in Dresden on March 27, 1926 under Fritz Busch, with Curt Taucher, a heroic tenor who later created Menelaus in Strauss' *Die Ägyptische Helena*—and Weill-Kaiser must have seemed to some a temporized expressionism. It lacks the form's demented contortions, true. Yet it harbors a fascination with insanity and violence in the sororicidal title character. Weill's brother Hans and Hans' wife, Rita, attended the premiere with their daughter, Hanne, very bright for her tender age, somewhat short of three. Rita later told Weill's biographer Ronald Sanders how Lenja, making conversation, asked Hanne how she was doing on this exciting theatrical night, and the tot replied, "I am very nervous."

But *Der Protagonist* was a hit, not only in Dresden but in other cities, and Weill celebrated by taking Lenja to Zurich, Italy, and the French Riviera for a belated honeymoon. A devotee of ocean bathing, Weill even managed to get into a vacation frame of mind and separate himself—somewhat—from his work. And Lenja discovered the casino. Suddenly, she became a merry addict of games of chance, now losing with the famous Lenja shrug and now calculating her bets with the concentration of a diamond cutter. This love of gambling, later translated into low-stakes card evenings with friends, stayed with Lenja all her life.

Weill had a love, too: of being successful. "My telephone never

---

* The generally uncelebrated Sym was influential in one respect: it was he who taught Dietrich to play the musical saw. This bizarre instrument is exactly what it sounds like: a saw that makes music when played by a violinist's bow. Dietrich used it as the opposite of a conversation piece. When guests became vexing, she would take it out and play till they left.

stops ringing," he proudly told his father—yet he was frustrated that the one-act *Protagonist* had to be paired with other composers' work to fill out an evening. What he sought now was a companion piece, *Pagliacci* to his *Cavalleria Rusticana*—but both works by Weill. Somehow he could not interest Kaiser in anything viable just then, so Weill did the usual Berlin thing when hunting for a new project in music or theatre: he went to the cafés. Schlichter's was a favorite, but the center of the circuit was the Romanisches Cafe, located across from the Kaiser Wilhelm Memorial Church (named after Wilhelm I, not the Kaiser of World War I, Wilhelm II) in the busiest part of town. The *Roman*, as it was called, offered a *Stammtisch*, or club table, to regulars of the various arts worlds, so that writers could meet publishers, playwrights and actors meet producers, and journalists meet anyone who could tip them to a story. Best of all, the *Roman* was where the establishment met the debutants, and many a penniless newcomer would foster his coffee all day in hopes of collecting somebody useful, springing for a soft-boiled egg (served in a glass) if a waiter started making faces.

It was at the *Roman* that Weill met his next librettist, in an introduction by Georg Kaiser himself: the poet and playwright Yvan/Ivan Goll. Bi-culturally Franco-Deutsch, from that disputed border region of Alsace/Elsass, Goll was the opposite of Kaiser in one important respect: where Kaiser was an old pro, Goll was a young Turk, filled with the ism ardor that had taken over French culture, from Fauvism to symbolism (though Goll stopped short at dada). Fluent in both French and German, Goll published in both languages and referred to himself as Johann Ohneland (roughly, Johnny Nocountry). He complained—or was simply stating—that he was "Jewish by decree of fate, French-born by chance, and German by passport stamp."

The first Weill-Goll collaboration was not a stage work but a sixteen-minute cantata for soprano, solo violin, and orchestra, *Der Neue Orpheus*. Indeed, this Orpheus is new, for the singer tells of the *Weltvarieté* (the Vaudeville House of the World), of gramophones and pianolas, of the Eiffel Tower and Gustav Mahler. To match all this, Weill gets almost playful, with moments of near-tonality and, at a reference to the "Pilgerchor" (the Pilgrims' Chorus, obviously the one from Wagner's *Tannhäuser*), the violinist slips in a phrase of it, but quietly—and not the most obvious phrase, either. It's not clear why Weill set the poem, for what he really wanted from Goll was a more or less comic libretto for an opera, to make an evening with *Der Protagonist*. This Weill finally did get, in a piece he and Goll entitled, in English, *Royal Palace*.

"I am gradually realizing," Weill wrote to his parents, "that my music is becoming much more assured, free, relaxed—and simple." It was Lenja's doing, in part: life with her made him, he said, "merry and less tense." Thus, *Royal Palace*, though not precisely comic, has its silly side. The orchestra includes a saxophone, that *Mischling* (halfbreed) of an instrument, part woodwind, part brass, and all impudence. Further, at one point Weill brings in an auto horn for a few notes. There's even a taste of jazz—or of something not unlike jazz—now and again. And because Goll favored the mixing of media in his plays, using masks and photography, the authors decided to narrate some of the action in film, for the first time ever in opera history.

Royal Palace's plot is rather what one expects of a symbolist poet. At a lakeside hotel, Dejanira entertains professions of devotion from her husband and from lovers of yesterday and tomorrow. Passionately unimpressed, Dejanira drowns herslf. The authors billed the piece as an opera, but it is something of an opera-ballet, in the old French manner, with prancing hotel waiters and other dance bits. Still, if the piece came off as a novelty, it did at least give Weill his first opera-world premiere in Berlin, at the Staats-Oper (as it was then spelled), with Erich Kleiber conducting and *Zaubernacht*'s Franz Ludwig Hörth directing. *The New Orpheus* was used as a curtain raiser, and Manuel de Falla's *El Retablo del Maese Pedro* (Master Peter's Puppet Show), a one-act opera in which Don Quixote wrecks a marionette theatre, filled out the bill. Weill also got his first experience working with a genuine diva, for Delia Reinhardt sang in both the cantata and as Dejanira (and the future operetta star Gitta Alpar took a small role).

However, the first night, on March 2, 1927—Weill's twenty-seventh birthday—was not a success. Worse, the following month Weill suffered an awkward scene at his publisher in Vienna. With Felix

Joachimson, Weill had written *Na Und?* (And Then What?), supposedly a comic opera, about which we know virtually nothing: for after
Weill played through the score for Universal's Emil Hertzka and
Hans Heinsheimer, they sadly refused to have anything to do with it.
Weill soon despaired of placing the work and put it in one of the bottom drawers that prolific composers never seem to run out of. And
now it is almost entirely lost.* If it was only the libretto that was
vexed, still the music must marry the words—and Weill was already
an active participant in the building of the texts that he was to enliven
with song. The composer, he once wrote, must "create for himself
the vehicle that he needs for his music." Thus, he writes not only the
sound but the letters. He seizes control of the art, and in this he is like
yet another of Weill's mentors, this one the oldest of all: Jacques
Offenbach, who died twenty years before Weill was born.

The two composers have a bit in common: both were sons of Jewish cantors in Germany and both became émigrés, though Weill
finally settled in the New World and Offenbach re-established himself in France. Further, while the career of Kurt Weill invents forms
of musical theatre, that of Offenbach centers on one form of his own
invention, *opéra bouffe*: "funny opera." The words are a French translation of the Italian *opera buffa*, but the format is entirely different. The
Italian form is sentimental and cute; *opéra bouffe* is zany, bizarre. In Offenbach, the classics are turned into sitcoms and people get into madcap
disguises or start yodelling for no apparent reason. It's life on the moon.
It's war with King Carrot. It is, in fact, the beginning of musical comedy as we know it, albeit in nineteenth-century guise.

Weill responded to Offenbach. He knew the classic titles from their
German versions in translation by Karl Treumann, an Austrian actor
who also wrote librettos for Johann Strauss and others such and whose
Offenbach German is still in use today. Weill would surely have
learned this repertory in his days at Dessau and Lüdenscheid, and he

---

* In 1960, the Weill musicologist David Drew caught up with the librettist and
asked him about the work, but Joachimson (who had emigrated and Americanized
his name to Jackson) only dimly recalled a plot about an Italian who strikes it rich
in America and returns home to find his betrothed about to wed someone else.

now realized that Offenbach's alchemy of high and low art—that is, legit music and sexy fun—could be reinvented in collaboration with a librettist from a crazy place. Not an opera poet. Not even a playwright like Georg Kaiser. Someone earthy, as Offenbach was earthy.

Like Goethe's Faust summoning the Devil, Weill met his trigger figure at the moment of need. This one was not a mentor: the two came together as equals. But he did help Weill move into the first of several styles that can be called Kurt Weillian. One of the enfants terribles of Weimar Germany, Weill now became one of the twentieth century's musical inventors: popular, protean, and one of a kind.

6

Mack The Knife

The Weill-Brecht partnership is central in modern art. Yet it lasted
only two years (with a resumption for one work a few years later)
and produced only three full-length works and no more than a hand-
ful of shorter pieces.

Further, the two men made a poor fit by temperament. Weill
was affable: reliable, professional, eager to trade ideas. Brecht was difficult: selfish, reckless, tyrannical, an exploiter of acolytes who assisted
him—sometimes fundamentally—on many titles credited entirely to
him. Weill was consistent if private, hard to know but easy to understand. Brecht was made of contradictions. He purported to use theatre
to expose defects in the social contract through writing that would be
direct and doctrinaire, yet he nevertheless examined the ambiguous
paradoxes of the human condition. He was a paradox himself, the fanatic communist who never joined the Party, a "Do as I say, not as I do"
communist: you get the police state and he gets a West German publisher, an Austrian passport, and a Swiss bank account.

There's more. Brecht bathed so seldom and smoked cheap cigars so
incessantly that he was all but unbearable in the physical sense. Yet
men and women alike found him personally magnetic. What was the

attraction? Oathed to the extermination of oppression, Brecht allied himself with the most oppressive regime of the century, and he lived by recognizing no one's rights but his own. Thwart his will in the slightest and you learned what the word "screaming" meant. He loved storming out of rehearsals, sabotaging rehearsals. True, German theatre was then ruled by the emotionally unscrupulous totalism of the Director Who Must Be Obeyed; German émigré directors in Hollywood subdued cast and crew in the wicked finesse of geschrei as if they were performers, too. But Brecht took it home. He cajoled and promised and, when you weakened and ceded him control, he bullied and abused you till you retreated and the cajoling began again; this was how he conducted his relationships.

Much later, when Weill had made a hit on Broadway and Brecht, rotting in California exile, schemed to revive *The Threepenny Opera*, Lenya warned Weill not to be drawn into Brecht's cavernous exploitations. "It's not surprising that somebody gets nice and soft when they are down and out," she noted. "But just let him be successful again and he'll be the old Brecht."

Lenja was one of the few who could resist him. She admired him, no more. But others, especially women, crumbled again and again. Or they would argue only to see their objections swept away by a combination of waterfall and Machiavelli. Brecht was like the Borg in *Star Trek*. Resistance is futile; you will be assimilated. He fought with allies and enemies, with actors and public. Scandals were his candy: an offended and raging audience, appalled notices, perhaps a detachment of police to keep order at the following performances.

Even worse was Brecht's predatory use of other people's writings—not just those of the besotted followers thronging his living quarters but published authors as well. This is not the recycling of public-domain tales that we find in the ancient Greeks and Shakespeare. This is theft. Now comes the famous Brechtian excuse, invariably recorded in English as "I have a fundamental laxity in questions of literary property." Yes, except his own. Brecht had a banker's worldview about his copyrights and a pickpocket's about everyone else's. In the standard Berlin joke, a bite of the *Schnauze*, two kibitzers meet:

HERR CAFEKERL: Who wrote that new play they're all talking
   about?
HERR SCHNAPSKLATSCH: It's by Brecht.
HERR CAFEKERL: Yes, but who wrote it?

 Here's the most famous version:

HERR CAFEKERL: Yes, Brecht steals—but he steals with style!

Even when those whose work he had exploited were in dire
need and Brecht was piling up gold in his counting house, he refused, again and again, to share even a pfennig. He demanded sacrifice like a rabid heathen god while palming small change off your
dresser. He drove Weill (and, after Weill's death, Lenja) crazy by
making deals with publishers and theatre companies concerning
Weill-Brecht titles without consulting the Weill half of the outfit—
and then pocketing all the profits. Throughout his career, from
Berlin into exile in, mainly, Scandinavia and the United States and
finally back to Europe after the war, settling in East Germany,
Brecht never stopped stealing, never stopped screaming, and never
stopped stooging for the totalitarian crushing of the human spirit,
as long as the crushing was performed by communists instead of
Nazis.

But then: how did Brecht get to be the top German playwright of
the first half of the twentieth century? If he was so dependent on various "secretaries" actually writing some or even *most* of many of his
works (as critics have lately asserted), if he made a shrieking shambles of
the rehearsal process, if he was such a hypocrite in his politics, how did
Brecht ever establish himself?

For one thing, it seems unlikely that all that much of the oeuvre
billed contractually as "by Bertolt Brecht" was the work of others, if
only because his voice, unmistakably, permeates his plays just as the
voices of George Bernard Shaw or Jean Giraudoux do theirs. When
Brecht switches format—from expressionism to the New Realism, for
instance—his characters always speak fluent Brecht, and even in exile

(for nearly fifteen years), no matter who the various secretaries are, the voice is Brecht's.

It's that touch of hangman's whimsey he slips into the direst situations, the sudden quirky changes of subject. Characters sometimes articulate free-associating nonsense. Extras create bizarre disturbances—for example, a woman hawking newspapers in a bar in *Trommeln in der Nacht* (Drums in the Night, 1922), Brecht's first produced play:

> NEWSGIRL: Spartacus revolution in the publishing quarter! Red Rosa [Luxemburg] speaks outdoors in the Zoo! How long till rioting begins? Where is the army? Ten pfennigs, Herr Gunner! Where is the army, ten pfennings.

Drums in the Night is largely concerned with the leftist uprisings in Munich right after the war. Yet Brecht billed the play as a Komödie. This lopsided humor—a tragedy of jokes—articulates what others only sense. Thus, perplexed by having a newborn in his life—his daughter Hanne, by his first wife, Marianne Zoff—he says, "There's so little one can do with children except be photographed with them." Even in mid-rage, he can be waylaid by an amusing discovery. "*Scheisse!*" (Shit!), he would cry, at a run-through. "*Es ist alles Scheisse!*" Then a well-wisher suggested that he tone down the assault. Why not simply criticize the acting as . . . pedantic? Unimaginative? Stylized? Tickled, Brecht took to halting rehearsals with "No, no, no, that is much too *stylized!*"

Then, too, how could so many unsung collaborators have counterfeited Brecht's idiosyncratic narrative flow? An aficionado of detective novels, Brecht dealt in action-logical storytelling so surely that, even in plays short on plot, each scene appears to create each next scene. *Mutter Courage* has no plot per se—no quest, no romance, no mystery to be unveiled—yet it unfolds as inexorably as anything by Sardou.

Salka Viertel, a Max Reinhardt–trained actress who rode the diaspora to Hollywood to run its primary German émigré salon, maintained that she had known only two geniuses—Arnold Schönberg . . . and Bertolt Brecht. Part of his intellectual power lay in the vivacity of his conversation, leaping from point to point while observing sociopolitical developments synoptically, as if he had already read histories of his era that would not be written for twenty years. Then he would cap all this with a quip, and another, at last to fall into laughter till he had to doff his glasses and rub his eyes with "*Ja, das Leben* . . ." (What a life it is . . .). And *then* he would pick up his guitar and accompany himself in song, his evocative lyrics set to his own rudimentary music. And the company was transfixed.

Everyone who worked with him knew that he brought out one's best. If he stole with style, he managed with genius. Simply put: he made the thing happen. Conducting an idea into a script and then a production, sparking the PR circuits with gossip and outrages, bullying the director when Brecht himself wasn't in charge, tapping the best talents around—Weill and Lenja among them, we notice—Brecht was the outstanding generator of theatre after Max Reinhardt's generation. A theorist in stagecraft, he showed you what he meant as his productions unfolded—like Stanislafsky before him, but more radically, fantastically. Yes, Brecht was a con man, but only among other things. One of those things was: a unique contributor to the body of theatre work in Western Civilization.

"This stupid Brecht," Lenja called him, while stiffening Weill's resolve to keep Brecht out of their lives during his years of exile. And "This Chinese-Augsburg *Hinterwäldler* philosopher." "Chinese" refers to the concept of the Chinese box, ornamentally subdivided into more or less secret cavities and thus Lenja's image of Brecht's double-dealing. "*Hinterwäldler*" (provincial) presumably conjures up the popular caricature of the Bavarian as an oafish lump who knows only two or three things, all of them wrong.

And Brecht was indeed Bavarian, and from Augsburg, which brings in a fourth major city to match Vienna, Zurich, and Berlin, for Augsburg is a relatively short train ride from Munich, and Brecht ceaselessly commuted between the two before he settled in Berlin. Augsburg was where he observed ties with his prosperous father, who spoiled him materially. But Munich was where Brecht made himself at home amid fellow creators, for this cultural capital of southern Germany was rich enough to support an artists' colony, in the district of Schwabing. Berlin is known as the *Spreeatem* (the Athens on the Spree), but Munich thought itself "the Athens on the Isar." The ruling Wittelsbach dynasty were art lovers, and they supplied their town with museums. "In 1885," writes the historian David Clay Large, "the Bavarian capital had more painters and sculptors than Berlin and Vienna combined." Munich was also the *Wagnerstadt*, where the composer who reinvented opera ran his command-and-control center—to the despair and outrage of the citizenry, for Wagner loved a scandal almost as much as Brecht did.

Munich's population was anything but cosmopolitan: extroverted among its own kind but hostile to outsiders, even German outsiders. Not surprisingly, Munich was the cradle of Nazism. Though it suffered several leftist coups after the armistice, the city was saturated with right-wing associations and conspiracies. Anyone planning sedition in hatred of the Weimar "traitors" up there in Berlin had a rich selection of outfits to join. Hitler chose the tiny German Workers' Party to expand into the National Socialist German Workers' Party—the Nazis— merely because he was attached to a Reichswehr intelligence unit in 1919 and had been ordered to report on the GWP. He did better than report. He took over the meeting—at a beer hall, typically—and ranted about the "Berlin Asiatics" and the "stab in the back" and the "Jew moneygrubbers." Anton Drexler, one of the GWP's founders, turned to the man next to him with (in Bavarian dialect) *"Mensch, der hat a Gosch'n, den könnt Ma braucha!"* (Man, does that one have a mouth we could use!).

Brecht was well aware of Munich's excitable political scene. Like many Germans, he found the Nazis—at first—more amusing than dangerous. This was partly because Hitler affirmed what was to become a twentieth-century rule: in their demented utterances and personal comportment, all tyrants, from Mussolini to Hugo Chavez and

Muammar el-Qaddafi, behave like clowns.* And just as Mussolini famously marched on Rome, in 1922, Hitler planned a March on Berlin. He launched it the following year in the aforementioned Beer Hall Putsch, so called because, apparently, any event in Munich not associated with a museum or opera house transpires near a large supply of beer. Stalking through the city toward a police detachment at the Feldherrnhalle (Field Officers' Gallery), a war memorial, the Nazis ran into their first taste of armed resistance by the republic. There were at least seventeen dead and, at Hitler's trial in March of 1924, judges sympathetic to fascism coddled him with five years of soft time, which he spent dictating *Mein Kampf* to paramilitary-loon-turned-secretary Rudolf Hess. Hitler was free by the year's end.

The Beer Hall Putsch may have been the reason Brecht decided to abandon Bavaria for Berlin. Two more of his plays had been staged: *Im Dickicht der Städte* (In the Jungle of Cities, originally entitled *Im Dickicht*, 1923), in Munich, and *Baal* (1923), in Leipzig. Like all Brecht's titles up to *The Threepenny Opera*, they flopped—but, again, they flopped with style, and were taken up by companies in other cities over the years. Brecht disliked losing access to indulgent Papa, for Berlin was all the way across Germany in Prussia. But he was ambitious; sooner or later, he would have to crack the *Weltstadt* Berlin. More immediately, though, he saw how fierce the Bavarian right had grown; southern Germany was dangerous for a writer as—to put it mildly—mischievous as Brecht. Fascists don't get mischief.

Lining up a position as *Dramaturg* for Max Reinhardt, Brecht waltzed off to Berlin in the summer of 1924. Of course Brecht worked in expressionism at this time: the art was mad because the world was

---

* Stalin is arguably the exception, as his paranoia compelled him to dial himself down to a setting of minus three in order to hide his purposes. Thus, his personality appeared perfectly uninflected. He had a wicked sense of humor, however. After Hitler attacked Russia, in 1941, one of the few Red Army officers who had been jailed rather than shot was freed to resume command. Stalin greeted the officer when he arrived at a staff meeting and asked where he had been all this time, as if he didn't know. "In prison, Comrade Stalin," said the officer. And Stalin replied, in a tone of mild sarcasm, "A fine time to be indoors."

mad, and audiences were born to be terrified, or at least insulted. *Baal* follows the escapades of an outlaw poet who whores energetically with both genders and murders his best friend, all in a rapt nattering that hides as much as it reveals:

BAAL: My soul, brother, is the groaning of the cornfields when they waltz in the wind, and the glitter in the eyes of two insects who want to eat each other.

EKART: A summer-crazed boy with immortal bowels, that's you. A potato dumpling that will leave the sky flecked with grease.

Then the New Realism swept in, and Brecht absorbed it in *Leben Eduards des Zweiten von England* (1924), a reworking of Christopher Marlowe's *Edward II*. His collaborator, Lion Feuchtwanger, got an acknowledgment in the text, though Brecht was soon to do away with such indulgent folderol. For that matter, there is much Marlowe in the piece—but also so much that is innovative and compelling that, in the 1960s, when Britain's National Theatre was playing the Old Vic while awaiting the construction of its South Bank home, the company programmed Brecht's *Edward II* rather than Marlowe's because Brecht gave them more to play.

Indeed, we see Brecht, for the first time, tearing up the stage in this *Edward*, with its musings on history, its sinister conspiracies, its eccentric characters too bold for their timeplace—exactly the qualities we note in the two marquee titles of Weill-Brecht, *The Threepenny Opera* and *Mahagonny*. Brecht's next play after Edward, *Mann Ist Mann* (One Man's Like Another, 1926), premiered in Darmstadt, is the first piece in Brecht's mature style, with its slippery fantasy-realism and gallows humor. In truth, most of the plays Brecht is famous for, from *Mutter Courage und Ihre Kinder* (Mother Courage and Her Children, 1941) to *Der Kaukasische Kreidekreis* (The Caucasian Chalk Circle, in English 1948; in German 1954), play as comedies, however serious their theme. For that matter, *The Threepenny Opera* and *Mahagonny* are very nearly farces. Note, too, that it was a radio performance of *Mann Ist Mann*, in 1927, that introduced Weill to Brecht's work. Thus it was

Brecht's blend of ideas and sardonic fun that inspired Weill to work with him: because Weill was made of just such a blend, striving to write *about* something even as his melodic style was ready to tilt from the intellectual to the sensual.

One thing about Brecht remained steadfast throughout his career: his byline. One often sees it as "Berthold Brecht"; this is an error. He was christened Eugen Berthold Friedrich Brecht, and his very first professional publications, when he was still a student, were signed as Berthold Eugen, without the surname. Nevertheless, from his first play on, he used the respelled Bertolt Brecht, sometimes shortened to Bert Brecht or even to Brecht, neat. Another thing about Brecht did *not* remain steadfast, though many think it did: his concept of Epic Theatre and its Alienation Effect.

Why the misunderstanding? Because *epic*, in this context, does not mean "grand" or "long" and *alienation* does not mean "offending." Brecht's intention was to override what he later disdained as the *"Oh-Mensch-Dramatik"* with a new form of writing designed for a new kind of production style. *"O Mensch!"*—to reword correctly the line from Friedrich Nietzsche's *Also Sprach Zarathustra*—captions Brecht's critique of plays offering "unreal solutions" to mankind's problems, especially that of warmaking by capitalist despots. The solution, Brecht was coming to believe, was to divest capitalism of state power, not—as Brecht described the then fashionable interpretation of Nietzsche—to present "a group of 'decent' people who can end war forever through moral condemnation." The remedy was revolution, and Brecht's theatre, from set design to acting style, was revolutionary.

"Epic Theatre" was in use before Brecht adopted it, and it belonged as well to the director Erwin Piscator, a Brecht associate who constructed multimedia stagings, to surround the spectator with stimuli. Brecht intended just the opposite: to concentrate the spectator's line of reasoning. Piscator exploded with theatre, like a salesman demonstrating a space-age vacuum cleaner; Brecht wanted his theatre already cleansed of flotsam. It sounds simple. Yet every time he explained it he varied the explanation just as he varied his production style over the years—especially after he settled behind the Iron Curtain. In East

Germany as in Russia, anything more advanced than nineteenth-century, fourth-wall realism was "formalism": a capital crime.

Before Brecht submitted to this tyranny, he effected the ultimate twentieth-century innovation: the smashing of the Wagner cult. Did this, too, attract Weill to Brecht?: Weill's theatre is also not only post-Wagner but anti-Wagner. In Wagner, one is less a theatregoer than a dreamer, transported into a darkness at one end of which myths of love and power are enacted. Each of Wagner's late works is a romance on one aspect of Western Civilization: *Tristan und Isolde* on courtly love; *Die Meistersinger von Nürnberg* on the making of art; *Der Ring des Nibelungen* on world creation, gods, and heroes; and *Parsifal* on Christian Redemption. If the magic of Wagner's transformative stagecraft functions properly, one sheds one's individuality and becomes one with each of these works, respectively: in mystical transcendence of "real" life; in nationalist community forbidden to the outsider; in the war of outsiders determined to enslave the community; in the agonized chastity of Belief.

Brecht refused to transport his public, and he mistrusted music unless it be self-contained intrusions into the flow of the script, punctuational devices. Distracting set changes and projected headlines announcing each next scene with plot spoilers were elemental in the Alienation—and Brecht refused to let his actors act. No impersonations—instead, presentations. One does not bring a character to life. One reveals the character's positions.

A quintessential Brecht moment is the very start of *The Threepenny Opera*, on "a fair day in Soho," with "beggars begging, thieves stealing, and whores whoring." A song: the world-famous Moritat, which we call "The Ballad of Mack the Knife." In the performance format typical of the raucous outer limits of Europe's ancient fairgrounds, a singer tells of an outlaw's capers while his assistant reveals illustrations supporting the saga. The shark and his teeth. Macheath and his blade. Corpses as the human shark glides around a corner. The victims: Schmul Meier, Jenny Towler, Alphonse Glitte the coachman, seven children and an old man in a fire. Now a burst of laughter from the whores as a man steps out of the crowd and crosses the stage: natty, charming, hard to read.

And the scene ends with what proved to be a cultural signifier of the twentieth century: Lotte Lenja coming forward to say, *"Das war Mackie Messer!"* (in the Marc Blitzstein translation: "There goes Mack the Knife!").

In fact, the coming together of Kurt Weill with Lotte Lenja and then of the two of them with Bertolt Brecht could be seen as more of the destiny—that is, of something more than pure happenstance—that Weill now and again bent to his will. It was he who sought out Brecht, and he had a collaboration in mind. Well, of course, you think—Weill was always looking for a partner among literary men, the better to experiment with form and content. German librettists didn't like to experiment; playwrights could be dependably unstable.

And this collaboration proved to be the turning point in the lives of Weill and Lenja, giving him an insight into the invention of melody while retaining his musicianly expertise. This melody can be jagged, wheedling, peremptory: it isn't the folkloric purity of Schubert. Yet it charms even so. And the orchestral settings can be abradant, ironic, jabbingly sweet. That's Kurt Weill: the new one, the songmaster who writes classical in a popular way, or who writes popular with classical technique, depending on how one views it. Gustav Mahler, perhaps, introduced this sophistication of elements into his symphonies. But in Mahler the use of songlike melody is folklike, less popular than basic, to put a brake on his apocalyptic wars of the senses. Weill's popular, however, is *popular*: made for sheet music with colorful come-on covers, made for whistling, for dancing, street stuff. There were very slight touches of this in *Royal Palace*, but nothing comparable to what Weill now made with Lenja and Brecht.

Yes, she was a part of what happened, because she was too much the music widow as Frau Weill: she needed work and a reason for being around him. And Weill was eager to incorporate his wife—his love—into his career. How could he not—for who else knew her as a singer? Today she is the Voice of Weill, but that didn't happen till after his death. How was it to get started if no one wrote music for her? And if not her composer-husband, then who?

Weill met Brecht in one of those networking Berlin cafés, of course.

Not the *Roman*—in Schlichter's, Brecht's personal hangout. The two made a truly odd couple, Weill's suit and bow tie, short, stocky frame, and soft demeanor nearly invisible next to Brecht's show-off costuming of leather coat over worker chic on his skinny build, with the wire-rimmed glasses of an academic, the three-day stubble of a gangster's stooge, and the cigar of a carousel mechanic. *Ja, das Leben.*

Both men were keyed up at the prospect of what they might accomplish together. After a private printing, Brecht presented the public with a book of poetry in this very year, 1927, entitled *Die Hauspostille* (The Domestic Breviary, generally called by its translation title of *Manual of Piety*). Designed to resemble those books of devotional reading that many households kept next to the Bible, the collection was actually a wicked spoof, with "lessons" on such subjects as the delights of the privy, "On the Love of Schnaps," and Brecht's favorite historical character, François Villon. Much of Brecht's poetry is a kind of concert prose, strong in imagery but devoid of rhyme or metre. *Die Hauspostille,* on the other hand, often feels like lyrics in search of a singer.

Weill was going to sing them, and he knew where: the German Chamber Music festival in Baden-Baden, which had commissioned one-act operas from four composers to fill out a bill for mid-July, a few months ahead. Brecht's psalm book gone wild offered as its fourth lesson a set described as *Mahagonnygesänge* (Mahagonny Songs), five poems on a more or less faraway place under a "schöner grüner Mond" (lovely green moon) with "keine Direction" (no authorities making laws). It's a tough place, a Wild West with the *Alles schwindel* of sharp Weimar operators, and Weill proposed to expand the five *Mahagonny* poems into a full-length opera, to startle high-toned *Musikfreunde* with disorderly conduct. This of course immediately appealed to Brecht, that flouter of bourgeois cautions. He had no use for opera per se, as I've said. But this sounded like anti-opera, meta-opera, potentially the greatest scandal of his career.

A *must!* But the two men decided to ease into the project with a half-hour piece made of the five *Hauspostille* songs by themselves: a study for the main work. They would stage it at Baden-Baden, scored for two violins, two clarinets, two trumpets, saxophone, trombone, piano, and percussion, to be sung by two tenors, baritone, bass, one soprano . . . and Lotte Lenja. Although the five songs didn't indicate character or plot, the sextet drew character billing as Charlie, Billy, Bobby, Jimmy, Bessie, and, for Lenja, Jessie, revealing Brecht's geographical pseudo-reality for Mahagonny: America. This world center of capitalist energy was a Brecht obsession until he actually got there (as we'll see). But then Mahagonny is less a place—however imaginary—than a sound Brecht found captivating, like "Mississippi" or "Benares," For he also tells us that "Mahagonny" is *"ein erfundenes Wort"* (a made-up word): its noise is its very geography.

There was no attempt to unite the work's free-standing numbers into a narrative, yet the whole has a strong formal presence. With the poems reordered, nine new lines of sung text, and short musical interludes, this song cycle for the stage (already an innovation—an oxymoron, in fact) created its own rough unity of attitude and tang. To round it off, it was set in a boxing ring, probably only because Brecht thought it both idiotic and charming that Berlin was boxing mad. But the cast performed in tuxedos, including the girls. As if the piece were not salty enough, Caspar Neher's projections against the back wall added mildly uncomfortable evocations. Then, in the last minutes, everyone carried strikers' signs, such as *"Für die Sterblichkeit der Seele!"* (Up with the death of the soul!) or *"Gegen die Civilis!"* ([a pun combining] Down with civilization! [and] Down with syphilis!). Lenja bore a sign reading, *"Für Weill!"* (Up with Weill!).

Some of the usual misleading factoids need correcting. One is that Brecht added explanatory spoken lines between the vocals: there were no spoken lines and no explanations. The songs were simply presented, take it or leave it, in a blunt realization that had its moments of shrugging humor, as when the men read newspapers while the women sang.

Another mistake is to sense a layered mystery in that titular word. Is Mahagonny a summoning term, a magic? Again: it's a noise, but above all it is Brecht's coining based on the term "the Browns," which is what the Nazis were called in the days before they seized power. In Munich, Brecht saw a great deal of the brown-shirted paramilitaries of the *Sturmabteilung* (Storm Division), the proletarian S.A., as opposed to the elite *Schutzstaffel* (Defense Squad), the S.S., who were uniformed in black. The Browns were mahogany (*Mahagoni* in German), and the respelled, "made-up word" Mahagonny was marching and murder and "*Heil!*" and "You were born to die for Germany!" It was Brecht's equivalent of Verdi's "*parola scenica*," the outstanding word that, properly set, encapsulates an opera's action.

Yet another of those misleading factoids calls this short work "the *Mahagonny Songspiel*." No: it was entitled simply *Mahagonny*, but *billed* as a *Songspiel*, a coining derived from the German for "play with songs," *Singspiel*. As *Singspiele* develop a storyline through dialogue between the musical patches and *Mahagonny* didn't, the authors emphasized its unique nature by terming it as not a "play with songs" but a "play *of* songs."

Further confusing the situation, this chamber piece is often called *The Little Mahagonny*. But the authors utilized two titles only—*Mahagonny* for the short piece heard at Baden-Baden on July 17, 1927; and, for the evening-length opera premiered three years later, *Aufstieg und Fall der Stadt Mahagonny* (Rise and Fall of Mahagonny City). Another factoid: most people think the opera is an expansion of the *Songspiel*. But our Weill specialist David Drew insists that Weill and Brecht had the big opera in mind from the start. The *Songspiel* came about mainly because Weill had an in with the Baden-Baden administration and because Lenja lacked the voice for opera singing but would suit the more modest demands of the chamber piece. The *Songspiel* was at once a study for the main work and a wedding present. Two years later, Garbo Talks! For the moment, Lenja Sings!

A common interpretation of Weill's life reads him as a shape-shifter, working in prestigiously "difficult" political art in Germany and then, in America, going commercial, as if the political were inherently prestigious—as if, in fact, Weill's German music must be special because Brecht is involved and Weill's American music is like something you pick out of a box of Cracker Jack.

However, a composer's work is not to be judged on the amount of collaboration with any particular writer. Further, Weill's first three

American shows *were* political, although equating politics with talent is idiotic in the first place.

Weill did undergo a change in mode—but it was not when he came to America, later on, in 1935. It was now, in 1927, on the verge of the first works that made him famous. Looking into the man's soul as best we can, it had nothing to do with politics. It had to do with Brecht and Lenja. Simply put, Weill suddenly starts writing sexy. He needed to be the Latest Thing in Music, and he at first had seen atonalism as the way in. But while atonalism is dramatic, it is by nature somewhat unmelodic, and there is just so much one can do in it, unless—as Alban Berg discovered in composing *Wozzeck*—the subject matter reflects the loony, agonized worldview that expressionist music conjures up. The form is limiting; Berg wrote only one other opera (*Lulu*, in Schönberg's twelve-tone style), although he did die young, at fifty. And *Lulu*, too, is loony and agonized. It's a closed system.

Weill realized that he could not make a career out of loony and agonized, and the Baden-Baden *Mahagonny* is when he effected his switch from atonalism to the above-all melodic forms in which he was to work from then on. It has been suggested that Weill was influenced by the unharmonized vocal lines that Brecht published for the *Mahagonny* poems in the *Hauspostille*, the barest outlines of song on a single staff. It was what Brecht termed (by reversing the vowels in the German *Musik*) "*Misuk*," and it unfortunately inspired another misapprehension about Weill: that Brecht composed some of *Mahagonny*.

Weill did not use Brecht's little musical doodles. One of them, the "*Benares-Song*," had already been used, by the anonymous composer of "There Is a Tavern in the Town" and by Puccini in "Un Bel Dì." However, Weill did adopt Brecht's suggestion for the verse of the "*Alabama-Song*" ("Oh, show us the way to the next whiskybar"), inventing his own tune for the chorus (at "Oh! Moon of Alabama").

"Benares" and "Alabama" were written in English, not German, and possibly by Elisabeth Hauptmann and not Brecht, though he of course signed it. Despite becoming a reader of English, Brecht didn't trust himself to speak it, while Hauptmann was fluent in it. Like many of Brecht's silent collaborators, she was besotted with him and thus manipulable—though, again, one notes a striking resemblance in these two songs to the whimsical despair and irrelevantly alluring images that trademark Brecht's voice.

Giving two of *Mahagonny*'s five numbers entirely in English may have been meant to map the work's exotic geography, or simply to startle, because neither Brecht nor Weill was willing to disappear amid the three other new pieces. These were: Paul Hindemith's *Hin und Zurück* (There and Back), in which a homicidal love-triangle plot stops at the halfway point to run backward (in music as well as action) to a happy ending; Darius Milhaud's slyly comic *L'Enlèvement d'Europe* (The Rape of Europa); and Ernst Toch's *Die Prinzessin auf der Erbse* (The Princess and the Pea), after Hans Christian Andersen. With four entirely new works to collect—in four different theatrical styles and musical autographs—the audience would be fatigued, and *Mahagonny*, third on the bill, was going to have to kick the house awake.

This it was bound to do. The boxing ring was sure to offend, with its reference to proletarian rowdies, sweat, and gambling. One recalls the house-wide booing tantrum that exploded at La Scala in the 1950s during a performance of a now utterly forgot new work simply because it brought a real-life automobile onto the stage of Italy's most holy place of art: a profanation.

Then, too, *Mahagonny*'s language had never been heard in classical precincts, not least in one number in which God presents Himself in Sin City and the populace jeers. By now, we've heard it all; in those days, even agnostics felt provoked. The Baden-Baden audience was progressive, but only in matters musical. *Mahagonny* was progressive socially. It wasn't avant-garde in the Alban Berg sense: Berg's *Lyrische Suite*, for string quartet, was heard in Baden-Baden the day before *Mahagonny* with such success that this partly twelve-tone work was encored in its entirety. No, *Mahagonny* was avant-garde in the confrontational sense, not least in the silken hoochy-koochy of the "*Alabama-Song*," whose English was probably a mystery but whose popularistic canoodling was, unmistakably, intended to outrage.

So *Mahagonny* was one of those risk/reward items: if it had ventured modestly, it would have enjoyed a modest success. If it smashed the Commandments in the gala setting of the Baden-Baden Festival, it could not fail in any real sense. Cheered or scorned, it must be the talk of the German music world.

Continental Europeans shout at shows they dislike. "*Pfui!*" and "*Das ist ein Affront!*" are popular. But most simply whistle, usually on their house keys. Anticipating a rumpus, Brecht handed out pocket whistles to the cast, and they did indeed get a chance to use them. Still, the risk earned its reward, and the evening's only victim was Hindemith, whose piece placed last in the running order, anti-climactically right after *Mahagonny*, Western Civilization's first taste of Weill-Brecht.*

"The sensation of the [Baden-Baden] opera evening was *Mahagonny*," Heinrich Strobel wrote, in the *Berliner Börsen-Courier*. "It is impossible to escape its magnetic attraction" was Max Marschalk's conclusion in the *Vossische Zeitung*, a newspaper so established it had a nickname, "*Tante Voss*" (Auntie Voss). And note how Strobel analyzed Weill's musical technics: "a blending of jazz, cabaret songs, and lyric elements."

That is: the sardonic turbulence of revved-up American dance-band recordings and the sweet vocalism of opera have now been laced into a form pioneered on the Berlin revue stage, the popular tune with topical content and roguish lyrics: the art of cabaret.

We know this word especially because of the eponymous Kander

---

* A famous anecdote finds Lenja and the *Mahagonny* troupe in a bar across the street from the playing venue, the Kurhaus, unsure how the work really went over. Then she feels a slap on the back as the conductor Otto Klemperer roars out, "Is here no telephone?," a line from the "*Benares-Song*." Whereupon the bar customers all break into the number, and Lenja knows *Mahagonny* made a hit. There's something odd here: the audience can sing "*Benares-Song*" from having heard it just once before? And in English, no less? This could not have happened—and it's all the more interesting in that, when the full-length *Mahagonny* was ready, Weill, desperate for a Berlin production, showed it to Klemperer, who ran the Kroll Opera, the most progressive of Berlin's three opera companies. And Klemperer, albeit with tearful apologies, turned it down. Klemperer's idea of opera was gods and heroes, or at least *Tiefland*. *Mahagonny*, as we'll see, is fornication, appetitive excess, and an all-out scorning of civilization's behavioral norms—again, a profanation.

and Ebb musical of 1966, which of course provided Lenja with her last great stage role. But that show's Kit Kat Klub represents only one aspect of Berlin's cabaret scene, the so-called *Tingeltangel* with its seedy clientele and more or less brazen showgirls. The term *cabaret* took in also the more upmarket variety shows produced by such as Erik Charell and Herman Haller to appeal to theatregoers who flocked to operetta; there were as well the intimate, worldly offerings emphasizing social and political commentary.

Typical of the last was the *Wilde Bühne* (Wild Stage), located in the basement of the Theater des Westens and founded by Trude Hesterberg, an actress with grande dame singing tone. The *Wilde Bühne* seems to have been the only cabaret to have featured Bertolt Brecht as a performer, singing his own ditties to his own guitar accompaniment, for a single week. At his debut, Brecht included "*Die Ballade vom Totes Soldaten*" (The Ballad of the Dead Soldier), in which a corpse is dug up to die all over again in the war about nothing. The criticism of hypocrisy masked as patriotism is scathing, and the audience reacted in fury. They liked their satire on the gentle side, as in Wilhelm Bendow's stand-up act as Lydia Smith, the tattooed lady. Wearing a body cast, Bendow would enlarge fancifully on the historical importance of his artwork, taking in, say, a depiction of Kaiser Wilhelm's new line of toiletries here and a view of President von Hindenburg noshing on a bialy there.★

The quality of the singing in much of cabaret was sketchy, and some of the music functioned simply to anchor the accents and rhymes. But at its best, cabaret created a level of songwriting without rival elsewhere in the West: music as news bulletins and cultural deconstructions. Call it "*Zeitgesang*" (songs of the day). One number, celebrating the aforementioned notorious place of illicit assignation, was titled "*Sind Sie der*

★ Somebody at MGM took note of Lydia, because the Marx Brothers film *At the Circus* (1939) offered Groucho in a number by Harold Arlen and E. Y. Harburg, "Lydia, the Tattooed Lady." One realizes how bold Weimar cabaret was in considering the rather humdrum illustrations *this* Lydia models, from "the wreck of the Hesperus" (alluding to a once-famous Longfellow poem) to "Nizhinsky a-doin' the rhumba."

Herr vom Fünf-Uhr-Tee?" (Are You the Man From Five O'Clock Tea?). It sounds innocent till we learn that he "stayed till breakfast." This was *Berlinersex: Kiss! Wow! Danke, Frau!* Or pugnacious little Claire Waldoff, more or less openly lesbian, would roar into "*Raus Mit den Männern!*" (Out With the Men!), a war cry determined to clear the Reichstag of men, because "if they can, *we* can!" Or American music becomes German music in "*Und Immer Noch Spiel'nse Blues!*" (And Always They're Playing the Blues!). To music of a simpering strut, the lyrics observe the many transitions of life: they renovate the Cafe Kranzler, keep on replacing the Republic's Chancellor. Hair and automobile styles change. Only one thing never changes: always they're playing the blues!

There were as well free-floating titles, concerned not with the sociology of Weimar but the eternal verities of love and courtship. These numbers often had an edge, as in "*Wenn die Beste Freundin*" (When My Best Girl Friend), from the aforementioned revue *Es Liegt in der Luft*. Marlene Dietrich and Margo Lion, in twin dark outfits topped by a huge carnation at the neck and a hat with a brim broad enough for the Vatican, sang of their special relationship. Oskar Karlweis scarcely got a line in this trio as Dietrich and Lion went on about how "lovely" and "sweet" the Best Girl Friend is.

Cabaret was the Peck's Bad Boy of Western song, and the Nazis closed down the workshop after the *Machtergreifung*, the seizure of power, on January 30, 1933. It was the usual fascist reasoning: anything that lives on freedom is dangerous to the regime. Worse, cabaret was artistic, the concept that supposedly led Hermann Göring to reach for his revolver.* Frequently composed in American dance rhythms and marketed with colorful painted covers on the sheet music, Berlin's cabaret songbook mirrored Weimar democracy in its racy, try-anything lifestyle and fascination with America. Its outstanding practioners were the composers Rudolf Nelson and Mischa Spoliansky, the

---

* The line is a common misattribution. It was introduced by the Nazi playwright Hanns Johst in *Schlageter* (1933), which was dedicated to Hitler. A diehard Versailles-hater engaged in sabotage in the Ruhr against the occupying French says, "When I hear 'Kultur,' I free the safety catch on my revolver."

lyricist Marcellus Schiffer, and the composer-lyricist Friedrich Hol-laender. All were Jewish and, like so many others in this book, all fled Nazism, though Schiffer killed himself in 1932 and Nelson, who had gone to Holland, was captured during the occupation and sent to Westerbork concentration camp, which he survived. Spoliansky settled in England, but Hollaender, like Weill and Lenja, went to America, perhaps to sample for himself the quirks and follies he had been singing about throughout the 1920s.

Hollaender's best-known work is the music for "*Ich Bin von Kopf bis Fuss auf Liebe Eingestellt,*" which we know as "Falling In Love Again," Marlene Dietrich's credo in *The Blue Angel.* In a way, it's the émigré's motto as well: the very sound of how Europeans who escaped the evil closeness of fascism discovered how much room there is in the United States, where *The Blue Angel*'s director, Josef von Sternberg, had already established himself and where he and Dietrich were to carve out some bizarrely autobiographical history as a living Beauty and Beast of erotic Hollywood film. When we last saw Dietrich, in *Cafe Elektric*, she was a nice little middle-class girl. In her American series with von Sternberg, from *Morocco* (1930) to *The Devil Is a Woman* (1935), Dietrich scorns various important yet impotent von Sternberg stand-ins in favor of sex with hunks. "Can't help it," she shrugs, in "Falling In Love Again," because the woman is a devil.

Cabaret fastened on piquant morsels of American life, just as Brecht picked through newspaper reports of Chicago crime in dreaming up his Mahagonny gangsterlands of the Browns march-ing and screaming and killing. However, behind all the headline fads, American culture was simply freedom culture. What Marlene Dietrich noticed about American life was that there she could live as she pleased.

My readers probably expect a report on how Lenja started her sing-ing career in this repertory. But there is no record of her having done so. Rather, cabaret liberated *Weill*, as the *Mahagonny* songs gave him something he had never before experienced: supreme musical power over lyrics like no others. "O moon of Alabama"—what helter-skelter imagery, with its "whiskeybar" and "good old mamma." It's like an uninvited guest presiding over your banquet because he knows all your secrets. But the song derives its power also when the pounding rhythm of the verse ("O show us the way") suddenly yields to wistful reverie. "Not quite so Egyptian," Brecht told Lenja when coaching her in how to present it. Apparently she had styled herself in the abstract, like a hieroglyph, while he wanted her styled as a prostitute who would clerk for a florist if only the world were as pretty as the moon.

Cabaret art proved so liberating that Weill even wrote lyrics as well as music for "*Berlin im Licht*" (Berlin Lit Up) a year later. But first, he had to take formal farewell of atonalism. Let Hindemith have it—though Hindemith, too, was to abandon it for more agreeable music-making. Comes now Weill's last major piece in his soon-to-be defunct style, *Der Zar Lässt Sich Photographieren* (The Tsar Has Himself Photographed). This was the little opera with a libretto by Georg Kaiser that proved too long for Baden-Baden; and as Weill wanted to pair it with *Der Protagonist*, he couldn't stray far from the atonal style of the earlier piece. Be careful what you wish for. At least Weill could cut a slice of cabaret into it, as the "Tango Angèle."

Angèle is the photographer of the occasion—but just before the Tsar arrives at her studio, terrorists take over with a false Angèle and a camera rigged to assassinate when she takes the "shot." Weill and Kaiser billed the piece as an "opera buffa"—Offenbach's form, and bizarre touches throughout do suggest an updated Offenbach. A chorus of old men in top hats and beards, seated in rows below and in front of the stage, punctuates the action with merry commentary, and farce overtakes the murder plot when the Tsar playfully decides to "shoot" the false Angèle himself and the two wrestle erotically for mastery of the scene. Here is where the "Tango Angèle" comes in, when she puts on a gramophone record. In the program book available at the premiere, in Leipzig on February 18, 1928, Weill, as always, enlarged upon his intentions: "I believed I could heighten [the moment] only by a complete change of tone color." From the generally frantic atonal style of the piece, Weill suddenly goes into the choppy languor of a cabaret tango, scored for saxophones and recorded for use in performances of *Der Zar* by the Dobbri Saxophone Orchestra.*

As so often in Weimar dance music, the tango is not just a tango but a study of the tango, an intellectual's tango, as if explaining something to Goethe. It does indeed heighten the moment, knocking the spectator out of the storytelling to demonstrate how the story is told: an act of neo-Classicism committed by jazz. This is why Weill's music becomes, from now on, increasingly difficult to describe because it is at once impulsive and observed, direct yet sophisticated. The melody appeals, but the composer has an agenda that is larger than melody.

Der Zar was to prove Weill's most popular stage work so far, but despite his attempt to pair it indissolubly with *Der Protagonist*, the two never became, so to say, an item. Even at the Leipzig premiere, it shared the bill with Nicola Spinelli's *A Basso Porto* (Low Flood, 1894), an obscure *verismo* piece. But *Der Zar* did mate with *Der Protagonist* at Altenburg two months after Leipzig, and the pair played the Charlottenburg Städtische Oper in Berlin six months after that, in October of 1928.

Yet by then Weill had put both works behind him, embracing his new meta-cabaret style, his new librettist in the cabareting of classical music, and his new leading lady in the singing of it. As Weill and Brecht worked on the full-length *Mahagonny*—the world's first cabaret opera—they paused to invent the cabaret play. The idea was so outlandish that its first-night audience sat in icy incomprehension for the first six numbers, then stopped the show with demands for encores after the seventh. All Berlin went mad for the work, all Central Europe. It has flopped repeatedly in Britain and America, but it has also resounded there uniquely. On the short list of definitive twentieth-century theatre pieces, it is, all the same, one of the strangest things ever written.

---

* Released commercially, the Dobbri's "Tango Angèle" was the first time Weill's music was available on disc.

7

"They'll Know Who I Am Tomorrow"

Ernst Josef Aufricht, a youngish actor with a rich father, decided to turn producer. He took a lease on the Theater am Schiffbauer-damm, located to the north of Berlin's entertainment district around Friedrichstrasse—in fact across the Spree from Central Berlin. As its name reveals, the Schiffbauerdamm originally housed Berlin's ship carpenters, and the theatre, though built in 1892, looked like a left-over from old Baroque Berlin, with the imposing entranceway, tower rising to a point, and ceremonial doodads of a town hall. It was a major house—Gerhart Hauptmann's *The Weavers* was premiered there—and now Aufricht was looking for something flashy to inaugurate his first season, starting in the summer of 1928. So of course he went to Schlichter's.

There he ran into Brecht, sat at his table, and asked him—as Aufricht put it in his memoirs—the *"Gretchenfrage."** As always, Brecht

---

* Literally "Gretchen's question," this common German idiom reflects how thoroughly high culture had permeated German life, as it refers to lines 3415–3417 of Goethe's *Faust, Part One*, when the heroine asks Faust, "Nun sag, wie hast du's mit der Religion? / Du bist ein herzlich guter Mann, / Allein ich glaub, du hältst nicht viel davon." (Now say, what meaning God has in your mind. / You seem a truly had a number of projects in process, but the one that engaged Aufricht was *Gesindel* (Riffraff), drawn from an eighteenth-century English ballad opera about a romantic highwayman who woos the daughter of an underworld lord.

A famous line cuts in here, as Aufricht tells us, *"Diese Geschichte roch nach Theater"* (The plot smelled of theatre). After a look at the partially finished script, Aufricht was ready to go to contract—but he had a stop in the mind over Brecht's choice of composer, who of course was Weill. In Aufricht's recollection, he went to the Charlottenburg Opera to hear that double bill of *Der Protagonist* and *Der Zar Lässt Sich Photographieren*, but, as we know, that bill didn't start its run till October of 1928, and we are now in the spring of that year.

Of course, Aufricht might have gone to Altenburg for the same pairing, but it's a sizable journey from Berlin. The only Weill recording available was that single 78 side of the "Tango Angèle." What, in fact, *did* Aufricht hear of Weill's style? Because it would have been the pre-cabaret, atonal Weill, too abstract and clangy for the popular hit Aufricht hoped to produce. He admits that he commanded his music director to whip up an arrangement of the original ballad opera's songs, just in case.

What Aufricht might actually have heard was another side of Weill, as composer of incidental music—atmosphere pieces, intermezzos, underscoring, and the odd vocal spot—for straight plays. Two such were running in Berlin at just this time, in March and April of 1928: Leo Lania's *Konjunktur* (Money Madness) and Arnolt Bronnen's *Katalaunische Schlacht* (A Battle in Catalonia). *Konjunktur* might well be where Aufricht heard his first Weill, for it was the more notable production, by Brecht's only rival as a theorist in stagecraft, Erwin Piscator, and be-

---

upright man, / But all alone, and not to God inclined.) It's a dicey moment, as Faust in fact is more or less agnostic in a credulous age yet needs to please this lovely maiden. The American equivalent of the *Gretchenfrage* would be the "sixty-four thousand-dollar question," but that lacks the essential nuance of the question's creating an awkward situation, being either difficult or embarrassing to answer honestly. Note, however, that Aufricht's *Gretchenfrage* created not embarrassment but opportunity.

cause *Konjunktur*'s heroine was played by Roma Bahn. It was Bahn who was called in to assume the heroine's role in *Gesindel* when Carola Neher stormed out of the job at the last minute. It can be surmised that Aufricht thought of Bahn because he had seen *Konjunktur*.

The Diva Walkout, along with The Other Diva's Refusing To Sing a Solo Because It Is Beneath Her, The Mechanical Failure of a Special Effect, The Risible Vanity of the Leading Man, and The Kibitzers at the Dress Rehearsal Who Gleefully Predict the Greatest Flop in History were all part of a milieu that Weill was entering for the first time. Composing incidental music for plays brings one into the theatre, yes—but composing an almost entirely new score for a full-fledged musical brings one onto the battlefield. For one thing, in the theatre world the director ruled; in the opera world that Weill had come from, the musician was in charge. Then, too, Berlin's theatre world introduced Weill to the backbiting and scheming typical of a community with no more than a few top slots for the ambitious; classical music reveled in an ever expanding roster of major names.

Further, Weill was at last entering the domain of his wife, to unite with her in the very act of writing for her. Remember, despite her participation in the *Mahagonny* one-act, Lenja was not yet thought of as a singer. At that, her role of Jenny in *Gesindel* was more spoken than sung, though when she met Aufricht, she told him, "Weill will write a song for me." Aufricht knew how some writers create opportunities for their paramours, but he had to admit that Lenja was a fascinating item. Talk about smelling of theatre! How, he wondered, had "little Weill" snapped up that trophy?

And so began the saga of *Gesindel*, which was later called *Des Bettlers Oper* (The Beggar's Opera) and *Die Luden-Oper* (The Pimps' Opera), and, finally, *Die Dreigroschenoper* (The Threepenny Opera). True, one could date the story from 1728, when John Gay more or less invented musical comedy in *The Beggar's Opera*. Yes, it was Offenbach who remixed it elementally with fantastical stories and music to match. Still, the musical as a form really starts with ballad opera. Gay wrote the words, but the piece has no composer as such: all its music was in existence before Gay conceived of a kind of low-down opera, with a cast of criminals, spoken dialogue, and Gay's lyrics set to popular tunes, the whole thing in English.

It was Elisabeth Hauptmann—once again, Brecht's chief exploited collaborator at this time—who brought *The Beggar's Opera* to Brecht's attention. A 1920 revival, with fresh musical arrangements by Frederic Austin, opened at a London theatre way to the west of the West End, the so-called Lyric Theatre, Hammersmith. In costumes fit for an eighteenth-century ball, from wigs and three-cornered hats to buckled shoes, the work enchanted London all over again—for 1,463 performances! And while it didn't spin off a spate of copycat productions throughout Europe, it was seen (in English) in Paris in 1921 and in Vienna, as *Der Liebling von London* (The Boy Friend of All London), in 1924. The latter production is perhaps the one that spurred Hauptmann to start a German translation of the 1728 original for possible use by Brecht. He was always keen to, so to say, liberate a classic in exhaustive revision. Using Gay's story and characters, Brecht added entirely new scenes and devised (with Weill) new song spots, till virtually nothing remained of the old work but one tune and a few spoken lines here and there.

Most important, *Threepenny*'s songs function in an entirely different manner from those in *The Beggar's Opera*. The older work is not only the "first" musical, but an integrated one: the songs bubble out of the script. Some of the *Threepenny* score does, too—but some of it crashes into the action at a right angle, observing the show, needling it, jesting at it. Further, some of the *Threepenny* music is classical, some popular, and some belongs to some gnomic echelon between the two worlds, as if Beethoven were working in a piano bar.

In short, *Threepenny* is the cabaret *Singspiel*. Besides changing Gay's text, Brecht so altered Gay's tone that his characters now reside, in effect, in the Berlin of the *Alles schwindel*. Gay's public were treated to a comic thrill tour. *Threepenny*'s public knew every character in the show personally.

For once, Brecht gave credit to a collaborator, billing Elisabeth Hauptmann for "translation," himself (by last name only) for "adaptation," and Weill of course for "music." François Villon and Rudyard

Kipling were also credited, for some of the lyrics. Unbilled was one K. L. Ammer, whose German translation of Villon Brecht had lifted. When Brecht's worst enemy, the critic Alfred Kerr, recognized Ammer's wording and went public with his discovery, Brecht had to split his 62 ½ per cent royalty with Ammer (who took 2 ½ per cent). Hauptmann got 12 ½ per cent and Weill 25 per cent.

The *Threepenny* cast was a sound but uncooperative one: they had the talent but didn't like their parts or the show in general. Harald Paulsen, of the operetta world, played Macheath with verve and glamor; Brecht saw the character as an apparently harmless gentleman who kills with money rather than a knife. A bank officer, say. When Paulsen accessorized his costume with a sky-blue cravat that he refused to give up, Weill and Brecht wrote the Moritat—the famous "Ballad of Mack the Knife"—to undercut Paulsen's exhibitionism.

But then, many of the cast were pulling stunts. The Mrs. Peachum—wife of the underlord who opposes Mack—was Rosa Valetti, the older woman we always see in the famous still of Marlene Dietrich in *The Blue Angel*. Dietrich is perched on a barrel and Valetti, to the right, is kind of skulking around. She's one of Weimar's most atmospheric characters—but she refused to sing her solo, "The Ballad of Sexual Enslavement." She found it too lubricious.

Nearly every *Threepenny* performer had some impediment to worry Aufricht with, for the relatively simple production had gone into ridiculous budget overruns and threatened to smash his managerial career at its inception. Helene Weigel, one of Brecht's several girl friends, was to have played Gay's Mrs. Coaxer, but was sidelined by illness. The Lockit (renamed Tiger Brown because the pun in "Lockit" wouldn't speak to a German audience even in translation) still had Gay's Lucy for a daughter, but that actress, Kate Kühl, couldn't get through her big scene, a mock recitative-and-aria in miniature, and it was cut.* Even the printer of the program created a problem when—as

---

* Modern revivals usually restore it, but it was dropped before Weill orchestrated it, and must be newly scored by others—one of his very few songs never to be heard in Weill's own instrumentation.

we know—he accidentally left Lenja off the cast list, throwing Weill into one of the few genuine rages of his life. Aufricht had to print a little insert reading, "Die Rolle der Jenny spielt Lotte Lenja." Either because the insert wasn't ready for opening night or because spectators didn't find it, the delicious mystery—who *is* she?—was the talk of the first intermission. By the second, those who knew had spread the word. Lenja's previously quoted "They'll know who I am tomorrow" may be one of the few understatements an actor ever made.

The final crisis was that of the prop horse which Kurt Gerron (the Tiger Brown, in another role as the Mounted Messenger) was to ride for his entrance in the show's finale. "It was a huge, galloping, dapple-grey beast with fiery nostrils," Aufricht tells us in his memoirs. The designer, Caspar Neher, had painted the rear of the stage as a huge organ, and a hidden door in the "pipes" was to open, allowing the horse to slide in on rails. Apparently the rails were skewed, and on the first try horse and rider crashed past the footlights into the auditorium. This was some four hours before the first-nighters were to take their seats, and nothing could be done.

"The horse appears or the piece will not be played!" Brecht insisted. He thought an extra could haul it on by hand.

Aufricht refused. "This is no children's show!" he said. "I won't have that hateful block of wood on stage at the finale!"

In the audience, Helene Weigel, recovered from her medical griefs, wrung her hands and cried, "The horse, the horse!"

Nominally, the show's director was Erich Engel, but—as always—Brecht had elbowed his way into the role of autocrat-in-chief. Was he merely creating his usual rumpus, or did he really think it necessary for the Messenger to be Mounted? He did nourish some half-baked (and, when he committed it to paper, utterly incoherent) notion that the bourgeois audience can't accept the deus-ex-machina unless it *sees* the machine. Everyone had a suggestion, but what could be done at so late an hour?

So "I have entered this theatre for the last time!" Brecht shrieked. Aufricht claims that Weill sided with Brecht, which seems unlikely. Caspar Neher, a Brecht buddy from earliest schooldays, did so as well.

They had all entered the Theater am Schiffbauerdamm for the last time.

To which Aufricht's assistant, Heinrich Fischer, replied, "Would the gentlemen give us that in writing?"

In the end, Gerron simply walked onstage as a plain old messenger, mounting no more than a little wooden step brought on by a minor player.*

And the show went on, on August 31, 1928, to a half-sold house that, from the first notes of the overture, sat on its hands. True, it surely wasn't ready to hear an eight-member jazz band playing the fugato lines of the overture's trio section. Was this classical music or pop music? But why did the public resist the Moritat, which directly follows the overture? It does make an odd first number: a Ballad Singer (Kurt Gerron again) simply turned a hand-organ crank to launch into a panegyric on loathsome crimes. And the organ didn't sound, because someone forgot to set the apparatus. Still, the tradition of the Moritat is an old one, surely known to *Threepenny*'s audience; and while Gerron had to deliver the number's first strophe a cappella, Weill had scored the music with the band joining in after the first four lines, so the accident proved momentary. The melody, simplicity itself, is twisted by the use of the sixth of the scale in the first phrase of each strophe. Every four lines, the melody is repeated, with the band offering variations in their accompaniment. All the world loves this tune. Not only the theatregoers of Western culture: everybody.

Yet *Threepenny*'s first nighters failed to respond to it, and the following book scene, a comic look at Mr. Peachum's industrialization of begging, could have been playing to an empty hall. "The rejection was unmistakable," says Aufricht. "Nobody clapped." Nor did anyone clap for the music, including Polly's party piece at her wedding, "*Die Seeräuber-Jenny*" (Pirate Jenny), today one of the score's most popular spots.

---

* On Broadway in 1933, a staging modeled on the Berlin original attempted the horse effect, and "the beast slowly emerges," said *The Stage*'s Hiram Motherwell, "with a dignity absent from any of the humans in the piece."

Then came the raucous, racist military duet of Macheath and Tiger Brown, *"Der Kanonen-Song"* (Cannon Song), and all of a sudden the audience got it. "There was bedlam," says Lenja, and the show went past hit status—past even smash status—into You're Socially an Idiot If You Haven't Collected It status. Dance bands jammed on the music. Journalists discussed it on every page. Someone opened up a *Dreigroschenoper-Bar* where musicians played nothing but the show's songs. Recordings proliferated—the *Tanzpotpourri*, of course, but far more than that. It was not unusual for musical productions of various kinds to leave an original-cast souvenir—Alexander Girardi or Fritzi Massary in Kálmán titles, even Lehár's original Merry Widow and her Danilo, Mizzi Günther and Louis Treumann, cutting five sides in 1906. So *Threepenny*'s Macheath, Harald Paulsen, recorded four numbers. *"Kabarett zu Hause"* (Your home cabaret), Homocord's ad promised. Carola Neher (no relation to the designer Caspar), who had walked out on the role of Polly but replaced her replacement, recorded two solos and a two-sided medley. Even Brecht got into the act—and when Weill prepared a *Threepenny* suite, *Kleine Dreigroschenmusik*, Otto Klemperer recorded four of the eight movements, further clouding *Threepenny*'s generical identity. Again, was it classical, popular, or—and this was always Weill's favorite slot, once he abandoned atonalism—an undiscovered stronghold located east of classical and west of popular? And then *Threepenny* got a sort of full-scale cast album, with Lenja and both first-night players and replacements, all switching around in various roles. These four twelve-inch Ultraphon (later Telefunken) discs, comprising thirteen selections introduced by Brecht's narrations (spoken by Kurt Gerron), may have been the first German attempt to record substantial chunks of a theatre score with something like its original cast.

So Berlin went—every writer says so—"*Threepenny* mad." Weill was made, Brecht was made, and Lenja—who proved that arguable old proposition that there are no small parts, only small actors—was made. Most immediately, Weill and Lenja could now move out of their pension into an apartment and buy a car. More broadly, Weill was no longer That Enfant Terrible Who Does the Kaiser Operas. He became instead the *Threepenny* composer: famous.

The nationalist press, by policy opposed to all work of Jewish or leftist authorship, denounced it, of course. But in fact many others, even today, do not enjoy the show. That narrative about the first night, however implausible (they really didn't like "The Ballad of Mack the Knife?" *Really?*), does tell us something about how unconventional this work is. Weill and Brecht combined playwrighting and cabaret into one unified piece with warring parts, a savage comedy, entertaining Machiavellianism. Like John Gay himself, *Threepenny*'s authors mean their underworld as a goof on the *nomyenklatura*: the Names of Power. Such a piece shouldn't be so much fun, but the dialogue is quite funny and the score is an adventure, because it never seems to behave the same way twice. That first audience didn't warm to *Threepenny* till its seventh musical cue because they were bewildered—first of all by Brecht's voice. Little of his work had been seen or heard (on radio) by the Berlin public by 1928. Second of all, the score is a paradox many times over: those songs rising out of the story followed by songs flipped out at the public like music-hall turns. Or that overture roving in from some sneering Philharmonic. Or the senior Peachums' "*Anstatt-Das-Song*," the "Instead of That" duet, which is completely sung yet sounds as if made of nothing but words. Or Polly's "Pirate Jenny." Why is Polly Peachum suddenly named Jenny (especially when somebody else in the piece *is* named Jenny)? And why does she want everyone killed?

Still, *Die Dreigroschenoper* quickly found a home in some two dozen other German cities, then in Zurich (where it failed), then Vienna (where it was a huge hit), then Paris. As *L'Opéra de Quat'Sous* (The *Four*penny Opera),* the stage work failed twice, in 1930 and 1937, though the film was popular. *Threepenny* traveled the continent generally but did not dare England (except for a radio broadcast in 1935)

---

* The change from three to four pennies reflects French usage: "*quatre* [or, colloquially, *quat'*] *sous*" is the French idiom for "cheap."

till the mid-1950s, as a direct result of the famous Theatre de Lys revival. The English hesitation was no doubt a matter of national pride, for *The Beggar's Opera* was still a performable classic and, it was thought, exempt from adaptation. More notably, *Threepenny* failed on Broadway, in 1933, in that aforementioned production modeled on the original but in a translation that (to judge by what little seems to have survived) was completely terrible, and at a time when New York's theatre critics were hostile to leftist art.

Besides winning material security for the first time in their lives, Weill and Lenja were now fully fledged personages in the German theatrical world; her acting career was established and he was never entirely "classical" again. In the world of symphony and opera, where Brahms listens only to Beethoven and Beethoven listens only to God, Weill had been, to his great displeasure, more or less indistinguishable from Hindemith. No longer: Hindemith didn't write musicals (though his one-act operas were edgy and even zany pieces). Weill would still pursue opera-house contracts; he was especially keen on getting a world premiere in Berlin. But from now on his "opera" would usually bear a *Threepenny* flavor—or, more correctly, a *Mahagonny* flavor, as it was this work that had set Weill on his new path.

He and Brecht maintained their collaboration in late 1928 and 1929 with *Das Berliner Requiem* and *Der Lindberghflug* (Lindbergh's Flight), both radio commissions. The *Requiem* calls for male soloists and Weill's favorite scoring platform, a wind orchestra, in settings of Brecht's poetry on death—a drowned maiden, the Unknown Soldier, and so on. *Der Lindberghflug*, also for male soloists but also with chorus, treats the famous aviator's 1927 flight across the Atlantic to Paris. "*Steig ein!*" the chorus sings excitedly at the start. "*In Europa erwartet man dich!*" (Step in! Europe is waiting for you!). Yet the piece is almost dreary, with too little of the Brechtian irony and whimsy; the *Requiem* is actually livelier. Perhaps it was incorrect for Brecht to try to hymn the courage of a man alone in the heavens. Brecht saw all human activity taking place within social norms, submitting to or defying them. And Brecht did not generally believe in courage. Even his favorite characters are without it—not only the ingenious Galileo but *Mother* Courage herself.

As for the music, Weill was so overworked at this point that he agreed to let Hindemith compose half of the piece. A bit later, Weill wrote his own versions of Hindemith's sections. This is the work that is heard today, with a change of title (by Brecht, in 1950) to *Der Ozeanflug*, because of Lindbergh's extreme pro-Nazi sympathies, not only before World War II but, without a morsel of shame, after it.

The *Requiem* was broadcast on May 22, 1929 and the *Lindberghflug* on the following July 27. In between the two airings, Brecht threw his harem into consternation by marrying (for the second time). Carola Neher might have thought herself first choice; in her actressy way, she was by far the most alluring of Brecht's liaisons. As Aufricht put it, "She had a great insouciance, covering the rattle of a broken heart." A professional femme fatale, Neher once asked the producer, "Do you love me?" And Aufricht answered, "Yes. On the stage."

Elisabeth Hauptmann might have thought herself indispensable, because of her hefty contribution to Brecht's output and because her fluent English gave him access to the sounds of the culture that obsessed him. He in fact predicted that, by the year 2000 or so, a form of pidgin English would be spoken all over the world.

In the event, on April 10, 1929, Brecht chose as his bride Helene Weigel, the least attractive of Brecht's Eves in every sense. A talented performer but an angry loon whose only content was communist fanaticism, Weigel was also the least sexual of Brecht's contacts, well-nigh motherly in her treatment of him. Neher enchanted him and Hauptmann enabled his work; Weigel kept house. Further, she knew and approved of Brecht's predatory business arrangements (and was insistently to pursue them in his manner after his death). It was a mating of the like-minded, sociopathic egotists who did it to everyone else but not to each other.

It crushed Hauptmann to the point of a suicide attempt, but it didn't stop her from contributing to the next Weill-Brecht piece. Indeed, this time Hauptmann appears to have written the entire script and at least some of the lyrics—and this is partly why this new show turned out so badly. It was not Hauptmann's fault, but Brecht's, but all the same it led to the single greatest debacle of Kurt Weill's career, and it all began when Aufricht let *Threepenny* fever overcome his judgment and welcomed to his theatre a piece so leftist it made Brecht look bourgeois.

The playwright was Peter Martin Lampel, the play was *Giftgas Über Berlin* (Poison Gas Over Berlin), and its subject matter, drawn from an actual event in Hamburg, treated an accident in the manufacture of chemical weapons that had killed civilians. Lampel did so little fictionalizing in the piece that two prominent *Reichswehr* officers, Hans von Seeckt and Kurt von Schleicher,* were to be represented by actors in masks. "Despite many dramaturgical weaknesses," Aufricht later wrote, "we were, as pacifists, fascinated by the theme." Aufricht even moved *Threepenny*—still selling out at the time—to another theatre to free the Schiffbauerdamm stage and thus make the new piece his own.

However, even in early 1929, at the height of the post-Inflation Weimar golden age, Berlin was under nationalist control. City fathers could loathe *Threepenny* but not close it: its comic facade disarmed assault. *Giftgas*, on the other hand, begged to be closed. Many on the left encouraged Aufricht to proceed with the play to challenge the very notion of state censorship, but *Giftgas* was too provocative. Aufricht gave it a closed performance with the security services in attendance and, just before the curtain, he caught a glimpse of Brecht slipping a bit of paper to one of the actors. Aufricht took hold if it: a demand that the army officers in attendance leave their sabres in the cloakroom because the actors didn't want to play before armed warriors.

Aufricht tore the paper up and no such speech was delivered. Someone in the audience created his own distubrance all the same, crying out, at the sight of the Prefect of Police, Karl Zörrgiebel, "Dog! Criminal! Abuser of workers! To the gallows with you!" This impulsive

---

* Von Schleicher, as much a power broker as a soldier, made the fatal mistake of supporting the ambitions of the frivolous Franz von Papen, who turned against von Schleicher when the latter was Chancellor, in 1932, and prevailed upon the senile President von Hindenburg to appoint Hitler in von Schleicher's place. This was how the Nazis came to power. Seventeen months later, on June 30, 1934, von Schleicher, whom Hitler regarded as his worst enemy, was murdered along with his wife and many other opponents of the regime.

pundit was then helped out of the auditorium. But it hardly mattered, because everyone in the house knew that *Giftgas* would be banned. It was. And Aufricht was now, as they say, in a spot. "You open your theatre with a *Welterfolg* [world success]," said Leopold Jessner, intendant of the Berlin municipal theatre system. "Your second piece is a vast political scandal made of newspaper banner headlines. No matter what you produce next, you're going to disappoint everybody."

And after a few fast flops, Aufricht realized that what he needed was another *Threepenny Opera*. Weill and Brecht again, that underworld theme, the same staging cohort, the jazzy little band. The same conductor, the same players. And surely another Jenny from Lenja.

But she was now a star of the Berlin stage and wasn't available. That may explain why the new piece, *Happy End*—thus titled, in English— has two woman principals, neither of whom is right for Lenja. *Happy End*'s heroine is a sort of Polly Peachum, and the villainess a Mrs. Peachum, so Carola Neher and Helene Weigel Brecht (along with Kurt Gerron) would be carried over from *Threepenny*, even if both women had missed the premiere. (And while Neher had eventually joined the cast, Weigel may not even have rehearsed her part.) As Lenja proved in recordings, *Happy End*'s best known numbers—"*Surabaya Johnny*," "*Der Bilbao-Song*," "*Der Matrosen-Song*," "*Der Song von Mandelay*"—are ideal for her. But then, Weill was now composing the music that is love—for Lenja's art but also, on some level, for Brecht's. Unless Weill was thinking up music for specific characters, he was writing Brechtian cabaret for Lenja.

Happy End doesn't have specific characters. It has *Threepenny* characters, basically gangsters and, a new touch, the Salvation Army, in the usual demented Brechtian Chicago-that-is-Berlin. The libretto credit is so imaginary that writers love to quote it: "A magazine story by Dorothy Lane/German adaptation: Elisabeth Hauptmann." The magazine was named as the "*J & L Weekly*, St. Louis," but there was no Dorothy Lane and no *J & L Weekly*. More important, Brecht may have deliberately sabotaged the show, for one thing by assigning to it songs that, unlike those in *Threepenny*, did not partner or even collide with the plot and characters. Brecht's biographer John Fuegi thinks Brecht was expressing irritation at his dependence upon Elisabeth Haupt-mann. Further, Brecht goaded a great actor, Heinrich George, into quitting the show during rehearsals (he was replaced by one of Brecht's Baals, Oskar Homolka), meanwhile feeding lines to the bizarre Weigel. Worst of all, Brecht failed with great determination to tidy up Haupt-mann's third act, which by all reports lay unfinished even on the eve of the premiere.

But was all this about Hauptmann? Brecht had only recently fin-ished working with Weill on the *Mahagonny* opera, and the playwright must have been aware of how much the music detracted from the—let us say—pristine glory of his words. That's the problem with opera: the singers and orchestra devour the libretto. When Berlin got *Threepenny* crazy, audiences saw the play once or twice—but the music was heard everywhere one went, not to mention *Kabarett zu Hause*. Brecht de-ceived and cheated as robins sing, and he would instinctively have made things difficult for Hauptmann—yet wasn't he really aiming his battery at Weill? In truth, an angry, open break in the Weill-Brecht outfit was in the near future. For now, however, Brecht would be con-tent with a scandal.

How, exactly, the *Happy End* cast (which included also Peter Lorre, soon to appear with Lenja in a revival of Frank Wedekind's *Spring's Awakening*) got through an uncompleted third act is unknown to chron-icle. But all writers take on faith Aufricht's statement that *Happy End*'s first night, September 2, 1929, was at first playing *"ebenso stark wie bei der Dreigroschenoper"* (as well as *The Threepenny Opera* did).

How can that be true? *Threepenny* is a rich piece in every way; *Happy End* is thin and nearly pointless, with less a score than a spate of cabaret inserts. The songs are very enjoyable, but the work as a whole is not an effective successor to the sheer artistic bravado of the earlier work, not even in *Happy End*'s if nothing else viable first two acts.

"And then," says Aufricht laconically, "came Act Three." The public grew restive at the lax—or, supposedly, nonexistent—writing. Were the actors extemporizing? Presumably at Brecht's connivance, Weigel suddenly began haranguing the spectators with propaganda. *"Was ist ein Bankenbruch gegen eine Bankgründung?"* (What is the robbery of a bank next to the founding of one?), Weigel cried, along with, says Aufricht, "other vulgar Marxist provocations." But who would feel outraged at criticism of banks? Perhaps it was Weigel's accusatory delivery that outraged, as if she had taken the audience for bankers and their stooges. Though an exponential Mother Courage in post–World War II East Berlin, Weigel was never anyone's idea of a charming performer.

Happy End closed quickly. It might have spelled the end of the Weill-Brecht collaboration, but the spring of 1930 found the two working on what they called a *Schuloper* (school opera) entitled *Der Jasager* (The Yes-Sayer). Based on an old Japanese No play, *Der Jasager* is short and simple, designed (as "school opera" warns) to be put on by schoolchildren, to a kids' accompaniment of strings without violas, two pianos, and harmonium, with other instruments added as available. The characters are schoolchildren, too, with one adult, giving an innocent feeling to what is in fact a foul piece of grownup propaganda: a child falls ill on a mountain trip and is asked if he will follow the "ancient custom" of being thrown off a height so the others can complete their journey without bothering with him any more.

Under Weigel's nagging regime, Brecht's progressive politics had devolved into a pure communist party line, and *Der Jasager* plays as an elaborated skit such as might be put on at a totalitarian "re-education" camp. The sacrifice of one life, two lives, millions of lives for some imagined Greater Good is built into the structure of communist regimes; it was also intrinsic to Nazism. "You were born to die for Germany!" was a credo of the cult among the young in the Nazi version of re-education camps, set up for the Hitler Youth.

In truth, discussions among the children and teachers staging *Der Jasager* revealed their anxiety about the tale, and after tweaking the libretto, Brecht prepared *Der Neinsager*, in which the boy rejects the ancient custom and his comrades bear him home. If Brecht expected Weill to set this text as well, it did not happen, and *Der Jasager*, by itself, remained a popular, if worrisome, item in school assemblies.

More Weill-Brecht was to come in Weill's incidental score to *Mann Ist Mann*, another fabulous Brecht flop, lasting 6 performances at Berlin's Staatstheater in 1931. More notably, Nero-Film, a subsidiary of the

German-American outfit Tobis-Warner, bought the rights to film *Threepenny*. As we'll see in the next chapter, Brecht pulled his usual stunt of attempting to take over the production and, failing, attempting to wreck it, which drew *Threepenny*'s authors yet further apart. At least Lenja got to preserve her Jenny—and the part was enlarged, giving her some interesting business in the first reel and transferring to her Polly's "Pirate Jenny" because her other music was cut. Whether Weill persuaded the film's director, G. W. Pabst, to give Lenja the number or whether Pabst realized that "Pirate Jenny" doesn't remotely suit the ebullient Polly but serves the grimly watchful Jenny as a character song, Lenja's "Pirate Jenny" remains the film's indelible memory: sung motionless till the last seconds, when Lenja makes one of those eloquently noncommittal gestures that we feel safe in calling "Brechtian."

Few of the *Threepenny* stage cast got to film their roles, but Lenja was now too big to overlook. *They'll know who I am tomorrow.* She appeared in *Die Petroleuminseln* (The Oil Islands, 1928) as Charmian Peruchacha, to incidental music by Weill. As if to emphasize how far she had come from her beginnings in Vienna and even from her development in Zurich, her biological father died during *Die Petroleuminseln*'s run, and Lenja did not miss a performance. It had also been a long time since she had seen her mother. *Be smart, Linnerl, and, if you can manage it, don't come back.* In 1929, Lenja played Ismene in an *Oedipus* cycle, returned to the Schiffbauerdamm for *Die Pioniere in Ingolstadt*, then moved to the huge Volksbühne am Bülowplatz to play Lucile in Büchner's *Dantons Tod* (Danton's Death), which is why she wasn't even in the audience for, much less playing in, *Happy End*.

Two odd notes in all this. First, on September 21, 1929, Berlin Radio presented *Grossstadt-Musik*, featuring works by the interesting combination of Offenbach and Weill, sung by a soprano, a baritone, and, so-billed, a "diseuse": Lotte Lenja. It was, in effect, her cabaret debut.

The other note: at the beginning of 1930, Weill went playgoing at the Berliner Theater, to see one of the American plays so popular at the time. Melodramas were favored—*Rivalen* (Rivals, originally *What Price Glory?*), *Der Emperor Jones*, *Anna Christie*. Even the intensely psychological *Strange Interlude* came over, as *Seltsames Zwischenspiel*. Lenja herself appeared in blackface in Michael Gold's anti-capitalist racial drama *Hoboken Blues*, retitled *Das Lied von Hoboken* (The Song of Hoboken). But the play that Weill saw at the Berliner was *Die Strasse* (The Street), a translation of Elmer Rice's *Street Scene*. At some point or other, Weill wondered what the piece would be like as an opera.

8

Kulturbolschewismus

S ome historians speak of the central convulsion of the twentieth
century as "the European civil war." J. M. Roberts warns that the
phrase is best understood as "a metaphor," because "the containment of
internal disorder [depends on] the fundamental presupposition of a
state." Europe was not a state, "and could not therefore in the strict
sense have a civil war."

However, Europe is nonetheless an entity of a certain kind and,
with its offshoots North and South America, it presents a "state" based
on shared beliefs, a single language family (for the most part: Hungarian, Finnish, and Basque are exceptional), and developments in technology, literature, and music unrivaled elsewhere. Europe claims as
well the unique evolution of human rights: to live free, to voice
unpopular opinions, to make subversive art, all understood by now to
be a birthright condition of citizenship in Western Civilization.
When President John Kennedy told the people of embattled West
Berlin, *"Ich bin ein Berliner,"*★ he was expressing a solidarity—almost

---

★ Here's another of those correctable factoids. "I am a citizen of Berlin" is properly
rendered as "Ich bin Berliner," while "ein Berliner" is a frosted pastry with a jelly

an ethnicity—across state borders in observance of the values of the West.

Comparably, literary critics emphasize a moment in the medieval poem *La Chanson de Roland*, set during the Islamic invasion of France. During a gigantic battle with the aggressor army, Frankish hero Roland tells his fellow Europeans:

> *Nos avons dreit mais cist gloton ont tort.*

or, in modern French:

> *Nous avons le droit, et ces gloutons le tort.*

and in English:

> *We are right, and these blackguards** *are wrong.*

It's a nativist mentality: we're right because we live here, and they're wrong because they're from somewhere else. But it's also a Crusader mentality: they're wrong because they're from a place of living and thinking that is different from the European—that is, Christian— way of living and thinking.

Thus, while Europe is not a nation-state, it *is* a civilization-state, and not till the twentieth century did it undergo a civil war in the broadest sense, one that virtually spanned the continent. All earlier wars were based on religious disputes, the need to stabilize borders, or warlords' conquest programs. Even Napoleon's attempt to seize control of European society and impose certain progressive reforms upon it is not ex-

---

or cream filling. Thus, many believe that Kennedy in fact said, "I am a pastry." In fact, "Ich bin ein Berliner" *also* means, "I am like unto a citizen of Berlin in sharing Berlin's concern about the Soviet menace," and no German-speaker would have failed to catch Kennedy's intended meaning.

* *Gloutons* does mean "gluttons," but the word is used by the Franks throughout *The Song of Roland* as an all-purpose and extremely offensive expletive, connoting someone literally disgusting.

ceptional: ultimately, the Napoleonic Wars were about Napoleon, not reform.

The European Civil War of the Twentieth Century was different—particularly in its second phase, the Hitler War. World War I grew out of Austria-Hungary's security issue with Serbian separatists. The Nazi uprising, however, was innovative in social and cultural terms, even biological ones: a fanatic repudiation of civilization's values in a worship of overlordism and mass murder. This time, "We are right and they are wrong" divided not Europeans from invading outsiders but one version of Europe from another. What was the *content* of Europe? Christianity and the arts and sciences—or the Nazis' industrialized primitivism? In Nazism's core belief, to love the self one must hate all others. What separates the two world wars is their very nature: the first was a conquerors' war and the second was a racial war, on the question of who was fit to run Western Civilization, who was to serve those who ran it, and who must be liquidated.

Ironically, this war among Europeans occurred at a time when Europe's different parts were in synch with each other as never before. We have seen how Weill welcomed radio, devoting some four years to a recurring column for *Der Deutsche Rundfunk* and accepting airwave commissions; we forget how, after the newspaper, radio constituted the major revolution in the spreading of information. Broadcasts from one nation were sometimes made available for broadcast to other nations. Movies, in the first years of the talkie, were often filmed polylingually, as when Garbo's first sound feature, *Anna Christie* (1930), was made on the same sets with two different casts and directors, one in English and one in German. Or think of it in terms of money: all Europe was banking in London, till many in authority thought that World War I was unthinkable simply because of the intricate interdependence of continental debit and interest. When one nation after another joined the war, bankers became the one thing bankers almost never become: flabbergasted.

Even so, banking is invisible to most people. However, communications touched their lives on a daily basis, and media not only united

Europe but, when the Nazis came to power, divided it with identity communications. A new idea: race was culture. You lived the life, expressed the wish-fulfillment, and made the art you were born to live, express, make. You were what you were. "We don't want German music," came the cry. "We want National Socialist music." Or "We don't want life-saving physicians. We want National Socialist physicians." Or "We want National Socialist newspapers, National Socialist scrambled eggs, National Socialist underpants."

And a National Socialist demagogue. *Dracula*'s monster-hunter Van Helsing tells us, "The strength of the vampire is that people will not believe in him." It was the German left that made that mistake, dismissing Hitler as a glorified street-corner shouter till he was on the verge of state power. The right found him easy to believe in: he persuaded the nationalists that his insanity was their insanity. This is the liar's universe, so consistent in its paranoia that the rest of us can't tell whether the demagogue believes what he says or uses rhetoric as a marketing upgrade. Discussing modern-day America's "truthers" and Holocaust deniers, Charles Krauthammer described such people as creating "a hallucinatory alternative reality in the service of a fathomless malice." This was what gave Hitler his base—not, as popularly believed, ties to the business world's power structure. Hitler mesmerized his followers because, quoting J. M. Roberts again, "He expressed the resentments and exasperations of German society in their most negative and destructive forms," all the while "working within a deranged logic which he . . . persuaded others to share."

Still, as Michael Signer observes in *Demagogue*, this figure is not a "self-contained demented or outright evil" character, but rather "a phenomenon endemic to democracy itself." The demagogue is a systemic problem, because democracy—even Weimar's compromised and stuttering democracy—is a rule by the people and the demagogue appeals to some portion of that polity. Thus, because the demagogue is inherently divisive, democracy has a sort of potential civil war built into it. And as Western governments become less oligarchical and more populist, the danger of upheaval within the West becomes more acute.

Kulturbolschewismus—"cultural bolshevism"—was a concept, a politics, a war cry, and yet another actuation, as a pseudo-legal description, of Hitler's rage. It purported to isolate art that offended nationalist attitudes, but it more truly invented the idea that art that wasn't "Aryan" must be "Jewish": biologically criminal. *Die Dreigroschenoper* was cultural bolshevism by that definition—but also because of Brecht's politics. What was worse than an Aryan who didn't take his place with the *Volk*? Another example was the Hollywood version of *All Quiet on the Western Front* (1930), for its "defeatist" view of war. The film even dared to begin with the novel's epigraph, which told (here again in A. W. Wheen's translation), "of a generation of men who, even though they may have escaped its shells, were destroyed by the war."

It's a superb movie, by one of the early talkie's most innovative directors, Lewis Milestone. *All Quiet* was made when regular sound production was but a year old, yet it admits of no technical handicaps as the camera roves through the story of the four comrades cut down one by one. Early on, Milestone presents a military band on parade in a town square before a cheering crowd, and the view then pulls back through a window into a classroom. We can't hear the teacher. Drowned out by the march music as he speaks, he appears to become one with the happy noise—and when we finally do hear him, he is urging his students to enlist. "You are the life of the fatherland, you boys," he says. But what he means is: You were born to die for Germany.

The film so enraged the Nazis that they closed it down by rioting in the theatre and bringing boxes of mice to set loose in the auditorium. President von Hindenburg dismissed it all as "The indignation of nationalistic youth," and the film was banned on the grounds that it would "endanger Germany's national prestige." Ironically, the Nazis did nothing to harass *All Quiet*'s German equivalent, *Westfront 1918* (1930), from the same director and studio that would film *Threepenny* one year later, G. W. Pabst and Nero-Film. Based on Ernst Johannsen's *Vier von der Infanterie* (Four Infantrymen), the film shares Remarque's scenario of comrades dying one by one and also focuses on one in particular. Home on leave, he finds his wife in bed with the butcher—not for pleasure but for the food he can bring her. The last of the four, he finally dies in the hospital, with the last words *"An allen sind wir . . . schuld"* (We are guilty of everything).

Perhaps the Nazis tolerated *Westfront 1918* simply because it was German. But what did they like?

They liked Fritz Lang, who directed movies that seemed national-ist and artistic at once; that wasn't easy to do. The two-part epic *Die Nibelungen* (1923; 1924) is extraordinary in every respect, blending myth and politics and design into history magic. In the opening forest sequence, primeval oaks jut out of a landscape clothed in mist, as if the earth hadn't yet finished its growth, and as the hero, Siegfried, travels into civilization, Lang presents vast, featureless castles made of empty spaces, dwarfing people who have not learned to master the environ-ment beyond the weaving and hanging of fabrics. These, too, are part of the eyeful, in designs ready for a rite of spring.

Modern audiences laugh at *The Nibelungs'* mechanical dragon, the one antique flaw in an otherwise timeless spectacle. This is, after all, a silent film, technically limited. Yet Lang is so resourceful he can ex-ploit the limitations. At the Cathedral of Burgundy (placed atop a flight of steps so gigantic that the building has to wedge itself in at the top of the screen), the rivals Brünnhilde and Kriemhild get into a fight, and Brünnhilde, winning, lets out a long and hearty laugh. Lang cuts to inside the church, where Kriemhild's mother, in prayer, raises her head in apprehension—as if Lang had made us *hear* a silent. The cast-ing, too, is sharp: the Siegfried, Paul Richter, seems like the winner of a national talent search, with his sleekly chiseled physique and gleam-ing skin tone. In fact, he was a regular member of the German acting pool, and had already worked for Lang as the *jeune premier* of *Doktor Mabuse, der Spieler* (Doctor Mabuse, the Gambler, 1922).

Most interesting of all is Lang's sly use of a bit of Richard Wagner's *Nibelungen* epic in a scenario otherwise drawn from a different source. Wagner's worldview was Hitler's, with shiny Nordic heroes, ugly, crafty underpeople who try to destroy the heroes, and an ending in the myth of Ragnarok: everybody dies. No wonder Hitler and his propa-ganda tsar, Joseph Goebbels, saw in Lang a potential master of Nazi moviemaking. When Lang ventured into dystopian science-fiction, in *Metropolis* (1927), his view of mechanized masses helplessly toiling in the basements of a wonder city exactly align with Hitler's vision of Germania, the planned renovation of Berlin. The famous long shot of Lang's Gotham is spectacular, a colossal miniature with tiny hordes moving in lockstep across a bridge as cars whiz by and, overhead, one plane makes a turn in the air, defying us to figure out how Lang filmed it.

Yet Lang's fascination with the criminal overlord who mesmerizes his prey—this same Dr. Mabuse—cannot have pleased Goebbels. It's a German theme: the Devil and his Faust. But it's also a Hitler theme. Lang devoted a talkie to his favorite criminal, *Das Testament des Doktor Mabuse* (1933), in which the evil mastermind makes notes on how to take over the world with a *"Herrschaft des Verbrechens"* (a ruling class of criminals). The strategy is to terrorize the populace with crimes that benefit no one, not even the criminal, thus to create a "state of anarchy" in which "chaos becomes the supreme law." Though Goebbels banned *Das Testament*, he realized how well Lang had understood the unseen heart of Nazism.

Of course, Bertolt Brecht did as well, especially in *Mahagonny*, for the full-length opera—once again, the reason Weill and Brecht had originally partnered up—finally had its premiere, in Leipzig on March 9, 1930. Now Brecht could enjoy having collaborated on the most radical of all operas—not only because of its savage social commentary but because of the way Weill weaves his cabaret into a musical fabric that is as rough and offensive as Brecht's images. Thus, after the opening scenes of the founding of Mahagonny—"which means City of Nets, set up to catch edible birds"—and the flocking of the prey, four loggers arrive to take it easy after seven years in Alaska. *"Auf nach Mahagonny!"* they cry, in one of the numbers first heard in the Baden-Baden *Songspiel*. To the words "Lovely green moon of Alabama," they swing into a kind of merrily vicious quotation of the Bridesmaids' Chorus from Carl Maria von Weber's *Der Freischütz* (The Marksman, 1821). This is the German National Opera, with its thrillingly haunted woodland, ambitious hero, redemptive heroine, and wise elders. *Mahagonny* turns all of this obscenely topsy-turvy, with a corrupt coastland, lazy hero, prostitute heroine, and gangster elders. *Der Freischütz's* Agathe tells the hero, "*Doch sündigt der, der Gott versucht!*" (But he who tests God is a sinner!). *Mahagonny's* Jenny asks the hero, "*Trage ich Wäsche unterm Rock, oder geh' ich ohne Wäsche?*" (Do you want me with panties or without?).*

Such irreverence was *Kulturbolschewismus* on the grandest scale, a trashing of *Völkisch* sentiments spit right into Nazi faces. Everything about *Mahagonny* is tilted into a sort of poetic rubbish, a lyrical tour through the underworld of Western society. The music is tremendously powerful, surely Weill's greatest work, and the libretto is bizarre, nasty, funny, and worrisome, possibly Brecht's most complete statement of how he views the social contract.

It's amusing to note that, for all Berlin's America fetish, with its love of Chaplin and Keaton and westerns and jazz, the really chic Berliners looked to upper-class England as the model in education, attire, drinking, and even names. Sometimes it seemed as if half of Berlin was called Bobby—men and women both. In his so-called "Berlin Stories," Christopher Isherwood typically named a gay bar the Lady Windermere. And Joseph Roth, in the novel *Rechts und Links* (Right and Left, 1929), tells us, in Michael Hofmann's translation, "Some went so far as to affect 'indeed' instead of 'ja,' and to take out subscriptions to English newspapers. [They] would refuse to acknowledge events if they hadn't read about them in English."

Brecht had no use for this in his pay-as-you-go paradise of Mahagonny. England was empire, which is why his Brits are imperialists in the East. America was money, which can buy empires. This made *Aufstieg und Fall der Stadt Mahagonny* the outstanding *Zeitoper*, something everybody knew about even if he hadn't heard a note of it. The *Zeitoper* absorbed trends of the day—especially anything American. Ernst Křenek's *Jonny Spielt Auf* (Jonny Starts the Music, 1927) was the most obvious example, with its black-musician protagonist and jazz-

---

* Lenja says that it was she who gave Brecht that line, when he wondered "what one of *those* girls" inquired of a trick, for it was his habit to pick up bits of life from everywhere, to authenticate his characters. Thus he forever toggles between the documentary and the fantastic till these two opposites merge into that unique attitude that is part of what is meant by "Brechtian."

stippled score. *Mahagonny* was a more devious example: timeless in its deconstruction of the profit principle but late-Weimar Berlin in atmosphere. Jenny's *"Denn Wie Man Sich Bettet, So Liegt Man"* (You'll Lie in the Bed That You've Made) was something new in opera, a scathingly cynical aria: arias heretofore were idealizations (such as Norma's *"Casta Diva"*) or confessions (such as Carmen's Habanera). *"Denn Wie Man"* is an attack. It's the perfect Lotte Lenja number, of course—but in the opera that Weill and Brecht wrote, as opposed to the *Mahagonny Songspiel* and later revisions of the full opera, Lenja temporarily lost her Jenny franchise. The role called for a legit soprano, even though it's an opera that behaves like a vampire movie. At least Lenja recorded *"Alabama-Song"* and *"Denn Wie Man,"* for the Homocord label.

Of a sort, *Mahagonny* tells of another of those Faustian bargains, in which mankind trades security and the orderly life for the rampaging fun of absolute materialism. The insidious Leokadja Begbick and her accomplices, Willy der "Prokurist" (Willy the "Bookkeeper") and Virginia-Moses,* create Mahagonny as a simple con. Yet they end in unleashing hungers that orderly societies keep in check: for Mahagonny's politics is fascist chaos.

The film director Pier Paolo Pasolini, explaining the painstakingly reckless snuffporn that he concocted for *Salò* (1975), spoke of the "anarchy of power" inherent in totalitarian rule. As the authority of tyrants expands beyond law and conventional morality, the very idea of government begins to define itself by its excesses, its outrages. It destroys ever more grandly and impulsively, even for no purpose other than the affirmation of absolute power over Christian teaching. Everything becomes its opposite: reason gives way to whim, expedience to passion, statecraft to mass murder. Only a few people die in *Mahagonny*, yet an

---

* He was originally *Dreieinigkeitsmoses* (Trinity Moses), but this proved too blasphemous for Leipzig. Actually, *Mahagonny*'s principal character names are as unstable as the town is. The male quartet carried over from the *Songspiel* and here filled out with personalities was designed to undergo name changes to suit each audience's culture. Johann Ackermann, Jenny's opposite, is often called Jimmy Mahoney (the surname accented on the first syllable, to match the scan of Ackermann), and his buddy *Sparbüchsenheinrich* (Bank Book Heinrich) also goes by Heinz and Bill.

air of lawless chaos permeates the action. In fact, the place has laws. Still, in a trial conducted like a show, with spectators admitted at "Fünf Dollar" a head, one Tobby Higgins get off in a murder rap by bribing Judge Begbick. *Mahagonny*'s hero, Johann/Jimmy, can't afford the bribe, is found guilty, and is executed.★

The intention, clearly, is to cut open the money-obsessed heart of unsocialized capitalism as Brecht sees it. Still, Mahagonny's criminal rulers and compassionless citizenry—even the hero's friends won't lend him the money with which to buy his life—seem to reflect the coming Nazi state more than any capitalist democracy. Certainly, the opera's final words, sung to the marching of an epic picket line, "*Können uns und euch und niemand helfen!*" (Cannot help ourselves or you or anyone!), distinctly suggest the joyless ecstasy of the hatreds that the Nazi state thrived on. Usually played as an expression of deadpan—i.e., "Brechtian"—despair, this finale really expresses a triumphant nihilism. Brecht strips away the science-superstition and masscult pageantry of Hitlerism as a warning. Those few who realized that the Nazis were more than a passing menace discerned in them the next helping of evil history. Walter Laqueur reports that in 1933 George Grosz told Thomas Mann that "Hitler would last not six months but six or ten years . . . that both Nazism and Communism were based on terror and slavery and that within a few years there would be an alliance between Hitler and Stalin."

The Nazis knew enough about *Mahagonny* to view it as a test case of their rising power—the year of *Mahagonny*'s premiere, 1930, was also the year in which Nazi electoral strength began to swell decisively. To the Nazis, *Mahagonny* was democracy's Witches' Sabbath, the Jewish-Bolshevik victory dance of surrenderism and war guilt and

---

★ Once again, toying with Berlin's Americaphilia, Brecht fastened on the internationally notorious execution of Ruth Snyder and her lover for the murder of Snyder's husband. The legal jurisdiction was New York State, whose only form of capital punishment was electrocution. A tabloid sneaked a shot of Snyder after the current was turned on and ran it on the front page. Though Weill was queasy about it from the start—Snyder was executed in January of 1928, not long after Weill and Brecht began work on *Mahagonny*—Brecht insisted on including this bit of Americana. We actually see Johann/Jimmy strapped into the chair.

reparations. And Mahagonny was the pleasure city while the Nazis needed to create a climate of obligation and sacrifice. The party was determined to stock the premiere audience with its usual riot squad.

Lenja was there that night, along with the senior Weills, who now lived in Leipzig and had, in a grudging way, accepted Lenja as a Weill-by-marriage. Witnesses at the *Mahagonny* premiere tell us that the evening crackled with tension. Outside the opera house, Nazi demonstrators established an atmosphere of insecurity. Not just of disagreement: of violence.

Incredibly enough, the first scenes did not set off a firestorm. *Mahagonny* played to a strangely quiet disturbance for the first two-and-a-half acts: mutterings, gasps, and so on. Still, as one critic noted, they were "small bubbles, as if . . . simmering over a fire that was slowly bringing them to a boil."

Then at some point—no recollection makes it clear whether it was during the last act or at its conclusion—fights broke out and the theatre became a seething war between agitators and escapees. The land had turned fascist, and this opera was exercising democratic rights: Weill and Brecht had become the lightning rods for the freedom of art. Leipzig's Neues Theater was forced to play the rest of *Mahagonny*'s run with the house lights on and a police detachment lining the walls, and Essen, Oldenburg, and Dortmund cancelled their *Mahagonny* productions. In Kassel, the show went on and there were no riots. There was, however, a great public outcry, fanned by Nazi journalists and city authorities. Braunschweig's *Mahagonny* was taken off after only two performances because of audience fury, though in Frankfurt, despite another riot, the management ran the piece for ten showings.

The *Mahagonny* Question, as the Nazis might have put it, made national headlines. But Weill-Brecht was still best known for *Threepenny*, because Nero-Film released its movie version early in 1931. G. W. Pabst directed a cast featuring Carola Neher's Polly and Lenja's Jenny, but Pabst emphasized the danger of Mack the Knife in Rudolf Forster's cooly murderous portrayal, utterly erasing the operetta charmboy that Harald Paulsen had played on stage. Again, showing how united Western art had become, Nero-Film had Pabst direct a French cast on the same sets in the same costumes; between the two languages, it was thought, the film could play throughout Europe and the Americas.

To its regret, however, the studio engaged Brecht to prepare a treatment. His habitual unwillingness to adhere to a contracted schedule delayed production, and what he finally offered them was overtly politicized and far removed from the stage *Threepenny* script, even in its plotting. Most perversely, Brecht wanted to give up that million-dollar title and rename the film *Die Beule* (The Bump on the Head). But then, Brecht really loved kicking everything in the teeth, including his own work: it was his personal version of "acting" in the Brechtian manner. The studio rejected his revision, so he sued it for a shameless Weimar reality show: Brecht in court! Brecht stomping out when he doesn't get his way! Brecht never acted in his plays because he acted in life, but he lost his suit. Weill, who also went to court, to prevent his music from being changed, won.

There are two things of note here. One is that the *Threepenny* film, excellent though it is, scants the score. The other is that Brecht's attempted sabotage of the script is always blamed on the incendiary Weigel, tutoring her husband in communist positions. Yet isn't it more likely that Brecht was rebelling against the Weill-Brecht that he found his fame locked into? Brecht didn't want a composer partner: he wanted a composer acolyte, useful but self-effacing, like Elisabeth Hauptmann.

Brecht's hostility to Weill broke into the open when Ernst Josef Aufricht arranged for a "theatre" version of *Mahagonny* in Berlin, at the Theater am Kurfürstendamm at the end of 1931. Trude Hesterberg, Lenja, and Harald Paulsen headed a *Threepenny*-like cast of singing actors with some opera people and an orchestra of thirty-five. The Kurfürstendamm house, too, was a big one, down on the main stem, so to say. Part of *Threepenny*'s charm lay in its booking that exquisite old Easter egg across the Spree, fit for classics; the Theater am Kurfürstendamm was just ten years old in 1931, part of the new wild Weimar Berlin of the 1920s, the perfect setting for the new wild *Mahagonny*.

Still, Brecht bristled at being little more than the librettist of what could be thought of, especially in Aufricht's *Threepenny*ish version, as

"Kurt Weill's musical." So Brecht let the fault line in his and Weill's relationship erupt in quake. When a photographer tried to shoot the two men together, Aufricht recalled, Brecht knocked the camera to the floor and shouted, *"Den falschen Richard Strauss werfe ich in voller Kriegsbemalung die Treppe hinunter!"* (I'll get on my warpaint and toss that phoney Richard Strauss down the stairs!"). Weill, who lived with the inner grace of one so sure of himself that he cannot be provoked by someone else's bile, held his tongue and walked away.

Weill's relationship with Lenja was becoming vexed as well, though none but them ever knew why. There was no anger in it, yet the pair underwent a certain estrangement of the heart. First of all, when Lenja had the opportunity to travel to Russia to make a film for Erwin Piscator, Weill encouraged her to go. She didn't like traveling except to the Riviera, and she was somewhat taken aback that Weill seemed so willing to carry on without her. But she went.

Piscator, of course, was Berlin's master of new-wave stage production, each show an assembly of spare parts on the grand scale: to contrast with Max Reinhardt's love of old-fashioned spectacle and Brecht's spare presentations. A Piscator movie was an enticing notion. As with Pabst's *Threepenny* film, two casts were to be recruited, to make separate but equal films, one in Russian and one in German. The source was Anna Seghers' 1928 novella *Der Aufstand der Fischer von St. Barbara*, on an uprising of Breton fishermen, written with great persuasiveness despite Seghers' lack of familiarity with either Brittany or fisherfolk.*

We have seen Lenja arriving in cultural capitals in the thick of their modern history, and the Moscow of the summer of 1931 was the perfect Soviet metropolis: everything was falling apart and police spies were as common as Morlocks after dark. There was a tremendous amount of waste: week after week waiting for a finished script because

---

* Though her name no longer means anything, Seghers was well known as writer and Nazi refugee in the middle of the twentieth century. Her best-known novel, *The Seventh Cross*, provided Spencer Tracy with one of Hollywood's best escaping-the-Nazis thrillers; Seghers made a harrowing escape from them herself.

of a shortage of paper, then the paper arrives and the crew comman-
deers it to roll cigarettes. Lenya's hotel was so squalid that, one night,
she awoke to the sound of a rat dining on Toblerone chocolate bars that
Weill had sent her and which she had left on a table—the room's one
piece of furniture besides the bed. Lenja threw a shoe at the rat; it went
right on eating. The next morning, she discovered that it had gobbled
up everything on the table, from the candy to the tin foil it had been
wrapped in. Generally, Lenja's Moscow experience recalls the old joke:
what happens when the Soviet Union takes over the Sahara Desert?
Nothing for fifty years. After that, there will be a shortage of sand.

Piscator was almost never around, even when everyone trained
down to Odessa, Ukrainia's major port city on the Black Sea, where
the shooting was supposed to take place. Odessa was no Riviera: and
there was no shooting. Piscator did make the Russian version, known
by Seghers' original title as *The Revolt of the Fishermen* (1934), but there
was no German version. "Dostoyefsky, I have come!" was Lenja's greet-
ing to Moscow, but in the end the Russian capital proved less an adventure than a look at a culture more or less sulking in terror. She enjoyed
herself nonetheless; she always enjoyed herself, wherever she was. Some
people know how to bring their own fun with them.

Returning to Berlin for the Kurfürstendamm *Mahagonny*, she was
surprised to encounter no theatre riots. There wasn't even a Nazi picket
line. Yet this was a more telling *Mahagonny* than the Leipzig original
had been, simply because the theatre-oriented cast had better diction
than the opera singers: the audience now could follow the action's bitter
insights from line to line. The show went over so well that Lenja made
a two-sided twelve-inch 78 medley of *Mahagonny* numbers with the
Kurfürstendamm pit orchestra. Further, Vienna saw a staging in April
of 1932, again at a theatre rather than an opera house, albeit in a shortened version. And here Lenja became yet more estranged from Weill,
for the tenor playing Johann/Jimmy, Otto Pasetti, became her lover
and broke up her marriage.

Pasetti, a serviceable rather than entrancing tenor, was handsome
in a limp-haired, thin-lipped way, and, like Lenja, he had a taste for
getting out and going crazy: gambling, late-night parties, racing

around, and all the other things that Weill had no use for. In a phrase, Pasetti was more Lenja's speed. Though Weill went on to buy a house for Lenja and himself—a brick rectangle in Berlin's western suburb of Kleinmachnow—she never really lived there. She was living with Pasetti.

Greatly saddened, Weill nonetheless believed that Lenja must eventually return to him, because what these two shared no one else could share—especially Pasetti, who, even Lenja admitted, was on the dumb side. And, as always, Weill had his music: his other Lenja, in a way. His alliance with Brecht at an end, he teamed up with Caspar Neher, the set designer of Weill's Brecht shows. For continuity? An attempt to maintain Weill-Brecht without Brecht himself? Unfortunately, Neher was no Brecht. The result, *Die Bürgschaft* (The Guarantee, 1932), is pompous and somewhat incomprehensible, an interminable harangue by stick figures devoid of character development.

The title echoes that of Schiller's famous poem about two friends who would literally die for each other. One, under capital sentence for attempted regicide, is allowed to attend his sister's wedding with his friend as the guarantee in his place. If the condemned man fails to return in three days, his friend will die. A storm and a brigand band delay him, but through force of will and prayer he returns, stunning the ruler into pardoning him with these words:

> *Und die Treue ist doch kein lehrer Wahn,*
> *So nehmt auch mich zum Genossen an!*

> *If good faith is so pure and strong and just,*
> *Then take me, too, in your loving trust.*

Note that, as in his use of Rilke for his tone poem of 1919, *Die Weise von Liebe und Tod*, Weill was treating national material. Of course, in the Nazi mania for discerning *Kulturbolschewismus* in the work of anyone Jewish, that made no difference. German-ness, so to say—or even the ability to appreciate the poetry of Friedrich Schiller—was a quality one was born to: it could not be attained.

Weill had written his own lyrics to "*Berlin im Licht*" (Berlin Lit Up), his slithery march of a theme song for a nocturnal light show as part of the Berlin Festival of 1928, and now Weill apparently collaborated with Neher on *Die Bürgschaft*'s libretto, though he took no credit. The pair incorporated Schiller's tale into their story, also using a parable by the Enlightenment philosopher Johann Gottfried von Herder that unfortunately bogs down the opera's action. It's central to *Die Bürgschaft*, but it manages to be uninteresting and daft at once: a man buys a sack of grain at a grain price, but finds gold in the sack. An honest man, he offers to return the gold; the seller refuses it. The king judges that the men's children be married and the gold passed to their union. Alexander the Great, a witness to all this, observes that, where he comes from, the state would execute the men and confiscate the gold.

Could there be a drearier basis for an opera scenario? It's almost math homework: if A sells a pile of cordwood to B, and if X percent of the wood be one hundred times its value, how much should B pay if $x = \dfrac{jp32y}{\pi}$? Worse, in keeping with the parable's gnomic nature, no character in *Die Bürgschaft* has any personal flavor. The two men are gruff bass-baritones; we are told that they're friends but they don't act like friends. They don't act like anything, even as the tale becomes dire because of war, famine, and the like; as a trio that constantly changes its occupations creates trouble; as the principals and chorus hector us about the meaning of it all. Oddly, this is very much the sort of program Brecht might have worked on—but he would have brought a playful quality to it, as well as establishing a personal connection between the two men.

The music, at least, is titanic and monstrous, as the subject demands. It is entirely tonal and melodic but it is also devoid of the cabaret style Weill had made his signature sound in theatre music. Except for some jazzy brass mayhem during one scene-change intermezzo and evilly boogieing tympani amid a war march, the score is starved for variety and fun. Each part of it sounds exactly like the rest of it.

Die Bürgschaft was the only one of Weill's full-length operas to get a Berlin premiere, in the Charlottenburg house, on March 10, 1932. The critics were very mixed about this new turn in Weill's style, and Brecht, still resentful, dubbed the piece *Die Spiessbürgerschaft*.* But then, except when he acceded to Ernst Josef Aufricht's plea for another *Three-penny Opera* and came up with *Happy End*, Weill seemed to demand that each new project be entirely different from the previous ones. Thus, he jumps from the overwrought *Protagonist* to the gossamer *Royal Palace* to the farcical *Zar*. Later, he follows a musical play (*Knickerbocker Holiday*) with a straight play containing three little operas (*Lady in the Dark*) and then writes his only pure musical comedy (*One Touch of Venus*).

In fact, Weill was already planning to write a musical comedy now, in 1932. The German form of the time, which we inadequately describe as "operetta," varied from the vastly lyrical romances of Franz Lehár to the so-called operetta-revues of the producer-director Erik Charell at Berlin's Grosses Schauspielhaus, which were sometimes very popular in the flavor of their music. Weill would have taken notice of how deftly Lehár integrated music and text in *Friederike* (1928), a fictionalized look at how the young Goethe (played by Richard Tauber) is forced by affairs of state to abandon his sweetheart. In particular, Lehár utilized a two-note melodic cell in various ways, now hesitant, now radiant, reaching a climax in the *Tauberlied* (as they called the big solo of a Lehár-Tauber evening), "*O Mädchen, Mein Mädchen*" and, almost directly after, as an agonized undercurrent running through the heroine's "*Warum Hast Du Mich Wach Geküsst?*" (Why Did You Kiss My Heart Awake?). This is the creative concept of the composer's composer, using but two notes to ennoble a work already thrilled by the presence of Goethe. Weill must have wanted to try something like this himself—and note, too, that Lehár lost no prestige working in the lighter form, eventually to see *Giuditta* (1934) premiered at the Vienna

---

* This untranslatable pun plays on *Spiessbürger*, literally "spit citizen," harking back to the middle ages, when middle-class householders bore spears or pikes (the "spits") in case they had to defend the town from attack. Over the centuries, the term was disarmed to denote simply "middle-class burger," especially one narrow-minded and suspicious of novelty.

State Opera, an extremely conservative house that normally wouldn't have let an operetta into its green room, much less take its stage. But then, as Tauber put it, "I don't sing operetta. I sing Lehár."

Further, Weill would have noticed the emergence on German-speaking stages of the Hungarian Pál Ábrahám with *Viktoria* (generally known by its German title, *Viktoria und Ihr Husar*, 1930), *Die Blume von Hawaii* (1931), and *Ball im Savoy* (1932). Ábrahám loved pastiche numbers. *Viktoria*'s peripatetic plot gave him the chance to run a musical travelogue, from "Meine Mama War aus Yokohama" to a French waltz, "Pardon, Madame." But the Hawaiian show is almost entirely a pastiche, the closest thing to Broadway ever heard in German, with a raving hot band in the pit and Harald Paulsen as Jim-Boy, a blackface singer in the Jolson style with such numbers as *"Wir Singen zur Jazzband im Folies Bergere."*

Weill, who could put on a musical style like socks, must have wondered what he could do in this form. Somehow or other, he and Erik Charell started talking about possible projects. Germany's Florenz Ziegfeld, Charell had recently conceived and produced one of the biggest hits in the history of the musical, *Im Weissen Rössl* (White Horse Inn, 1930). It was big also in the physical sense, with a staggeringly huge cast and scenery that extended beyond the proscenium into the auditorium. Yet the plot as such was small, a sort of sunny *Little Night Music*, the rotating couples here placed in a lakeside Austrian resort. Charell was thus able to fill out his production with anything that caught his fancy—a yodeller, a slap-knees-and-hop men's dance group, a train, a rainstorm, acrobats. *White Horse Inn* went to every major city, often in its original spectacular staging.

However, Charell was not the right producer for Weill. Thinking spectacle and variety the essential elements of the musical, Charell went in for grab-bag scores by a team of writers, with his house composer, Ralph Benatzky, "arranging" out of the public domain or supplying the core numbers. It worked well in *Casanova* (1928), drawn from lesser-known Johann Strauss and providing a "new" operetta standard in the soaring Nuns' Chorus, for the heroine and a sororal choir. But *White Horse Inn*, for all its fun, was the opposite of what Weill expected of musical theatre: innovation, consistency, and above all a love affair between words and music.

Still, Weill and Charell tossed some ideas around. Shaw's *Caesar and Cleopatra* is mentioned in one of Weill's letters, and there was also talk of adapting the horror film *The Cabinet of Dr. Caligari*. It's an odd notion, for the *Neue Sachlichkeit* had all but terminated fantasy horror, especially the expressionist kind. But expressionism was the summoning term of Weill's erstwhile collaborator Georg Kaiser, and in due course Charell had bowed out of the talks and Kaiser bowed in. He and Weill decided to team up again; oddly, the piece they settled on was in its barest outline comparable to *Die Bürgschaft*: another parable with a socially progressive moral framework. In its execution, however, the new work was utterly unlike *Die Bürgschaft*, and would prove to be the third and final masterpiece—after *Threepenny* and *Mahagonny*—of Weill's German years.

Overworked and, in personal relationships, often disappointed, Weill was in need of a turn of fortune, and the year 1932 was the worst yet in Weimar democracy. The world Depression had mashed the German economy badly enough for Hitler to propose himself as the nation's fixer, facing the incumbent, Paul von Hindenburg, in the presidential election that spring. It was virtually a two-man contest, Nazi versus Nationalist, for the other two major parties, the Social Democrats and the Center Party (representing Roman Catholics), realizing what a disaster a victorious Hitler would be, fielded no candidates at all and advised their constituents to vote for Hindenburg. Only the communists insisted on intruding on a race that essentialized the fault line running through Weimar's fragile democracy: the homicidal rage of the losers of the war about nothing. Operating under Moscow's orders and locked into Moscow's worldview, German communists thought of themselves as the classic revolution from below, the answer to a post-Kaiser Kaiserism, the old Bismarckian empire surviving war and democracy with its hierarchies intact. The left failed to understand that the Nazis were an alternate revolution—not the counter-revolution of the hierarchies but a revolution from below *of a different kind*. It was a threat that Marx and Lenin had never anticipated. With the country once again in chaos, more and more voters, impatient with Reichstag bumbling, gravitated to the Nazis.

The communists' Ernst Thälmann drew enough votes away from Hindenburg to necessitate a runoff, which Hindenburg won, on April 10, 1932. Still, the Nazis became the largest party in the Reichstag, and pressure was building to let Hitler into government. At the age of eighty-five, Hindenburg was fading. Worse, he was surrounded by what every historian likes to call a "camarilla" of plotters and schemers who beguiled him into accepting Hitler while thinking they could subordinate Hitler's participation.

All this was in train while Weill and Kaiser worked on their new piece, which, on the allegorical level, reflected the state of the nation. It was a fairy tale, and so they subtitled it: "a Winter's Tale." The cold is hard times. There is a castle, a refuge: the democracy that Germany tried to make a home in. And there is a lake, a barrier to one's escape when monsters take over the castle. But for those with hope, the lake freezes over and leads on to new life: "*Wer weiter muss, den trägt der Silbersee*" (Whoever must go onward the silver lake will carry).

It's the kind of solution that artists dream up when what is most dear to them is in danger. And that was Weill's marriage. Somehow, Lenja never quite moved into the new house in Kleinmachnow as Frau Kapellmeister Weill. As in Zurich, she remained outgoing, energetic, and a bit unreliable. But she had changed her look from the *Wienamödel* of her youth to a more worldly turnout *à la mode*. When Elisabeth Bergner crossed paths with Lenja in Berlin, she stared with one of those "Don't I know you?" looks.

"*Ja, Sie haben schon recht, ich bin's wirklich*" (Yes, you guessed right, it's me), Lenja told her. "It's Linnerl Blamauer!"

Lenja loved that moment. It became one of her favorite story-tells, because it proved how far she had come.

She not only looked different, and had not only been graduated from ballet dancing to principal acting roles: she was one of the most versatile actresses on the Berlin stage. Because in her later American years her accent limited her, we tend to think of her as difficult to cast. Back in Germany, Lenja could move from the classics to the most modern writing and from meek to aggressive through instinct, a rich imagination, and a love of taking direction. We see her in Sophocles, Büchner, Feuchtwanger; in tragedy and satire; in a comedy on the housing shortage, Valyentin Katayef's *Kvadraturya Kruga* (Squaring the Circle), translated as *Die Quadratur des Kreises* and a sort of Russian *Private Lives*; in various roles in *The Threepenny Opera* including Mrs. Peachum; and, as I've said, in the role of Ilse opposite Peter Lorre in Wedekind's *Frühlings Erwachen* (Spring's Awakening).

And of course she had her new boy friend, Otto Pasetti. True, Lenja was always having boy friends. But Pasetti was different. The others were most often drawn at whim from Weill and Lenja's professional loops in Berlin, from the world of writers and artists. The Pasetti idyll seemed overtly physical, less a dalliance than an infatuation of the lingering kind. In their letters, Weill and Lenja were still Weillili and Tütilein or Pünktchen and Littichen, respectively. Still, at some point, Weill realized that he might have to face losing his love to a cuter guy. Later on, he told Lenja that he never had the slightest doubt that she would come back to him. Still, one never knows how the heart will speak. And one day he found in his mailbox a note asking, "What is a Jew like you doing in a nice place like Kleinmachnow?"

9

Punch And Judy
Get A Divorce

The new Weill-Kaiser work, *Der Silbersee* (The Silver Lake), was not a musical, after all. Yet it wasn't an opera, either. In a letter to Universal, Weill called it a *"Zwischengattungs-Stück"* (a piece in a format between formats). Looking back on his three one-act operas, the stage works with Brecht, and *Die Bürgschaft*, Weill concluded that opera was too much music and not enough theatre, but that musical plays like *Threepenny* were enough theatre but not enough music.

In other words, opera singers can't act and actors can't sing. Again and again, Weill shifted the balance between the elements of song and drama to try to harmonize them as effortlessly as Offenbach seemed to. In fact, none of Weill's truly major stage works, from *Threepenny* and *Mahagonny* to *Lost in the Stars*, is Offenbachian. Weill ended up being influenced by Weill: he avoided professional librettists as mediocrities, working instead with playwrights to conjur up eccentric Weillian formats, to make the most music possible in a strictly theatre-oriented environment.

Thus, *The Silver Lake*'s "format between formats" is that of a spoken play punctuated by songs, underscored dialogue, and incidental music, all designed for singing actors, some of whom would possibly be opera people and others of whom might be theatre people. The songs would return Weill to his cabaret style, if on a more "classical" plane than in *Threepenny* and *Happy End*. And, above all, there would be a role for Lenja.

The Silver Lake's story is set in hard times in a parable that is also documentary: Germany in what increasingly appeared to be the last days of Weimar democracy. Policeman Olim shoots the starving Severin while he is stealing a pineapple. Then, in a typically preposterous Kaiserisch turn of plot, Olim wins the lottery, buys that symbolic castle, and takes the embittered—in fact, crippled—Severin there to care for him.

Of course, in Kaiser such opportunistic plotting is not an expedient but elemental in his worldview: Kaiser believes coincidence is simply destiny wearing a party mask. To add to the fun, Kaiser populates Olim's castle with stock villains, a greedy pair who blackmail Olim out of his property and a young girl, Fennimore (the Lenja part, apparently), with surprising depth of personality. To entertain Severin, she animates two bananas on the dinner table to Weill's hopscotching dance strain—an hommage to Charlie Chaplin's dance of the bread rolls in *The Gold Rush*, a sensation in Berlin. Fennimore follows the banana dance with a complete reversal of tone in the grimly epic "*Cäsars Tod*," generally known in English as "The Ballad of Caesar's Death." But Fennimore is a visionary, too, and it is she who points the way to Olim and Severin as they struggle along in the snowfall of this winter's tale. They must find the silver lake and walk across it to a new life together. Whoever must go onward the silver lake will carry.

As so often with Weill's playwright-partners, Kaiser wrote too many words and insisted that civilization would crumble if a single one was cut. Still, Kaiser's lyrics, filled with piquant insights, charmed Weill into trying to top himself, and the *Silver Lake* score is marvelous, as magical as the castle and the lake and as dense as the psychology of Olim and Severin, the enemies turned buddies.

With Brecht, Weill was sardonic and mischievous. Now, with Kaiser, Weill is as bizarre and otherworldly as the inhabitants of the *Kaiserisch* universe. The transition from Olim the gun-toting cop to Olim the pacifist, a turn of conscience, is executed by the simplest of means, an offstage chorus repeatedly chanting an accusatory "Ohhhhh-*lim!*" as he ruminates over his guilt. Lest the scene get too introspective, the authors insert a solo for the Lottery Agent who presents Olim with his check. Weill cast the character as a tenor, pushing him into the difficult *passaggio* of the voice, to suggest the desperation of greed, powerlust, and a love of spending all at once—the sound of a deranged, homeless banker. "*Zins*" (interest), he cries, and "*Zinzeszins*" (compound interest), all to a dizzy tango with a tom-tom beat that marks a potent link with *The Threepenny Opera*. The melody even echoes the "*Zuhälter-Ballade.*"

Further, we should note Fennimore's performance piece, "Caesar's Death," a brutal march on how the anti-democratic *duce* of ancient Rome sought to rule by the sword but was taken down by a knife. The allusion to Mack the Knife is obvious—but the song as a whole recalls the "Pirate Jenny" that Polly Peachum sang at her wedding: homicidal storytelling by a young woman we had thought of as having no more than a young woman's concerns. With its "damn the torpedoes" aggression and slithery turns of phrase, it sounds exactly like Weill-Brecht: as if that partnership created a business model so compelling that even Kaiser adopted the style. "A city was called Rome," it begins, "and all the Romans had hot blood in their veins." It's tough-love history with a touch of trivia when the conspirators strike and Caesar of course utters his "*Et tu, Brute!*" Why in Latin? the song asks. Ah: "Because that was the language of the place!" Weill responded to Kaiser's goading strophes with slashing chords in a relentlessly stalking gait, less a requiem than a warning to tyrants.

This marks *The Silver Lake* as a *Zeitoper*, that *Weimarisch* term that, once again, denotes operas that bore affinity to the times, whether in a crossover use of jazz (meaning, really, American popular music in a dance-band idiom) or in allusions to events of the age. Perhaps a better term for this form would be *Zeitgeistoper*: in sympathetic union with the worries of Germany's arts community.

Yes: for even as *The Silver Lake* was in rehearsal in three different productions—in Leipzig, Magdeburg, and Erfurt—President von Hindenburg announced the end of German democracy by appointing

Hitler as Chancellor. The Nazis were now in power, and the work of *Gleichschaltung* began: the "coordination" of public life by Nazi dictates, with one-party rule, one-party thinking, one-party biology. Hans Heinsheimer, the man at Universal who was closest to Weill, urged him to get out of Germany; Weill's very existence there was now life-threatening. The language of the Nazi press after *The Silver Lake*'s three premieres, all on February 18, 1933, was not simply antagonistic to the sound of Weill but outright hate speech. After menacing Leipzig's stage director, Detlef Sierck,* and its conductor, Gustav Brecher, one F. A. Hauptmann in the *Völkischer Beobachter*, the official Nazi Party daily, defined *Der Silbersee* in terms that were by now piling cliché upon Pelion: "One must approach a composer such as Weill with mistrust, not least when he, a Jew, makes use of the German opera stage for his anti-German goals [*für seine unvölkischen Zwecke*]." Analyzing *The Silver Lake*'s musical dramatization in terms so irrelevant he could be describing the Trapp Family Singers, Hauptmann then declares, "Ugliness and sickness—this creates the style."

Politically, it was impossible to anticipate what might happen in Germany with Hitler as Chancellor, because so many governments had been set up, so many cabinets formed, so many chancellors appointed. Some of them had lasted about as long as a decent revival of one of Schiller's second-division titles. Yet there was a feeling among those of Berlin's arts community who traveled with Weill and Kaiser to Leipzig for *The Silver Lake*'s premiere that the arts world was enjoying its last night out before the revenge of the Browns engulfed it. Why did Goebbels even allow *The Silver Lake* to open—to give it a show trial by a prosecution of Party music critics? *Der Silbersee* was the last work, one might say; this was where the termination of Weimar art began. Ernst Busch, who had played Severin in Magdeburg *als Gast* from Berlin, recorded two songs from the score just in time for release

---

* In the familiar pattern, Sierck emigrated to Hollywood—but his was one of the success stories. As Douglas Sirk, he directed a series of big-budget weepies that were among the most successful films of the 1950s, from *Magnificent Obsession* to *Imitation of Life.*

before the legalized terror started up systemically. Lenja, too, recorded two numbers: too late. The disc was never pressed, and the masters were apparently destroyed.

In fact, Lenja wasn't in any of the three *Silver Lake* premieres, despite Weill's having had her voice in mind for Fennimore. Instead, she was on vacation with Otto Pasetti and still estranged from Weill in a certain way but, like Cynara's lover, faithful in a fashion. The Weills were in constant contact by post; "Regards to Pasetti," Weill would add when signing off to his "Zybelinerl" (a play on her given name and the German for the fortunetelling sibyls of the ancient world). Weill even paid off the gambling debts Lenja and Pasetti incurred when she became an addict of the casino.

So Lenja missed the last work of Weimar, and also the first work of the Third Reich, on February 27, 1933: the burning of the Reichstag. This momentous happening is often misunderstood, because the apparent culprit was a lone man, a Dutch radical named Marinus van der Lubbe, and most people assume that the arson was political theatre, a Nazi plot to frame the left and initiate mass arrests, torture, and executions. After all, staging an act of "sabotage" was typical Nazi behavior, and how could one man alone burn down an entire building?

This is the popular view of it, but, first of all, the Reichstag was not burned down. Practically speaking, stone buildings can't be destroyed by fire; even after the Battle of Berlin that ended the European War in 1945, when the Russians shelled what remained of the bombed-out Nazi capital till its center was little more than a cemetery of contentless facades, the Reichstag was one of the few structures left standing, wounded yet more or less intact.

So no one "burned down" the Reichstag: the *interior* was gutted, because, after starting small fires in the exterior rooms that burned themselves out, the culprit ran through the assembly hall igniting the wall draperies and creating an inferno at the heart of the edifice. The damage was more symbolic than substantial: but the political results were absolute, for the way toward Nazi totalism had now been opened: to counter this supposed act of revolutionary insurrection. One can imagine Hermann Göring, as he arrived on the scene to watch the Reichstag's great canopy collapse, exclaiming, "Why didn't *we* think of this?"★

The day after the fire—February 28, 1933, exactly four weeks after Hitler was appointed Chancellor—the government assumed emergency powers, and with the passing of the Enabling Law, on the following March 23, effective the very next day, the constitution of the Weimar Republic was in effect dissolved and Germany now a Nazi dictatorship.

Brecht had already stolen off to Prague; had he been at home the day after the fire he might have been taken in the roundups. There was even a bit of hugger-mugger at the last minute, for the railroad stations were being watched, and no one was more recognizable than skinny Brecht with his short-cut hair style and leather jacket. (He literally owned no other.) Presumably Brecht affected at least some mild disguise, for he, Helene Weigel, and their son, Stefan, made it off safely. (The Brechts' daughter, Barbara, was staying with the senior Brechts in Augsburg.) Then Brecht launched an exile that was to last for fifteen-and-a-half years, during which his career—though not his writing—came close to a standstill.

It will be a familiar story in these pages: the problem that many artists must solve when cut off from the culture that nurtured, inspired, and understood them. For all his intelligence, Brecht was not adaptable—not because he tried to work his way into alien creative at-

---

★ Conspiracy theories about Nazi involvement in the Reichstag's burning proved so stubborn that various German governments after World War II attempted to address them, always hoping that evidence implicating the Nazis would turn up. Unfortunately, the evidence pool has been so tainted by Soviet disinformation that the case will likely never be resolved for certain. In 1967, a West German court reduced van der Lubbe's sentence to eight years—idiotically, as the Nazis had executed him in 1933. Another court reversed this decision the following year. Yet it has become a German article of faith that the Nazis set the fire using van der Lubbe as a stooge, even though the crucial fact about the Reichstag fire is not how it happened but how Hitler used it as a pretext for a nationwide termination of civil liberties that lasted twelve years. Still, mesmerized by the dogged hysteria of the conspiracists, Germany exonerated van der Lubbe in 2008.

The World of Kurt Weill and Lotte Lenya:

a picture essay

Fascism or Freedom?
Fritz Lang's film *Die Nibelungen* (1924) glories in Nordic power. A model for nationalist art—or a warning to those who think for themselves?

Berlin. Waisenbrücke und Märkisches Provinzial-Museum

From Berlin . . .

Critics blast prewar Berlin as ugly and crowded, but it was actually very airy, with an architectural rhetoric blending fairyland (the redbrick Regional Museum, above left) with Classical Tone (the Reichstag and the Victory Column, below).

Berlin. Der Reichstag

The AUTOMAT *as famous as the New York Skyline itself*

. . . to Broadway

To newcomers, America was not only the land of the free but a nation of gadgets, such as the Automat, an eatery with space-age food dispensers. Its promotional postcard gives us the Manhattan that Weill glimpsed as his liner docked in the Hudson. After Berlin's roomy layout, New York was utterly crammed. Humble dwellings were mashed up against lordly public buildings, including the most important edifice in Weill's life, the Manhattan Opera House (below), where Weill's Biblical opera *The Eternal Road* was staged: the reason Weill came to America.

Weill's Broadway

Most of Weill's shows were experimentally unique. Right, *Johnny Johnson,* in 1936, was, all at once, a musical for actors, a pacifist treatise, a black-comic fantasy, and a picaresque with each scene written and played in a different style. Note the presence of the Statue of Liberty, which appears in the piece. Is it nationalist art of another kind? Below, two years later, everyone could sing in the political operetta *Knickerbocker Holiday*—except the star, Walter Huston (center, as a peg-legged Pieter Stuyvesant, with Jeanne Madden, in the "Dutch Dance").

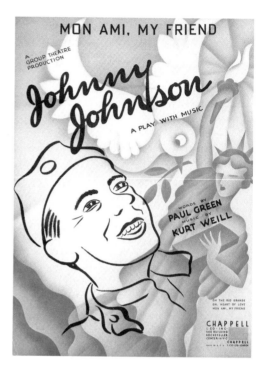

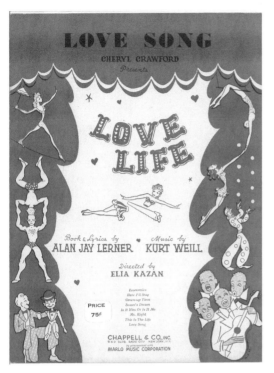

In the 1940s, Weill toyed with the very structure of the musical. Below, *Lady in the Dark* is actually a straight play diddled by dream operas. (In the Circus Dream, left to right: MacDonald Carey, Gertrude Lawrence, Victor Mature, Bert Lytell, Danny Kaye.) Left, the later *Love Life* anticipated *Cabaret* with a slew of vaudeville numbers commenting on the story line.

Weill's Favorite Collaborators
Left, Maxwell Anderson and daughter Hesper, circa 1937, at what used to be called a child's "play station." Note Anderson's gala three-tone shoes. Above, Bertolt Brecht with the inevitable cigar and monkish haircut.

Freedom Conquers Fascism

Two signs that the Nazis are over:
Above, a British soldier adds his graffito to the Reichstag. The Russians
have already signed in; note, northwest
of the Tommy, the signature of one V.
Myelnikof, "From the Volga to Berlin,
1941–1945." Right, *The Threepenny
Opera*, banned by the Nazis, can be
performed in Germany again. (Stefan
Lisewski as Mack the Knife.)

The Lenya We Love

Here in *Cabaret*: Left, tough with enemies (Peg Murray), but below, soft with allies (Jack Gilford, who has just presented her with a pineapple). "It makes me blush," she admits.

titudes but because he refused to work his way into anything. Everything else must work its way into Brecht.

Weill would adapt splendidly, because of that love of varying his materials that always kept him keen. Strangely, he did not flee Germany at once, though he must have known that his name was on many a Nazi's list. He may have had a warning phone call from a friend in the government; we know that he did leave Germany one day before the vote on the Enabling Law. And of course, legend celebrates the picture of Lenja by Weill's side as they desperately drive to the French border, checking behind for a tail, anxious about what hazards await them with the border guards.

Or so the story ran. In fact, Weill left Germany without his wife. Caspar and Erika Neher drove him to safety. Why Lenja stayed behind is unknown. One wonders if it relates to the quandary of the character Lenja played some thirty years later in *Cabaret*, the helpless widow engaged to a Jewish man at just this time in history. She has no politics; it's all Nazi Schmatzi to her. She wants only to like everybody and stay out of trouble. What would you do?

The subject of Lenja's being separated from Weill at this direst time of his life was so tender a matter that they never spoke of it to each other. We know this because, after Weill's death, Lenja tried to learn exactly how Weill left his native land. She must have had an inkling, because she wrote to Caspar Neher (who had survived life under Hitler with no interruption of his career) asking for any details he could share. Lenja was apparently not even certain when Weill departed; didn't she have access to his old passports? Or did the Nehers conduct him to a suitably deserted spot and let him out to sneak into France on footpaths? (For this, too, is part of the legend, in an alternate text.) Lenja was instrumental in helping to defend Weill from Nazi scrutiny, cleaning the Kleinmachnow house of documents that could have incriminated colleagues and friends, shipping furniture and music to Weill (including scores that the Nazis would subsequently not only ban but try to eradicate to the last copy). Everything else she sold.

Still, for all Weill knew, the political upheaval might easily drive him and Lenja permanently apart. It was an eventuality that he could not bear to consider, for Lenja really did not come right after his music. Lenja *was* his music. Still, for now, Weill had to turn to the new art that so many like him had to acquire: surviving.

Many went to Prague, like Brecht, because it was very much a German-speaking city and politically anti-Nazi. Most went to Vienna, some to Zurich. However, Paris was the magnet, because Paris was the cultural capital not only of France but of all Europe. Since the late eighteenth century, Paris had been the one place where a composer could forge a civilization-wide reputation, and by about 1845 the Paris Opéra held all Western music in fee. From Verdi to Wagner, creators hated the place, its audience, and its idiotic regulations—especially the one forbidding composers to conduct their own music, despite the uninspired and at times incompetent house *corps de bâton*. Yet only by conquering Paris could one assume the role of a musical grandmaster in European society.

By 1933, when Weill arrived, Parisian culture was more unified than that of Berlin, for the *tout*-Paris—literally "all Paris," meaning all those who mattered—encouraged a great deal of intermingling among the avant-garde, the nobility, and the wealthy. You could say that salonistes ran society, or rich lesbians promoting the arts, or even couturiers. In *Fireworks at Dusk: Paris in the Thirties*, the historian Olivier Bernier records the serious facetiae of the visual themes Elsa Schiaparelli wove into her dress designs: "The map of Normandy, surrounded by gamboling pigs on a midnight blue crepe dinner suit . . . a fabric printed with a collage of her [press] reviews . . . the dark blue satin dress embroidered in gold below the waist with a violin, a French horn, a tuba, and a harp."

But that was society. Politically, the city—like the nation itself—was divided. Half the public supported a democracy as inept as that of Weimar; every two or three months, the government fell, to be succeeded by another government with more or less the same leaders. The press dubbed them "corpse cabinets." The other half of the public openly touted a return to the monarchy or outright fascism. The National Assembly of deputies was so hated that the new hip insult in Paris was "*Espèce de député!*" (roughly, "idiot congressman!").

By the mid-1930s, says Bernier, "It was becoming clear that there really was no such thing as France." There were right-wing riots at the appearance of bold art. In 1930, Luis Buñuel's savagely anti-Church *L'Age d'Or* (The Golden Age) was treated much as Weill's operas had been across the frontier, with shouting, stinkbombs, and attacks on those who expressed appreciation. The state even confiscated the film, in deference to "family, country, and religion." Further, known liberals were physically assaulted on the street. And when, in 1936, Hitler made his first belligerent move in marching his army into the Rhineland in a defiance of Versailles, France did nothing, though it had Europe's largest army. In fact, Hitler had been terrified that France might oppose him, vexing his insecure relationship with the German Army and imperiling his regime. But France would not fight. And that's when the French lost the European Civil War, says Olivier Bernier: "It merely took them four years to realize it."

This was the place that Weill entered into on the first leg of his exile: a kind of Weimar *en français*. At least he was not unknown. Besides the 1925 world premiere of the Violin Concerto, already mentioned, there was on December 11, 1932 at the Salle Gaveau a double bill of *Der Jasager* and yet another *Mahagonny* confection, the original *Songspiel* expanded by four numbers from the opera. There really is a kind of bundle of works that we loosely call "*Mahagonny*"—because it seems that, all too often, someone uses this title to front for a new and faithless reading. For that matter, even the Leipzig premiere was compromised before the first night because of the work's outspoken look at how civilized cultures make commerce of sex. This Paris *Mahagonny* is something like the sixth edition, after the *Songspiel*, the opera as written, the opera as originally performed, the Berlin "theatre" version, and the shortened version for Vienna. Yet to come are the Berliner Ensemble's disgraceful spoken version of 1963, with bits of Weill tipped in like mezzotints in a folio, and the post-Beatles rescoring seen off-Broadway in 1970.

But at least Paris had heard Kurt Weill in his cabaret mode—and while a staging of *L'Opéra de Quat'Sous* had failed, the French print of the Pabst film had scored a great success. Thus, cut off from the world he had made for himself, Weill was nonetheless *un personnage*. Important. The screams of Nazi barbarism echoed behind him all the while even so; less than a month after he arrived in Paris, the German government staged book burnings throughout the Reich, on May 10, 1933. "By destroying Jews they are persecuting Christ," wrote Joseph Roth, now another émigré in the pack, though he had been in Paris since 1925. "We have sung Germany, the real Germany! And that is why today we are being burned by Germany!"

Brecht and Remarque were among those honored by this intellectual terrorism; so was Ernest Hemingway, in translation. Weill cooly turned his back on the country of his birth, and he never changed his attitude till the day he died. Putting up in hotels, he urged Universal in Vienna to work out a disposition of his royalties from German marks into Austrian schillings so he could exchange them for French francs, but the process hit a snag and failed.

Then luck—or, again, the espionage of destiny that sometimes edged Weill forward and sometimes let him lead—struck immediately. It started, as so much in art does, with an eccentric millionaire. Though he was gay, he was besotted with his lesbian wife, a dancer, and he now proposed to capitalize a ballet company for her. Top of the line, with arguably the greatest choreographer of the century; he'd call it *Les Ballets 1933*. And as ballet had been the art of choice in Paris since the seventeenth century, the affair smelled of prestige the way the very notion of *The Threepenny Opera* smelled of theatre to Ernst Josef Aufricht when he ran into Brecht in Schlichter's in 1928. And what if this Maecenas wants Weill to compose? What if the work is a "*ballet chanté*"—sung while danced, and sung by Lenja? And what if Weill adds Brecht into the project to write the verses?

No question, Weill had had his fill of Brecht's megalomania, his delight in making trouble, and his kleptomaniac writing habits, not to mention the stink of his stubbornly unwashed body. Nonetheless, Brecht was the best at what he did, and Weill went with the best as a rule. We have seen this again and again in the collaboration of words and music—with the temperamentally unsuited Gilbert and Sullivan, with the sensitive Hugo von Hoffmansthal and the personally coarse Richard Strauss, with the professional Richard Rodgers and the off-a-maying Lorenz Hart and then with the increasingly misanthropic Rodgers and the life-loving Hammerstein. You don't mate with nice. You mate with genius.

The gay Maecenas of *Les Ballets 1933* was Edward James, his lesbian wife was Tilly Losch, and the choreographer was Georges (so spelled at the time) Balanchine. The company's other dancers were, mainly, Tamara Toumanova, Roman Jasinsky, and Pearl Argyle. Weill's fellow composers on the bills included Darius Milhaud, Henri Sauguet, and Mozart and Schubert, in arrangements run up for the occasion.

And the Weill-Brecht piece was *Les Sept Péchés Capitaux*, though of course Brecht wrote the libretto in German as *Die Sieben Todsünden* (The Seven Deadly Sins). Caspar Neher (billed as C. Rudolph Neher) designed set and costumes, the former consisting of seven doors, each labeled with one of the titular sins. The Weill-Brecht-Neher-Lenja collaboration suggests a *Threepenny* reunion, but in fact Brecht was, this time, a near-nonentity. This was a rush job. The commission materialized like a genie's *poof!*, so there was none of the luxurious "writing vacation" that Weill and Brecht enjoyed at the beach resort of Le Lavandou while creating *Threepenny* and *Happy End* (though the reckless Brecht crashed his car on the latter jaunt, leaving Weill to enjoy sun and surf on his own). We note, too, that Brecht—who had to travel to France around the corner of central Europe to avoid setting foot on Nazi soil—would have had none of his "secretaries" on call. *The Seven Deadly Sins* is perhaps the purest work in the Weill-Brecht canon: no one wrote it but Weill and Brecht.

In the event, *The Seven Deadly Sins*—Weill's second-to-last work in German and his final full-scale collaboration with Brecht—is one of the pair's best works. Two sisters, each named Anna, troll for payoffs through another of Brecht's capitalist American wastelands. Four men sing the roles of the sisters' family—the mother included—who remain back in Louisiana, "where the water of the Mississippi flows under the moon." As always before, Brecht falls in love with the—to him—exotic American names of Memphis, Philadelphia, Baltimore, San Francisco, and of course the family is evilly greedy, right? Yet all they want is a house to live in. There's no Enron depravity in the piece.

A small corps of dancers assisted as Balanchine took the two girls on their tour: a manipulator and a naive who together form a single con woman with pathological excuses: the seven ways of being human. "*Nicht wahr, Anna?*" (Right, Anna?), Lenja would ask Losch. And Lenja would reply, "*Ja, Anna*" (Right, Anna). The two are one.

By now, Weill was absolutely in control of his gifts, Julien Sorel as an artist rather than a seducer. Everything Weill wrote bore a particular style of his choosing, a melodic content of his choosing, a dramatic density of his choosing. He has become the jazz Mozart. Thirty-five minutes long, *The Seven Deadly Sins* stands among his most concentrated and ironic works, very reminiscent of *Mahagonny* in the part writing for the male quartet especially. Yet it is exhilarating as sheer music-making, with, of course, the voice of Lenja analyzing the adventure. In 1933, she was still working in her gin-joint soprano, not the gravelly speak-sing lower range she so famously used later on. "My sister is pretty," she tells the audience, "and I'm practical." It could almost be Lenja speaking of herself and Weill: the magnetic performer and the achiever merged in that music that is love. *The Seven Deadly Sins* is perhaps as strange as their marriage was, for despite its sardonic edge it is intensely appealing. It is, in fact, a paradox: how the beauty uses the brain to succeed, but how the brain uses the beauty to live. As Balanchine told Lenja, much later, "If I'd understood it at the time, I'd never have done it."

Unfortunately, the ballet—and James' company in general—did not go over. One problem, surely, was the German text. The French are the least venturesome people in Europe in the matter of language: they love theirs and scorn all others. Oddly, the names of each sin on the set's seven doors were in French; on the first night, June 17, 1933, at the Théâtre des Champs-Elysées, Weill came out for his bow through the one reading "Luxure," to a mix of applause and boos.

James took his troupe to London in July, now billing the work as

Anna Anna. The premiere was sung in German, thereafter in translation—Lenja's first stab at singing English to an English public, though of course she had already tasted the language in sections of *Mahagonny*. The critics found her odd but fetching: outside German-speaking lands, she was something of an acquired taste. *Anna Anna*, however, failed to generate interest.

Of course, Lenja had an affair with Tilly Losch, but she was still with Otto Pasetti (who was in *The Seven Deadly Sins*' male quartet), and this is when Lenja divorced Weill. Those who knew them both thought it a capricious and even cruel act. Weill did not contest it, because he loved and forgave her and, further, he believed that she would tire of Pasetti and her various Losches and come back to the music. The Weills of the world always have that one overwhelming piece of artillery in duel with the Pasettis: there is nothing more powerful in the life of a performer than the work that defines and ennobles one's talent.

The divorce was finalized on September 18, 1933, and as Weill didn't want to homestead himself without his wife by his side, he had been guesting ever since he'd arrived in France. At times he put up in hotels; he also stayed with the Count and Countess de Noailles, where he lived while writing *The Seven Deadly Sins*. Patrons of the arts, les Noailles didn't support culinary entertainment but did support the boldest innovations; it was they who presented the aforementioned Buñuel film, *L'Age d'Or*, that was shut down by the government—or, rather, by a feeble government response to pressure from right-wing thuggery. The count was actually asked to resign from the Jockey Club over the incident, a tremendous humiliation by Birth and Breeding aristos of one of their own. The countess was even more imposing than her husband, a beauty and a poet from one of the grandest families in France. "Though still alive," wrote Janet Flanner in *The New Yorker*, "she is regarded as immortal."

That this singular couple invited Weill to live with them (and allowed him to dedicate *The Seven Deadly Sins* to them) suggests how well—how instantly—Weill had made his connections in the French arts world. By the fall, Weill had found a new publisher, made his

French radio debut with a wild new work, and, finally, leased, a home.

The publisher was Heugel et Cie. (Heugel and Company), a major house with a thriving business in popular music. Universal, Weill's former publisher, not only didn't publish popular music but didn't like its composers writing any. This had created a simmering tension between their doctrinaire thinking and the always experimenting Weill. His manager at Universal, Hans Heinsheimer, still saw Weill as the house's answer to Paul Hindemith, ensconced at the rival house of B. Schott's Söhne, headquarted in Mainz. Hindemith's idea of popular music was a Bach chorale; why did Weill have to write that cheap cabaret twaddle? "An ugly little asshole," Weill called Heinsheimer, pouring "holy water over himself." Worse, Universal, even in still democratic Austria, was accommodating the Nazi regime in its war on Weill.

The wild new work for French radio tantalizes us today, for *La Grande Complainte de Fantômas*, heard on November 3, 1933, has vanished—the last of Weill's major pieces to do so. Fantômas is a master criminal of the kind that obsessed Fritz Lang, and indeed, Fantômas was the protagonist of a thirty-two-part movie serial in the early 1910s. In a plot contrivance still in use today, the invincible Fantômas enrages Inspector Juve of the *Sûreté* and teases an ambitious journalist; the character was thought worthy of revival by Paul Fejos in early talkies. Now, only two years later, Weill and his collaborator, Robert Desnos, created a brief yet monumental tribute to Fantômas with a gigantic cast, David Drew reports, "of cabaret and music-hall artists, buskers, accordionists, whistlers, and clowns—with a few opera singers and recitalists thrown in for good measure."

Weill's new home was a flat in the Parisian suburb of Louveciennes, far to the west of the *tout*-Paris, directly north of Versailles and near enough to a loop of the Seine for Weill to hear the noise of the boats on the river. This was not a temporary *pied-à-terre* but Weill's new address, on a three-year lease, and he then set about effecting a reunion with his pet Alsatian, Harras, left behind perforce when Weill fled Germany. The dog arrived in a crate, which made quite a show for the neighbors, because when the wooden slats were pulled away Harras' first act was to surrender to an epic urination. Then, overjoyed to see his master again, Harras became Weill's shadow, though he suffered an agonizing first night in his new home because of the continental habit of segregating man and best friend at sleeping time: the animals are usually locked up outside or in the scullery like Cinderella. Disoriented from his long trip, Harras howled all night, repeatedly drawing Weill downstairs to console him.

Weill's sending for Harras is a tell, along with the sedentary implications of a three-year lease: he believed he would be able to grow new cultural roots in a country that was frankly as politically perilous as Weimar Germany had been. Or perhaps Weill—like many others—still expected the Nazi regime to implode under the density of its countless manias, allowing exiles to return. Still, signs that France was now as divided between democrats and fascists as Germany had been were everywhere. Most immediately, in November of 1933, Maurice de Abravanel conducted a concert featuring three numbers from *Der Silbersee* sung by Madeline Grey. These are distinguished names. Abravanel, who dropped the "de" on *his* exile, in the United States, became Weill's favorite conductor of his music, and Grey made an album of some of Joseph Canteloube's *Chansons de l'Auvergne* that became a classic of the 78 era. Weill's music went over quite well, but after "Caesar's Death," the French composer Florent Schmitt shouted, *"Vive Hitler!"* and a few others of a like mind joined in. "Enough music by German refugees!" was Schmitt's conclusion.

The bulk of the audience fought back by demanding an encore and rewarding Weill with an ovation, but the press sided with Schmitt. Weillians today dismiss Schmitt as "a mediocrity," though in fact he is the third of this concert's distinguished participants, not a terribly original composer but a good one, in the Debussy mode, with one acknowledged masterpiece—a setting of Psalm 47 for soprano, chorus, organ, and orchestra—and ballets on Salome and Antony and Cleopatra whose suites are still heard today.

The incident itself, catcalling and abuse in the holiest of sanctuaries, a home of music, should have warned Weill that he had not arrived at a safe place. He may have been misled because, unlike Germany, France had no charismatic demagogue to unite the destroyers. But France did have a Jewish rogue to inflame anti-Semitism: Serge Stavisky, whose collossal bond swindles compromised government officials on the very highest levels. Stavisky's trial was postponed over and over while he roamed free and actually put together yet another swindle: almost seventy-three million dollars' worth of fantasy bonds all together. And, of course, given the intolerant tenor of the times, Stavisky would have to be not only a foreigner but Jewish and a dishonest finagler in the sale of money.

As Janet Flanner wrote in *The New Yorker*, "To keep up with the Stavisky scandal—i.e., the French government—anyone would have to read the newspapers three hours a day, which is what everybody does." It was a national mystery—not so much what Stavisky did but how he got away with it when the authorities clearly knew what he was doing. One might have expected a brace of resignations; instead, Premier Edouard Daladier fired the Prefect of Police and the head of the Comédie-Française, for having staged Shakespeare's incendiary *Coriolanus*.

Meanwhile, Stavisky committed suicide. Really? And a judge deeply involved in Stavisky coddling, Albert Prince, was found run over by a train. He had been tied to the tracks, but—respecting the Wonderland tone of *Staviskyisme*—the police ruled this, too, a suicide. *Paris-Soir*, France's biggest newspaper, commissioned the mystery writer Georges Simenon and the Scotland Yard inspector Sir Basil Thompson to solve the Stavisky puzzles as France looked on in cynical amusement.

Writing to Lenja—who was in San Remo with Otto Pasetti, indulging in her passion for casino gambling—Weill asked if she was following the Stavisky story. "It's all terribly exciting," he said, "a pure gangster story." Actually, it was a sort of Dreyfus affair, except this time the protagonist was guilty. In the middle of the scandal, on February 6, 1934, the fascists attempted a coup, staging an assault on the Chamber of Deputies. The police beat them back, they regrouped and charged again, and finally the cops opened fire; sixteen were killed and more than six hundred injured. The police suffered one thousand wounded and terrible assaults on their horses, for the fascists had attached razor blades to walking sticks and slashed frenziedly at the animals' legs. As so often before, the government fell like a soufflé in an earthquake.

Weill buried himself in work. On assignment from the Princesse Edmond de Polignac, he produced his last major non-dramatic work, a symphony that he termed "Number One." Thus, Weill believed he had suppressed for all time the student symphony he had written for Busoni. This new piece belongs to Weill's post-*Mahagonny* mode, laid out in a three-movement structure with sturdy echo texture in which melodic cells are varied in subtle and at times almost indiscernible ways. Tuneful yet acerbic, the work is a kind of *Zeitsymphonie*, commenting on the political storms wrecking the peace in Europe. Begun in the fateful month of January, 1933—the "Hitler month," one might say, of the seizure of power—the symphony was first performed in Amsterdam under Bruno Walter on October 11, 1934, to be rejected by press and public. Walter took the work to Vienna, thence to New York, where it was given a title as *Three Night Scenes*, though the two outer movements do not remotely suggest anything like a nocturne.

At least a new side of Weill was emerging: that of what we might call the Song Dandy, creating impressive samples of his cabaret art on demand. This was crossover music before the term existed. Weill composed two numbers for Marlene Dietrich (on texts by Erich Kästner and, it is believed, Jean Cocteau) and then, at Heugel's request, two for the French singer Lys Gauty on texts by Maurice Magre, "Complainte de la Seine" and "Je Ne T'aime Pas." Dietrich, typically, bustled about Paris, frantically trying to get hold of Weill to commission her two numbers, then didn't sing them. Gauty, however, liked the Seine number, with its dense imagery of the rubbish and sorrow that live at the bottom of the river, and requested "Je Ne T'aime Pas" as a companion piece for a recording. And she made it, too.

Today, Weill is celebrated for unusually theatrical songs with moody, juicy lyrics—"Pirate Jenny," "Surabaja Johnny," "That's Him." But in

1934, no one knew what Weill should be known for, other than *Die Dreigroschenoper*, and mainly through Pabst's film, with its truncated score. The Symphony could only complicate his public identity, and in fact it really was the last of Busoni's Weill, the concert-hall Weill. Yet wasn't it Busoni who urged Weill never to disdain the appeal of sheer melody? Busoni meant this generally, but Weill had been specializing his melody as a kind of cabaret *Meistersinger*: for his work with Brecht had taught him the value of composing around lyrics of satanic glitter—words too smart for music yet, once set, conclusively musical. Think of "The Ballad of Mack the Knife": if you had never heard the music, you might take the verses for a jeering little set of black jokes, as uninterested in music as a limerick. But let Weill add his primitive tune, with its absurdly wistful rising sixth followed by a sardonic falling seventh, you realize what Brecht had been missing. The two men were a bad mix, but they had a beautiful marriage.

Weill suffered some terrible marriages for the next few works, starting with the French playwright Jacques Deval. Just the year before, in 1933, Deval had produced a hit boulevard comedy, *Tovaritch*, that seemed bound to conquer the stages of the West, as indeed it did. A spoof of that endemic Parisian irritation, the White Russian émigré, *Tovaritch* was good character writing and even had some serious political content. This was Weill's territory, crafting the unique out of a popular form, and he and Deval teamed up for a play with music, *Marie Galante*.

The problem with Deval was laziness. He didn't have any difficulty writing; he just didn't want to. Worse, *Tovaritch* was going to make him rich, so now he *really* didn't want to. Based on his own novel, *Marie Galante* concerned an attractive young woman shanghaied from Bordeaux who ends up in Panama, working her way around various abusers and even an Asian spy while trying to return to France. Her name is Marie Basilde, but because of all the attention she gets as a potential sex toy, Deval ironically dubbed her *la galante*. The noun refers to, among other things, the erotic life. It's like saying Garbo Galante, Marilyn Monroe Galante. To stretch the pun, there is an island called *Marie Galante* in the lesser Antilles, just southeast of Guadeloupe.

Weill's music would comprise songs and incidental music, and he decided to execute the entire score in a "French" voice he had never used before. The relentless hectoring by critics at the way Weill supposedly changes his style from uniquely German to stereotypically American ignores the central fact that he changes his style *from work to work*, both while he is in Europe and, later, in the United States. Yes, Weill was a shape-shifter: but *throughout his career*, not just when he crossed the Atlantic. Creativity, to him, was not a system but an adventure.

Perhaps this was why Weill worked so often with the impossible Brecht: *he* was an adventure, too. Deval wasn't even a rainy weekend in Boulogne. "The worst of all the literary swine I've met" was Weill's view of Deval, because work didn't matter to him. Weill nourished a dream of having a hit with *Marie Galante* the way Deval was having on his own with *Tovaritch*, with a German-language *Marie Galante* starring Lenja. Weill was banned in Germany, of course, but Vienna and Zurich were available; Lenja was known in both cities to some degree. In fact, when Weill began work on *Marie Galante*, in August of 1934, Lenja was appearing at the Corso Theater in Zurich—and here we quote the posters—"*in der grossen Schwank-Operette*" (in the great musical comedy) *Lieber Reich Aber Glücklich* (Better Rich But Happy). The show's composer was Walter Kollo, who never internationalized his name as did Johann Strauss or Franz Lehár, but was thought of as the essential *Berlinisch* voice in light opera. (His son Willi also composed, and Willi's son René became a prominent opera tenor.) This was a distinguished booking for Lenja. True, the jester was the star: Otto Wallberg, "the comic," those posters tell us, "of the hundred thousand laughs." But Lenja, "Jenny in the *Threepenny Opera* film," was billed right under Wallberg in comparably large type. Huge type, even: they outbilled the show's title, and poor Kollo was lost in the fine print.

Still, Lenja's career had not prospered. She should have been singing Weill, not Kollo. Of course, Weill's coterie despaired of the whole Lenja thing. His dogged loyalty to her felt pathetic. Did he hope to re-eroticize their relationship with the catnip bait of a great part? A title role, in fact, which would have been Lenja's first ever in a new piece—and with just enough songs to make the show utterly her own? Lotte Lenja *is* Marie Galante!

But the play flopped. Opening on December 22, 1934 at the Théâtre de Paris and starring the mononymous Florelle (who had played Polly in the French version of the *Threepenny* film), the production had vanished in a few weeks.* Today, everyone blames Deval, though his lyrics, at least, are quite good. They certainly inspired Weill, even if he did track in some of the *Happy End* music, having assumed that its scandalous first night had locked the score up forever. Among *Marie Galante*'s incidental pieces was a tango that Heugel brought out, much later, in a vocal sheet as "Youkali," with words by Roger Fernay. But *Marie Galante*'s "hit," if it had one, was "*J'attends un Navire*" (I Wait For a Ship), Marie's life's dream, set to a lightly pounding beat, to return to France. She gets her wish, but ironically: when her homebound ship finally docks, it is to transport her lifeless body back for burial. Coincidentally, "*J'attends un Navire*" shares an affinity with the life's dream theme song of a later Weill heroine, Liza Elliott of *Lady in the Dark*: "My Ship."

More important, "*J'attends un Navire*," like all Weill's vocal music to French lyrics, offers another instance of how quickly Weill absorbed the sounds around him and the styles he drew on. It has the tang of French cabaret even as it influences French cabaret. We hear echoes of Weill *à la française* in the generation of composers clustered around Édith Piaf, especially Marguerite Monnot, in "*Milord*," "*Salle d'Attente*," and "*La Goulante du Pauvre Jean*" (known in English as "The Poor People of Paris").

Of course, it was Lenja whom Weill was so to say listening to as he

---

* This did not stop Hollywood from filming the story in 1934, without the slightest taste of Weill's score. It's an anticipation of the bad luck Weill was to have in his repeated attempts to establish a niche in the movies. Henry King directed the film, with Spencer Tracy and, as Marie Galante—this was now her full name, and the film's title—the French Ketti Gallian, whom the historian David Shipman calls "Fox's entry in the Garbo-Dietrich stakes." Helen Morgan, still famous for making *Show Boat*'s "Bill" her personal property, sings a couple of numbers.

wrote down the notes; it always was. And they were still interacting, from afar. At the start of 1935, Lenja finally sold the Kleinmachnow house, and then she was in Paris, undergoing surgery for a delicate gynecological problem. Weill was in London at the time, fretting by post, but her operation was a success, and Weill once again made a destiny-defying choice that necessitated his staying over in London: he had decided to enjoy a mad success in the West End theatre world with an operetta in the zany Offenbach mode.

It didn't start that way. The London show, *A Kingdom For a Cow*, was in fact Weill's very last German-language work. As *Der Kuhhandel* (The Cow Deal), it began with the appearance in Paris of Robert Vambery, who had been Ernst Josef Aufricht's dramaturg when Aufricht was running the Theater am Schiffbauerdamm. Vambery offered Weill a libretto for a comic opera about an American munitions salesman trying to start a war between two banana republics. While lampooning the Hitlerian bombast of the "strongman" General Garcia Conchas, Vambery did not neglect what used to be called "heart interest," and a young romantic couple, Juan and Juanita, supplied the title in that all they own is a cow that the government wants to confiscate.

The scenario really does recall Offenbach, not only because of Vambery's madcap plotting but because the juxtaposition of a resourceful pair of sweethearts and a corrupt state is a central Offenbach premise. We see it in most of his best-known *bouffes*: *La Belle Hélène* (1864), *Barbe-Bleue* (1866), *La Grande-Duchesse de Gerolstein* (1867), *La Périchole* (1868), and even *Orphée aux Enfers* (1858; expanded 1874), though the "government" is divine rule on Mount Olympus and the sweethearts Orpheus and Euridice hate each other's guts. Further, Weill contrived for *Der Kuhhandel* a score not only melodious but broken into diverse parts in the Offenbach manner. Think of Périchole's famous Letter Song, in farewell to her love—touching, poetic, concise. The utmost in the stripped-down French version of sentimentality. Yet virtually all the rest of the score is crazy marches, waltzes, parodies of grand opera, running around, giggling, and even a "tipsy" aria.

Offenbach is essentially a lot of everything going off at once. Weill's habit, however, was to *concentrate* his scores, create a series of interlocking parts till all the numbers blend in perfect cohesion: a pane of glass. Think of the tone of *The Threepenny Opera*, so even throughout that Weill can frame the whole with two aberrant pieces in classical mode, the Overture and final chorale, heightening the effect with the intrusion of a mad scene, the sometimes omitted "Lucy's Aria," in between.

In all, *Der Kuhhandel* would be a rich mix, even giving General Garcia Conchas a fandango just as Offenbach would have done. Yet one wonders why Weill thought a German work useful at this point in history and in his own career. In his letters, he varies from statements of fear that the Nazis and Germany are a marriage made in hell to expressions of hope that he is simply alarming himself. What future was there for a work by Kurt Weill in German beyond a few play dates in Austria and Switzerland? True, Weill was even then trying to interest Aufricht in producing a German-language tour of *Marie Galante* with Lenja for those two countries and the Netherlands. But wasn't Weill's future now that of the émigré, writing in translation?

So *Der Kuhhandel* was turned into an English musical. It looked promising: both Erik Charell and Charles Cochran seemed so positive after hearing Weill play through the score that he told Lenja he feared "the envy of the gods," for the ancient Greek deities were reputed to destroy mortals enjoying good fortune. Was Weill using the new work to move, with Lenja, yet farther from Nazi terror? The divisive politics and inflammatory rhetoric of French public life suggested that the nation was unwilling to withstand German belligerence.

That's the best and worst quality of democracies: they don't like fighting even when their enemies do. Perhaps it was Weill's idea to give Charell or Cochran a smash hit, thus to relaunch himself as the new voice in London's musical theatre. Still, was Weill's sound at all suitable for the West End audience? There was a BBC radio performance of *The Threepenny Opera* while Weill was in London, on February 8, 1935—the first time *Threepenny* was heard in England—and the critics excoriated it.

"It was the worst performance imaginable" was Weill's opinion. But reviewers were reacting more than anything else to *Threepenny* itself. *The Musical Times* concluded that Weill "has thrown away the well-loved tunes [of the 1728 *Beggar's Opera*] and substituted his own post-war jazzy inanities." Of course, Weill hadn't "substituted" anything: *Die Dreigroschenoper* isn't a version of *The Beggar's Opera* any more than *Oklahoma!* is a version of *Green Grow the Lilacs*. It's a different work.

In any case, the English theatre in 1935 was the last place in the free world that Weill could have claimed as his patch. While the mercurial form of the American musical was (despite Depression capitalization problems) always subject to experimental reinvention, the English musical was locked into strait formats. The farce about class starring Jack Buchanan. The instant–Masterpiece Theatre operette of Noël Coward. The incipient Ivor Novello love-and-adventure spectacle cycle, starting with *Glamorous Night* (1935). The snappy American importation: *Gay Divorce*, with Fred Astaire and a Cole Porter score. The lushly lyrical American importation: Jerome Kern's *The Cat and the Fiddle* and *Music in the Air*. And a ton of operetta. Neither Charell nor Cochran went to contract on *A Kingdom For a Cow*, the mock-Shakespearean title given to the translation of *Der Kuhhandel*. Reginald Arkell and Desmond Carter adapted and translated the book and lyrics, respectively, and the producers were two unknowns. Billed as a "musical play" and opening at the Savoy Theatre on June 28, 1935, the piece got a good press but failed to draw a public and closed in a few weeks.

Thus, as with *Happy End* and *Marie Galante*, the *Kuhhandel* music on which Weill had lavished so much thought and inspiration was—as far as he could tell—to be confiscated by history. Residing at the typical émigré's unreliable address of Please Forward To Nowhere, c/o Western Civilization, Weill was in no position to protect his work when it failed to impress. At that, he had not quite finished *Der Kuhhandel* when revising it for London, so the original German piece was incomplete and the English piece a distortion. And there Weill helplessly left it: modern revivals of his only essay in true Offenbachian musical farce are reconstructions of a work that does not entirely exist.

Some artists are raft riders, floating on wind and current till their work is less chosen by them than happening to them. Weill always chose, and with an impressive comprehension of the *contexts* in the world of music theatre, the forms and their possibilities. This is why he was always looking for something bizarre to do: only mediocrities write normal.

So it is most odd that Weill's next project was not of his choosing. It *happened* to him, at that partly because Max Reinhardt, still the grandmaster of European theatre, was Jewish and thus could not produce in Germany. (Three years after this, Austria, too, would be forbidden him after the *Anschluss*, though Reinhardt resided there, in a baronial mansion near Salzburg, with whose festival he had been closely associated since its founding, in 1920.)

Now Reinhardt, too, must consider emigration out of harm's way, and Reinhardt has a plan: a spectacle for London with music by Kurt Weill. Not any old spectacle, but the biggest spectacle that ever lived—and Reinhardt was known above all for spectacle, for his individualizing of actors in crowd scenes, his painterly compositions, the flow of narrative and power of mime, all timed to music.

There were drawbacks to Reinhardt's plan. For one thing, he was open to any idea except someone else's. The playwright he had in mind, Franz Werfel, was an egomaniacal hysteric. And the designer Reinhardt was to end up with, Norman Bel Geddes, was as self-important as Reinhardt and a reckless crazy as well.

Well, so far so good. At least it was another chance for Weill to try to secure a place in the English arts scene. But at some point in the planning, the playing venue was changed to New York, because the financing was in the hands of an American named Meyer Weisgal, and his American backers were not willing to pay a fortune to enhance the theatrical season in London. *Der Weg der Verheissung* (The Way of the Promise), though written and directed by Central Europeans, was to be an American offering.

The Way of the Promise! A generation after all this, Jean Kerr's fifties collection of humorous pieces *Please Don't Eat the Daisies* mentioned in passing a budding playwright who wants to make a musical based on the Bible. (This was retained for the Doris Day film of the same title, in a supporting role for Jack Weston.) It tells us how forgot *The Way of the Promise* was by then, because Reinhardt's spectacle was in fact a musical—or, really, an opera—based on the Bible. Threatened by one of those periodic surges in European anti-Semitism, a Jewish congregation seeks refuge in a synagogue, where its rabbi inspirits his people with Old Testament retellings, which are then enacted: Abraham and Isaac, Joseph, Moses, Ruth, David, King Solomon.

What Meyer Weisgal had in mind was a celebration of Bible mythology as a kind of anti-Nazi manifestation, but what Reinhardt and Bel Geddes were preparing was what Berlin theatre-world slang termed a "*Schinken*." The word literally means "ham," but in this usage it denotes something colossal, not only in size but in prestige. A career marker.

The Way of the Promise, however, was above all colossal in size. It came of a genre that had ruled Western stages for about eighty years, and this one was to be the last: the spectacle that was at once a play, a visual sensation, a "cast of thousands," a talk-of-the-town event. Some of my readers might think of the *Spider-Man* musical of 2011, but *Spider-Man* is on the concise side compared with the spectacles raised in theatres the size of opera houses in the days before microphones and computers, so that a vast audience has to sit absolutely still to follow pageants created by not technology but human endeavor. These spectacles played to a public innocent of arena stagings and cinematic special effects. New York even had a theatre, the Hippodrome, built exclusively for spectacle and seating some 5,200. Its last major booking before it was demolished, the circus musical *Jumbo*, opened in this very year, 1935. New York had other such venues, and the Manhattan Opera House, built by Oscar Hammerstein I (grandfather of Richard Rodgers' Oscar Hammerstein), was where *The Way of the Promise* was headed.

Weill fell into this project in the summer of 1934, a full two-and-a-half years before the show finally opened. Meeting with Reinhardt and Werfel at Reinhardt's estate, Weill had to control his irritation at Reinhardt's lord-of-the-manor pantywaisting—and Werfel, clearly, was going to be another of those writers who goes into shock at the suggestion that a single letter of text be cut. "About the most obnoxious and slimy literary pig I've ever met" was Weill's opinion of the latter. And while he admired Reinhardt's ability to shape theatre like a sculptor, "his veneration of money makes me want to vomit."

Bible stories were really out of Weill's line, for though he identified with Judaism culturally he held few if any religious beliefs; to Weill, the spiritual was to be encountered in a symbolic humanist piece like *The Silver Lake*. Furthermore, Weill must have known that the previous Reinhardt–Bel Geddes spectacle, *The Miracle* (seen in New York in 1924), a medieval pantomime about a runaway nun, virtually silenced *its* composer, Weill's old teacher Engelbert Humperdinck. With hundreds in its cast, the unprecedented cost of something like half a million dollars, and a design that made the audience feel as if they were inside a cathedral, *The Miracle* and its visuals overwhelmed all else, and the music evaporated as it was played.

At least the new work was no pantomime. Setting Werfel's text—which, on stage, would be heard in English translation—Weill believed he was composing his first grand opera. That is: no "format between formats" but an old-fashioned blood-and-guts Big Sing music drama, with solos and choruses dressed to thrill.

That suited Weill's need to dare the unique in each work: never before had he tried anything so pungently vast, and he would never do so again. But something more significant was in play. The weight of history was bearing down on Weill and Lenja, yet, for once, instead of Weill's choosing his destiny, destiny pointed at Weill and said, "*You.*" Weill *had* to go with Reinhardt to America, not only because he had achieved all he could as the composer of Brecht, of Berlin, of *Kulturbolschewismus*, but because The Promise was his own salvation and its Way led to America. Reinhardt retitled the work *The Eternal Road*, probably because Bel Geddes designed a tiered set, rising from the synagogue along a pathway angled along a mountain ever upward to . . . safety? Did Weill have any inkling, as he and Lenja joined Reinhardt, Werfel, and Weisgal on the S. S. *Majestic* on September 4, 1935, that he would never see Europe again? He had no wish to: eleven days later, Germany made public the Nuremberg Laws, which not only deprived all Jewish citizens of their citizenship but whose racial psychosis eventually banned them from the professions; from owning pets, bicycles, radios, record players, shavers; from theatre- and moviegoing; even from walking on major Berlin streets. As if they could live on air.

Weill didn't know it yet, but he was headed for relief from Europe's ancient war on Jews, from synagogues filled with the victims of the next pogrom. He had only fifteen years more of life, but they were extremely productive ones. Whoever must go onward the silver lake will carry.

10

Sailing To Byzantium

The first thing Weill and Lenja did was visit Hoboken, across the river from Manhattan in New Jersey, because, as I've said, one of the plays that Lenja had appeared in during her Berlin stage career was *Das Lied von Hoboken* (The Song of Hoboken), in 1930. This was a German translation of Michael Gold's *Hoboken Blues* (1928), an offering by one of Broadway's communist troupes, the New Playwrights Theatre. While these radical outfits dealt almost entirely in propaganda, they also delighted in experimentation, though the Party, following the Moscow line, would soon outlaw anything other than black-and-white "socialist realism."

On Broadway, in *Hoboken Blues'* original staging, a huge cast of whites in blackface played the tale of an idealist who leaves Harlem for Hoboken, only to return to find his old neighborhood corrupted on capitalist money hunger. The critics excoriated it, *Variety* observing that, but for support from the arts philanthropist Otto Kahn, "one would suspect [The New Playwrights] were pulling a Cherry Sisters"—a reference to a notoriously bad vaudeville act and a buzz term of the day.

How this quaint theatrical footnote made it to Berlin's

Volksbühne—the home of super-director Erwin Piscator, no less—is unknown; presumably someone was attracted to its deliberately clashing elements of surrealism and social commentary. The Berlin staging appears to have outclassed the New York original, which was lambasted as amateurish, and Wilhelm Grosz, one of the best of the new composers, gave *Das Lied von Hoboken* its incidental score. In fact, Grosz's *Afrika-Songs,* a chamber cycle on lyrics by black American poets, made him, like Weill, a *Jazzkomponist.* Certainly, Lenja did not reject the experience. Still, despite the German cast playing in blackface, something must have been lost in the translation, for Lenja believed that Hoboken was the center of northern black culture, which is why she and Weill ended up in Hoboken and not, more properly, Harlem.

Obviously, both were eager to experience at first hand the high-tech fancies of American life that so permeated Weimar's Americaphilia. A spoof of Weill-Brecht in the revue *New Faces of 1968,* "Das Chicago Song," speaks of Brecht's favorite American city as "a magic town where the drug stores never close." That was the America that Weill and Lenja had heard of: not only the New World but a World so New it had entered the Space Age in a push-button culture obsessed with gadgets of all kinds, from the automat to this week's movie star. America's ability to absorb technology, leisure, and ethnicity into an ever-changing New and Improved America was a relief from the torture-chamber bigotries of the Old World. The Nazis' concept of *das Volk* limited membership in the community to Aryans—and not only to them but to those among them who thought alike, thought "German." When the future comic and then producer-director Mike Nichols came to the United States, at the age of seven, in 1939, he and his younger brother stepped off the *Bremen* to be met by their father. Almost immediately, Mike saw Hebrew lettering on the sign of a Jewish delicatessen—a sight forbidden in the Germany he had just left.

"Is that allowed?" he asked his father.

And his father answered, "It is, here."

What impressed young Mike was the sheer openness of the United States, the abundant amusements of that gadget culture, whether it was the latest dance that, somehow, everyone instantly picked up or the snap-crackle-pop of Rice Krispies, the fizz of Coca-Cola when ice blocks were dropped in.

"We had never had food that made noise," Nichols later remarked. "It was great."

We have reached the latest of our cultural capitals, New York. After Vienna, Zurich, Berlin, Paris, and London, Weill and Lenja, like Lincoln Steffens, have stepped "over into the future, and it works."* Because here they will find the fulfillment that, thus far, has eluded them both. It will take Lenja some twenty years to get acclimated: performer émigrés had a more difficult time going native—because of their accents—than creator émigrés. Weill will make a place for himself relatively quickly, because American culture is enjoying a love affair with the *Zwischengattung* that he himself finds irresistible: the marriage, really, of art and pop, a crazy yet sublime marriage, like his with Lenja. It's in the air: as when Walt Disney fashions the masscult "funny animals" cartoon into *Snow White and the Seven Dwarfs*, or when George Gershwin scores a crap game with conservatory counterpoint in *Porgy and Bess*. We've seen classical composers absorbing "jazz" in Weill's Germany, true. But in Europe, it was a stunt. In America, it's music.

The ideal Next Project for Weill would have been a commission from the First Address in American music, the Metropolitan Opera. Yes, another of those museums, where song, not theatre, reigned. Nevertheless, it might have placed Weill as a pro among pros. Up to the end of the 1934–1935 season, the Met's General Manager, Giulio Gatti-Casazza, had been obsessive about putting on new operas by Americans. But Gatti retired and his successor, Herbert Witherspoon, abruptly died, leaving the Met in the hands of one of its tenors, Edward Johnson. While Johnson heavily Americanized the roster of singers, welcoming many more native artists than Gatti had done, Johnson hated new operas by Americans. As recently as 1934, Johnson

---

* Steffens made the statement after a trip to Soviet Russia in its early days. It is commonly misquoted as "I have seen the future, and it works."

was forced to assume the tenor lead in Howard Hanson's *Merry Mount*, a tuneful and extremely dramatic piece that enjoyed great success, not least because of a titanic performance by Lawrence Tibbett as a Puritan preacher maddened by lust. But *Merry Mount* is virtually an opera for baritone and chorus. The soprano has relatively little to do, and the tenor—Edward Johnson—virtually nothing. Worse, he had to show up in a dream orgy dressed as the devil. As the Met's new manager, Johnson unofficially banned *Merry Mount* and would have been in no mood for any *Zwischengattung* from a refugee German composer.

Thus, as Weill waited for *The Eternal Road* to reach the rehearsal stage, he and Lenja found themselves in the typical émigré position, trying to restart their lives while cut off from the culture that had nourished and stimulated them. Would Weill ever have found his way to Mahagonny if he had not been living in Weimar Berlin, entranced as it was with American myths of get-rich-quick business ethics and assembly-line crime? Would Weill have composed *Der Silbersee*, with its almost specifically anti-Nazi escape from reality?

Refugees found it difficult not only adjusting to American life but finding work in their metier. It was the myth of the Russian archduke driving a taxi in Paris: and it wasn't a myth. Then, too, there had already been a European influx into American culture, especially in Hollywood during the late silent era, when there was no language barrier between actor and public. Foremost among many others, Greta Garbo gave the movies an extraordinary acting style combining the Grand Manner with something comparable to pre-Method realism, all from within a glamor of such radiance that it is difficult to imagine Hollywood without her.

Some émigrés, one might say, had all the luck. Coming to Hollywood, like Garbo, in the mid-1920s, Ernst Lubitsch, too, fit into silents easily—yet he found his self-definition in the talkie. True, Lubitsch was the most "silent" of sound directors, doting on how his actors passed through doorways, revealed evidence in a drawer, or traded whispers. Yet such Lubitsch films as *Trouble in Paradise* and *One Hour With You* (both in 1932) revel in dialogue, and Lubitsch knew how to spark his players' delivery. *Paradise* offers Herbert Marshall's least wooden performance ever—he's as sexy as a willow—and when, in *One Hour With You*, Charles Ruggles asks why his butler got him up as Romeo for a party that is strictly black-tie, the butler replies, with a shameless smirk, "Oh, sir, I did so want to see you in tights."

A very few émigrés had so established themselves internationally that it didn't matter where they lived. "Where I am," Thomas Mann declared, "there is Germany." He, too, landed in Southern California. Brecht got there later, having traveled through Russia and across the Pacific, and he did not find Germany in Los Angeles. "Tahiti in the form of a big city," he called it. It certainly lacked a *Luft*.

There was enough of this crowd to form a community headquartered at Salka Viertel's salon, a Little Berlin from food to language, as if they were all at the *Stammtisch* at Schlichter's café. Weill, who often visited Los Angeles in pursuit of composing jobs in the movies, made no secret of his contempt for the entire gang, living in a past that Hitler had eradicated and scorning anything American.

The "*Mumienkeller*" (Mummies' Den) was his term for the gatherings at the Viertels'. It was not just their contempt for the nation that had saved their lives that shocked him, but their arrogance—the sheer failure to understand that their old medals, so to say, were useless in the new military. Arnold Schönberg felt post-German enough to re-spell his last name as Schoenberg. Yet when MGM considered commissioning a soundtrack score from him, he told Irving Thalberg that the actors must deliver their dialogue in the *Sprechstimme* (the ghoulish pitched recitation) that accompanied twelve-tone music. The notion of utilizing a flamboyant artistic affectation in the "natural" medium of cinema is so bizarre that one wonders if Schoenberg had ever seen a movie. Of course he wasn't hired.

Some of these émigrés in Hollywood got cagey and blended their innovations into prevailing moviemaking recipes. Many think Josef von Sternberg was one of the Hitler-era refugee group, but he spent some of his youth in the United States and was a Hollywood veteran before the Nazi takeover. Even so, the six films he made for Paramount with Marlene Dietrich from 1930 to 1935—sequels, culturally speaking, to *The Blue Angel*—are rife with the one quality that has long separated European cinema from Hollywood movies: atmosphere. From design to casting, these six Paramounts are continentally flavored—logically so, as Paramount was a directors' studio just as MGM was a producers' studio and Warner Bros. a leftwing writers' studio.

Some writers derogate von Sternberg—but then, says the film historian David Thomson, he "made it easy for us to dislike him, and his tone is one of disdain." Critics invoke the old saw that art too obviously striving for greatness fails in greatness. Yet Beethoven's Ninth Symphony, *Ulysses*, and *Long Day's Journey Into Night* are incontestably great partly because of the grandeur of their agenda. Besides, von Sternberg's films strive less for greatness than for a compulsive iconolatry of the unavailable woman, the opposite of Goethe's *ewig-Weibliche*: a *niemals-Weibliche*. Goethe's personal lady of the sonnets inspires man. Von Sternberg's teases and scorns, despite the Paramounts' blatant sensuality.

Thus *The Scarlet Empress* (1934), in which Dietrich is married off to the heir to the Russian throne, revels in innuendo and display. One of the most bizarrely entertaining movies ever made, it proves that an émigré (of sorts) could corral a major Hollywood studio into letting him make a European movie. *The Scarlet Empress* breaks every Hollywood rule, not least in the casting of the romantic element. Sam Jaffe plays the incipient tsar as a grinning, infantile idiot; for contrast, von Sternberg opposes Jaffe with John Lodge, barbarically long-haired and absurdly tall, with the kind of smile that goes with a honeymoon cascade. Jaffe is the von Sternberg double, Lodge the male equivalent of Dietrich: sensualized and beckoning yet never yours. Someone at Paramount must have put a foot down, for in the midst of all this is the middle-American Louise Dresser as the *tsaritsa*, a grouchy old buzzard out of *Mother Carey's Chickens*.

Von Sternberg was, in effect, the émigré who never emigrated: his career started in California. Fritz Lang not only emigrated but fled, after Joseph Goebbels offered to put Lang in charge of German cinema despite Lang's being half-Jewish. Having seen *Die Nibelungen* and

Metropolis, Hitler himself predicted that Lang would "give us great Nazi films!" In fact, Lang's work deteriorated in America. It's not that the films are poor: most critics prefer them to his German titles. But they are films that virtually any other director could have made. The pictorial narration that makes *Die Nibelungen* an animated storybook is gone, as is the Mephistophelian hocus-pocus of the crime films. Lang assimilated himself into American culture by reading comic strips and chatting up gas jockeys and waitresses. Perhaps he assimilated too well. *You Only Live Once* (1937), Lang's take on Bonnie and Clyde, with Henry Fonda and Sylvia Sidney, actually contains a cutesy routine about a cop lifting fruit from an apple vendor. Another critic's favorite is *The Big Heat* (1953), the one in which Lee Marvin throws boiling coffee into Gloria Grahame's face. Dashing Glenn Ford plays a detective out to break up a crime ring—and that isn't Lang. His detectives are plodding fat guys and his criminals are magicians out to rule the world. Dragged down by stock acting and bland decor, *The Big Heat* never imagines anything. It's slick product, the last thing one expects from a director who, in the 1920s, had revolutionized cinema.

So there were very few genuine success stories among these émigrés, though one achieved tremendous success by changing not his art but his medium. Erich Wolfgang Korngold, a prodigy who saw his operas staged at Munich when still a teenager, composed theatre scores so elaborately narrative that if the cast got laryngitis you could still follow the plot from what the orchestra said. Moving to Hollywood, Korngold gave up opera for the movies: and invented the Hollywood soundtrack.

He called his movie scores "opera without singing," because he was in effect musicalizing narratives at Warner Bros. just as he had done in the opera house. Of course, background music in film was hardly a novelty when Korngold made his first visit to Hollywood, to score Max Reinhardt's *A Midsummer Night's Dream* (1935), co-directed with another émigré, William Dieterle. From earliest silent days, a piano or small group played along with the action in even the smallest cinemas, and major releases in big cities boasted symphony orchestras, sometimes playing original scores commanded from Victor Herbert or Jerome Kern. Nevertheless, most of what was heard truly was background music, usually cobbled out of the classical or popular repertory.

Consider MGM's *Grand Hotel* (1932), which took the Best Picture Oscar for its innovation of the all-star ensemble—the two Barrymore boys, Wallace Beery (the only one in the whole film with a German accent, though most of the characters are Germans), and both Greta Garbo and Joan Crawford (who never appear in the same frame together for even a second). The studio had financed the smash Broadway adaptation of Vicki Baum's bestseller precisely to start with a property oozing cultural prestige, and every MGM department was encouraged to paint the film with the utmost in style. Looking at Garbo's scenes with John Barrymore today, one realizes why MGM's couturier Adrian said, when Garbo retired, "Glamor is over."

And yet *Grand Hotel*'s soundtrack music is the very opposite of glamor: continental favorites bought off the rack and barely fitted to the action at all: Strauss and Rachmaninof, "Vienna, My City of Dreams," and the English pop hit "The King's Horses and the King's Men" in jazzband mode for Lionel's drunk scene. Nobody wrote this music as a movie score: the "composer" is an arranger.

Thus, when Hollywood began awarding Oscars for Best Score, in 1934, the composer, if there even was one, would be named but the award itself went to the studio's music department head. Korngold "won" for *Anthony Adverse* (1936), but the certification in fact went to Leo Forbstein. Two years later, the rules were changed and the composer himself was the honoree—and Korngold was the main reason. He didn't fit music to a film's action: he propelled the action, timing his effects so precisely with the screen that the music was the story. After *Grand Hotel*'s mechanical waltzing, Korngold brought surprise to the art, even to the point of matching words of dialogue to notes of music. Detractors like to denigrate Korngold's postwar symphonic works—he refused to compose for the concert hall till Nazism was defeated—by calling it "movie music." It's the opposite: Korngold made movie music sound like symphonies, "classicizing" the popular.

And isn't that what Kurt Weill was doing in the various manifestations of his *Zwischengattung*? There is little in German art between Beethoven and kitsch. But American art, again, revels in crossover forms. Democracy is flexible, protean, open to compromise, and the *Zwischengattung* is a compromise in genre: anything goes.

German artists who did not emigrate found themselves with a communication problem. Paul Hindemith's magnum opus, the opera *Mathis der Maler* (Mathias the Painter), had to be staged in Zurich. All the major European cities, from Paris and London to Budapest and Prague, sent reporters to cover the event, but not a single German newspaper fielded a correspondent. And as the first night occurred on May 28, 1938—two-and-a-half months after Hitler's troops had marched into Austria for the *Anschluss*—Vienna joined the Nazi blackout.

Hindemith's difficulties with the regime lay partly in his having married out of the *Volk*. (His wife was Jewish.) Worse, his enfant terrible 1920s had tasted of jazz, in which Hitler discerned the very bloodflow of *Kulturbolschewismus*. By the time *Mathis der Maler* was performed, Hindemith, too, had gone into exile, and it is touching to report that this opera asks what kind of life an artist should have in time of epic turmoil. Who will defy tyrants if not the artist, the most free of all citizens because of the power of creation? There actually was a Mathis, in the sixteenth century. His masterpiece, the altar at the church in Isenheim, in that disputed Franco-German borderland of Alsace, depicts events in the life of St. Anthony. Hindemith sees Mathis as a kind of Anthony himself and a kind of saint as well. The opera is virtually a musical expression of the Isenheim artwork, yet it wonders what art is to be made amid a totalist uprising, with the usual atrocities and bookburnings, the totalist's anti-art nihilism. As Goethe's Devil puts it, *"Ich bin der Geist, der stets verneint"* (I am the spirit that says no).

Many of Hindemith's countrymen made art in anti-humanist times. Werner Egk even included a touch of jazz in his opera *Peer Gynt* (1938), encountering no trouble, and Carl Orff enjoyed great success with two storybook operas, *Der Mond* (The Moon, 1939) and *Die Kluge* (The Wise Woman, 1943). Lenja, when she finally encountered *Die Kluge* after the war, was outraged, claiming the whole thing was stolen from *Die Bürgschaft*. (It wasn't, though Orff's use of three vagabonds to push the narrative along does recall a comparable trio in Weill's opera.) And of course Germany's most prominent composer, Richard Strauss, continued to develop his opera catalogue, even if he did offer one work, *Friedenstag* (Day of Peace, 1938), that, if not "defeatist," is powerfully anti-war. Further, it was premiered in Munich during the summer of the Czech crisis, a bold act for a man who had a rickety relationship with the regime.

Bold acts were rare, but some did agree with Hindemith that an evil age demands reply. Ernst Jünger, whom we last saw writing love letters to war in *Storm of Steel*, published in 1939 a short novel called *Auf den Marmorenklippen* (On the Marble Cliffs), a timeless parable in which someone called the Chief Ranger grabs power and maintains it through terror. Characterized as both majestic and ridiculous, intransigent and cunning, he is clearly Hitler, and Jürgen's book is so anti-Nazi that it is amazing that it was published at all.

While the Nazis politicized art, they also made art out of politics. Hitler's biographer Joachim Fest suggests that Weimar's leaders failed in part because they didn't dramatize the issues. Hitler brought politics into the world of entertainment with—in Richard and Clara Winston's translation—"his endless obfuscations, his theatrical scenarios, the storms of ecstasy and idolization. Those vaults created by massed searchlight beams [at party rallies] were the fitting symbol for it all: walls of magic and light erected against the dark menace of the outside world."

Weill and Lenja's first shock in acclimating themselves to daily life in the United States was the complete absence of a concept of *das Volk*. "Folk" pertained to quaint dances and antique ditties, to tall tales and household remedies for common ailments. It wasn't just that America wasn't totalitarian. It was that the feeling of the nation was ecumenical, that "American" was an inclusive, not a segregating, category, especially in the liberal communities of New York music and theatre that Weill and Lenja moved into. In fact, there were plenty of American nativists, some quoted prominently in the news. But the evidence of immigrant or minority acculturation was everywhere: in Garbo and Lubitsch, Stokowski and Toscanini, Joe DiMaggio and Ethel Waters.

So Weill and Lenja felt welcome, though there was one amusing glitch. Chieftains of New York's arts tribe, aware of the Telefunken *Threepenny* records and even the Pabst film, started inviting Weill and Lenja to parties, and the couple's first big one, apparently, was in George Gershwin's apartment. A showplace, of course: fourteen rooms on two floors at 132 East Seventy-Second Street, walled with Gershwin's impressive art (including his own really quite wonderful paintings) and taking in a gymnasium, a sleeping porch, a garden, and even one room just for the exhibition of Gershwin's life-and-work souvenirs. In the usual cavernous living room was the grand piano with Gershwin playing it, for "Gershwin at the keyboard" was a fixture of New York social life at the time—so much so that a Cole Porter musical that opened just a week or two after this party, *Jubilee*, featured a likeness of Elsa Maxwell singing about a dance she's planning. " 'Twill be new in every way," she explains, "Gershwin's promised not to play."

At some point or other in the party I speak of, Gershwin finally took a break and was introduced to Weill and Lenja. Gershwin, too, knew the *Threepenny* records, and duly congratulated Weill—but Gershwin did have one problem. He didn't like the leading lady.

Lenja!

Of course, Gershwin had no idea that the singer he was denigrating was standing in front of him. As she always told the story, Gershwin said she sang "like a hillbilly." Then she'd pause for dramatic effect— now that she finally knew what he meant. "A hillbilly, you know?"

In the more famous version of the tale, Gershwin complains about the "squitchehdickeh voice." And, yes, in 1928 Lenja was using her soprano register and it was a bit on the scratchy side.[*]

The main thing about that party at George Gershwin's was George's sibling Ira, a combination collaborator, pep squad, and brother's keeper. Ira and his wife, Leonore, lived just across the street, and Ira was always

---

[*] The story travels around: Lehman Engel, who had already conducted a little-known production of *Der Jasager* and who would conduct Weill's first Broadway musical, *Johnny Johnson*, said he did precisely the same thing to the Weills, in slightly different words. "In my young life," he explained in his memoirs, "I held pear-shaped tones sacred."

at George's, not only to write shows with him but because he loved and revered him. Ira was to prove one of Weill's most constant writing partners, but this night he served another purpose: he invited Weill to a rehearsal of *Porgy and Bess.*

This is what I mean about America completely lacking a *Volk*—or how did one of its artistic masterpieces end up a Broadway opera by a southern gentleman and two Jewish upstarts on a black subject directed by a Russian? We don't know whether Weill saw a runthrough in street clothes, a dress rehearsal, or something in between, but we do know that he was stunned by the music: here was the *Zwischengattung*, not in some obscure bohemian corner but at the center of the commercial theatre structure, with intense media curiosity following it as if readying the atmosphere for a *Time* cover story.* In an interview with the *New York Times,* Ira recalled that Weill turned to him and said, "It's a great country where music like that can be written—and played."

That is, not only can you create this art, but no one will try to stop you from making it public. Weill had not come to America—he thought—to emigrate. He had come for the production of *The Eternal Road.* He and Lenja didn't even try to find an apartment; they stayed at the Hotel St. Moritz. And yet he must have been considering his options. As we've seen, he was a man who kept a firm grasp on destiny's lapels: no, you'll do what *I* tell *you.* He still had the house in Paris, though the political climate in France, insistently anti-Semitic, was leaning toward détente with the Nazis. Weill had made contacts in London, even as his show there had suffered terrible failure. And while he was getting along very well in English—Lenja, with the usual comic malapropisms, was struggling—Weill had no plans to settle in the United States.

On the other hand, *The Eternal Road* was suffering delays, mostly because of designer Bel Geddes' impossible demands. He was virtu-

---

* Gershwin actually got his cover on July 20, 1925, at an odd time in his life, just after his most ignominious Broadway flop, *Tell Me More,* and five months before the premiere of his Concerto in F. It must have been a slow summer. "Famed jazzbo," *Time* called Gershwin, in the chatty but syntactically louche wording it favored back then.

ally rebuilding the interior of the Manhattan Opera House. According to Lenja, on one day, four colossal columns arrived, and after the crew erected them in place on stage, they sank through the deck into the basement, and were never bothered with again.

Other mishaps followed, such as the announcement that the multi-tiered playing area could scarcely contain the vast company of actors, singers, and dancers, so Weill's orchestra would have to play backstage, to be piped into the auditorium. Just as Humperdinck had been overwhelmed in Reinhardt's *The Miracle*, Weill's very players would vanish into the status of canned music.

Worse than the grandiose Bel Geddes were Weill's more immediate collaborators, Reinhardt and Werfel. As a professional genius, Reinhardt was bound to act at least a little crazy, but his daily vacillations irritated Weill, as erratic behavior always irritates the steady temperament. Werfel, however, was proving truly outrageous. Lenja thought he looked like a composer rather than a writer, and she didn't mean that as a compliment: "a drooling mouth, always wet, thin straggly hair, greasy looking, ready to burst into tears at the drop of a hat." Was any of it for real? she asked. And what about Werfel's wife, Alma? What a prize, that one! A collector of prominent men, she had married Gustav Mahler, then the architect Walter Gropius,★ and now Werfel. Two of the three husbands were Jewish, yet Alma was, Lenja thought, a thoroughgoing anti-Semite.

What Lenja—and Weill—didn't yet realize was that Reinhardt and the Werfels were what you put behind you when you leave Europe: the high-strung egomaniac offering talent instead of manners and noise instead of class, who relishes his time-honored bigotries as if they were accessories of culture, and has no idea how loathsome everybody finds him. One can almost hear Lenja saying, "All the comforts of home, you know?"

As *The Eternal Road*'s premiere seemed ever further in the future,

---

★ There is a slight connection with Weill here, as Gropius founded the Bauhaus architectural school, in Weimar. Harassed by local authorites, it moved to Dessau—Weill's family home. After a second move, to Berlin, the Bauhaus was dissolved shortly after the *Machtergreifung*.

Weill cast about for something to write. New York's theatre world was vast, yet everyone seemed to know everyone else—especially the influential names at the top of its success loops. And they loved bringing talents together. True, one had to work around the established feuds—Eva Le Gallienne hated Helen Hayes; playwrights hated the Theatre Guild; and everyone hated Jed Harris. But otherwise, parties led to lunches, and lunch conversations led to ideas for a show. And lunches with experimental talents led to experimental ideas. And that has to be why Kurt Weill has fetched up in New York. It is not for that European leftover *The Eternal Road*. It is to write a Broadway musical.

True, it's an odd musical. All experiments are odd. Gustav Mahler's symphonies are odd; the Beatles' White Album is odd. The Group Theatre was odd: and they were going to produce Weill's show. It was to be their first musical, because the Group wasn't a musical outfit. The Group was socially progressive and entirely non-singing (though in its summer communal retreat the Group's exercises included some work in dance). Nevertheless, the chance to write, in effect, an American *Threepenny Opera* was something Weill could not turn down.

So Weill tossed ideas around with the Group's three directors, Group drama guru Harold Clurman; Group acting coach Lee Strasberg; and Group den mother and managing director Cheryl Crawford. Strasberg, who directed most of the Group's plays, was the headstrong one, though nothing like the raving tyrants of the Berlin theatre. The other two were rather easy to work with; Weill was to write two more shows for Crawford later on. Clurman did affect a bit of the grand manner—one night, years later, his wife, Stella Adler, gave him a rap on the ear, saying, "Don't sleep like a great man. Just sleep!"

A congenial management, then: but everyone was telling Weill that he couldn't have arrived at a worse time, because of the Depression's drain on Broadway's operating capital. In the mid-1920s, the number of musical productions tallied at about forty-five a season. By 1934–1935, the total fell to fourteen, and it was to slide to eleven in 1935–1936, at the start of which Weill had arrived in New York.

Yet Clurman, Strasberg, and Crawford were undeterred, even though their very limited budget would be savaged by the demands of a musical, with the orchestra's salaries and all that scenic decoration. Straight plays scraped by on the cost of an Irish boiled dinner. Further to hearten Weill, the Group was a relief after the vacillations and extravagances of *The Eternal Road*'s crew. To a man like Weill, whose sociopolitical identity as a citizen of Europe had been ripped from him, the very reliability of the Group's triumvirate was inspiring.

Now, what should a Kurt Weill–Group Theatre musical be? Weill suggested adapting Jaroslav Hašek's novel *The Good Soldier Švejk*, an international bestseller about an amiable ne'er-do-well who outfoxes authority with a cluelessness so impenetrable that not even army officers can regiment him. Weill may have thought the work's European atmosphere would open up an opportunity for Lenja; her only job since their arrival had been a two-piano concert of Weill's music just before Christmas that did not go over well. However, the Group did not cast outside the company, as it constituted a uniquely trained ensemble, wedded to Strasberg's theories. At that, a piece as continental in flavor as *Švejk* would have strained the deeply personal coordination of performer and character that Group acting demanded. A mannered European comedy would be just the thing for the Theatre Guild (of which the insistently all-American Group was, ironically, an offshoot). But the Group could approach *Švejk* only if the material was transplanted, the characters and themes viewed in American terms.

And that is how Weill and the Group came up with *Johnny Johnson*. Hašek never made it clear whether Švejk is genuinely idiotic or an inspired fake, so Weill and his collaborator, Paul Green, invented a protagonist neither foolish nor devious: a naif with good intentions and, in his unassuming way, a hero. Enlisting in the war about nothing, he sees his patriotic ideals shattered, tries to end the conflict by treating the Allied High Command with laughing gas, is incarcerated as a lunatic, and is finally released nourishing a new ideal, pacifism.

Note that Weill was working, once again, with not a musical-comedy librettist but a playwright. As in Germany, Weill sought to find theatre in music while making music out of theatre—but too often those playwrights just want to find theatre, with a little music here and there. Something like *Peer Gynt*, so one might delete all that Grieg and still have My Wonderful Play. Nonetheless, the story conferences that Weill had with Green and Cheryl Crawford promised a lively and unusual piece. Weill thought Crawford "terrific," probably responding to her genuine respect for creative talent. Throughout her later career as an independent producer, Crawford constantly backed works with no certain commercial potential simply because she found them interesting. "It's astonishing," Weill told Lenja, "how much she understands."

Green was a bit less agreeable, for he kept hogging the center of the writing, leaving the score at the edges of the narration—a bizarre number for Johnny's sweetheart's mother at her sewing machine, a celebration of tea for British soldiers, an American private recalling his cowboy past, a psychiatrist's history of his profession. Musical-comedy numbers are supposed to define and develop the principals and spend little time with minor characters. There's no reason for anyone's mother to sing to us, especially when this one confesses, "I once dreamt a duke had made me his queen," which makes us curious about a character who then abruptly vanishes from the story.

Yet the two authors (and Crawford) worked closely, and both Weill and Lenja took the opportunity to pull off characteristic feats: he got lost and she had an affair with Green. A North Carolinian, Green invited Weill to journey down by rail to Chapel Hill for a writing vacation, instructing him to count the stops and get off right after Durham, or wherever. Weill enjoyed the trip. Sleeping through the night, he looked out, the next morning, at beautiful geography tinted for late spring; it reminded him of the south of France. Getting off at what he thought was his stop, he found himself on a siding, deserted except for "a few dilapidated Negro shanties," as he put it. It turned out that Green hadn't warned Weill about this seldom-used railroad Brigadoon; Weill says he "finally talked a young man with a Ford" into driving him the rest of the way to Green's.

As for Lenja, her liaison with Green might have surprised a few people even in the tolerant milieu of the Group Theatre, but by now Weill and Lenja were as sure of each other as courtly lovers in a medieval romance. They were meant to be together the way he was meant to compose: as something natural, unhinderable. The two remarried less than a year later, on January 19, 1937—but this was no more than housekeeping, to observe the legalities, from hospital visits to testamentary security.

"A play with music" is how the Group billed *Johnny Johnson*, admitting that it wasn't anything like a musical, or simply euphemizing the cast's lack of ability in song. (The playbill designated the show as "a legend," distancing it yet further from the everyday of Broadway song and dance.) Remember, too, that there were no microphones on Broadway at the time (except at the Center Theatre, the musical's equivalent of Radio City Music Hall). Oddly, for someone so protective of his scores and his orchestrations, one who refused to allow stagings that altered his intentions in any way, Weill was very comfortable with performers' use of a song for dramatic rather than vocal expression. It's the Lenja ideal, perhaps: less tone but more personality. Weill even went up to the Group's summer seminar retreat—in 1936 it was in Trumbull, Connecticut—to coach everyone, using the *Threepenny* movie and the Telefunken discs. Much later, talking with Foster Hirsch for his *Kurt Weill On Stage*, Phoebe Brand (who played opposite the Johnny of Russell Collins as his sweetheart, Minny Belle) recalled how Weill wanted them singing on "your attitude, your character." Noting the play's original billing, Brand emphasized that *Johnny Johnson* "isn't exactly a musical . . . It was realism, and as in all the other shows [the Group] worked on, it was the acting that was all-important." Indeed, hadn't Weill come to the theatre to escape the lifeless affectations of opera-house acting?

The Group was game for the experiment, for while musicals were thought dramatically unworthy, this one was not only politically interesting but artistically innovative. If too much of the score gives solos to minor characters, that does support Green's kaleidoscopic approach: except for Johnny, the show consists of an ever-changing dramatis personae. Highlighting these starry bit parts, Weill gave them pastiche numbers—a smutty tango for an army captain, a French *café conc'* specialty for a nurse, and that "Cowboy Song," also entitled "Oh the Rio Grande." Weill was so eager to assimilate into American life that he changed the pronunciation of his surname to "while"—but this was window dressing. For a man who lived within his art with Weill's quiet intensity, there was no way to be American till his music was.

Thus, sorting through the sounds he had been hearing since he had stepped off the boat, Weill sought out the various American ethnicities. He was to re-use melodies from his European works almost to the end of his career, but he eagerly absorbed the sounds of his new native land—for surely he realized, just about now, that he had not, after all, simply made a visit to New York for professional reasons. Yes, he was here for *The Eternal Road*, all right, the real one of wandering exiles. This wasn't a visit: this was the new address. And what better way to celebrate than with a "Cowboy Song," its verse banged out in hoofbeats and its chorus pure open-hearted lyricism? The Weill-Brecht cabaret hadn't closed, but it was under new management.

Unfortunately, no matter how well the Group players acted their songs, they were boxing above their weight in musical terms, and director Strasberg gave them no help. It was mandatory at the time for anyone with intellectual pretensions to scorn musicals as meretricious, and Strasberg apparently could find his way through *Johnny Johnson* only by pretending that it was a play *without* music. The songs looked like dialogue by other means—but songs, even in a work of social inquiry like this one, aren't supposed to look like dialogue. The cast was so lost in trying to put its music over that, as Lehman Engel recalled, one night Sanford Meisner gave up on Captain Valentine's tango verses and just whistled his way through the music. When Engel chastised him at the next intermission, Meisner slapped him.

With *Johnny Johnson*'s premiere set for November 19, 1936, Weill and Lenja would have noted that Erik Charell's *White Horse Inn*, in yet another replica of its Berlin original, was just about to take over the Center Theatre. With Kitty Carlisle and William Gaxton heading the cast (a nearly twenty-two-year-old Alfred Drake was in the chorus) and Charell directing, *White Horse Inn* could be seen as a reminder of what Weill might have done with his talent had he gone into conventional musical comedy—or into any conventional form of music theatre. Weill's works, from *Mahagonny* and *The Silver Lake* to *Lady in the Dark* and *Street Scene*, do not startle us today because we have got used to the works conceived under their influence. When new, they were the one thing *White Horse Inn* wasn't: absolutely original, as was *Johnny Johnson*.

This same November of 1936 also gave Weill and Lenja the chance to look upon their first full-scale manifestation of American democracy as the nation went to the polls on November 3 to choose their next president. Franklin Roosevelt's first term saw such sweeping changes in the government's power to shape the country's economic and social life that his run for a second term was bitterly contested by Republicans and the turncoat Democrats of the Liberty League (including Roosevelt's mentor and a former presidential candidate himself, Al Smith). The Republican choice for president was the spectacularly uncharismatic governor of Kansas, Alfred M. Landon; further, the nation had already seen what a Republican does to cure Great Depression in the immobile Herbert Hoover. Roosevelt's Postmaster General, James A. Farley, predicted that Roosevelt would carry every state but Maine and Vermont.

And that is exactly what happened: Roosevelt collected, by some eleven million votes, the greatest plurality in American history. Weill and Lenja must have noticed in particular the lack of fascist undertow in the currents of American politics. The Spanish Civil War had broken out that summer—in effect, the first battle in the continuation of the European Civil War, now with a totalist agenda, a war of annihilations. Yet the United States contained its dark prophets. The most dangerous of them, Louisiana's Huey Long, had been assassinated in 1935, and the infamous "radio priest," Father Charles Coughlin, was at this time more a critic of Roosevelt than a spokesman for anti-Semitism and other crazes of the far right. Most important, there was no attack on the bloodlines of art. The haters had no conception of cultural bolshevism; they tended to hate what you believed in far more than they hated what you were.

Certainly, Weill and Lenja would have heard a great deal about politics during their time with the Group Theatre; progressives talk The Social Order the way evangelicals talk God. But with Weill, the work came first: leave the social order to others while we fix the show. And

Johnny Johnson was in trouble from the moment the production "put in" (as the parlance has it) at its house, the Forty-Fourth Street Theatre, ideal for the big singers of spectacle shows. True, when it opened, as Weber & Fields' Music Hall, it hosted somewhat modest-sized entertainments, albeit built around the two star comics' extravagant, eye-filling visuals. But this was a Shubert house, and after Weber and Fields broke up and the theatre was renamed, it was filled with the Shuberts' favorite thing, operetta. And operetta is really what belonged there. As the Group couldn't afford the usual out-of-town try-out, it gave a few previews to audiences so uncomfortable with the cast's inability to project the music that the walkouts started within a few minutes of the curtain-up, and continued throughout the running time.

This has always seemed unbelievable to me, though we have the tale from more than one trustworthy witness. What exciting lives these spectators must be enjoying if they have something better to do than hear the Group's take on the Broadway musical! Very few shows gave previews at all in the 1930s, so these were presumably friends of the company, guests at an important undertaking, the first on their block. What were they going to do when they left the theatre? Have sex with Beatrice Lillie? She was rehearsing *The Show Is On* just then; she would have been free that evening.

In the end, *Johnny Johnson* did fail, though not so very badly. The reviews were mixed and the run lasted 68 performances, enough time for the curious to attend. If the show has a flaw, it is Green's verbose book. Cut back to emphasize the wonderful music, cast with true singing actors, and assigned to a director with show-biz acumen, the piece would play beautifully. With its odd combination of jest and sorrow and, above all, its lashings of irony, it is probably better suited to post-Beckett theatregoing than it was to that of its age.

The Eternal Road, on the other hand, was one of the last of its line, for the spectacle as a form now seemed as antique as a staging of *Ben-Hur* with a simulated chariot race, or the annual Hippodrome pageant, theatre as a tourist stop. True, Billy Rose had made spectacle momentarily valid in *Jumbo*, at this same Hippodrome, in 1935. Most people today think of this as a Rodgers and Hart musical. In fact, it was a circus with snatches of plot and some songs.

Kurt Weill thought of *The Eternal Road* as his opera. But, as I've said, the composer disappears in a staging of this kind, as Max Reinhardt develops pictures so absorbing that one is watching more than listening. Lighting strikes down from on high on an intimate scene, setting it within the halo of revitalized myth; vast crowds undulate, attack, cringe in turn-on-a-dime timing. Lighting even created the show's "curtain," for the Manhattan Opera House had been stripped of the tradiitonal opening and closing of the public's view by the raising and lowering of a barrier. Instead, in an effect common today but unknown in the 1930s, the lights, aimed at various parts of the gigantic set, controlled the sightlines.

Spectacle was of course Reinhardt's forte, but he also knew how to talk to actors; even the intimate scenes would play well. So, between Reinhardt and Norman Bel Geddes, there was little room left in which Weill could emerge with his score, fierce and tender as befits a piece centering on not only faith but on oppression and massacre. After all, *The Eternal Road* is really set in modern times. Its ageless picture of a folk fearing an imminent pogrom was Europe Today—not only its Jewish population but the Polish leadership class, liquidated by the Nazis, and the Russian peasants burned alive in barns by the Nazis, and the seven million of occupied countries kidnaped for slavery in war factories by the Nazis.

The Eternal Road almost didn't open on January 7, 1937: because the fire department found hazards in Bel Geddes' geography that afternoon. Weisgal got hold of Mayor Fiorello La Guardia, who was on splendid terms with firefighters because of his obsessive habit of joining them on the job. Not in the firehouse: at fires. Under the Mayor's arbitration, *The Eternal Road* would comply with the department's demands on the morrow, and the premiere would proceed with a detachment of firemen bearing extinguishers.

At least Lenja had a role—two of them. Weill had wanted her to play Ruth, who has a heartfelt solo beginning "Nay, where thou goest," drawn right from Testament. But Reinhardt assigned Ruth to

Katherine Carrington, who had no accent, fielded a dependable soprano, and claimed a Broadway track record including ingenue leads
in *Face the Music* and *Music in the Air*. Lenja—who Americanized her
billing to "Lotte Lenya" with this appearance—played Miriam and,
in the Saul sequence, the Witch of Endor.

The reviews were fabulous. Brooks Atkinson called it "a glorious
pageant of great power and beauty." And the reconstruction of the
Manhattan Opera House had won so much press and talkabout that
the production, already physically huge, got even bigger, as Event Theatre. The auditorium seated three times what the average Broadway
house could accommodate, yet at first the place was selling out: and
losing money, because the running costs were so high. After 153 performances, Weisgal closed it. It had always been a not-for-profit undertaking; Weisgal's backers wanted to dramatize the plight of the Nazis'
Jewish victims as elaborately and prestigiously as possible, and they had
succeeded.

After Weill remarried Lenya (the marriage license bore a name
that must have seemed almost biblically antique: Karoline Charlotte
Blamauer Weill, of Paris, France), he set off alone for Hollywood,
staying for five months, through June of 1937. While there, Weill
caught a performance of *Johnny Johnson* put on by the Federal Theatre
at Los Angeles' Mayan Theatre. With a young, personable Johnny in
Brian Morgan and a cast of singers, the show played as Weill had never
heard it before: not just a "play with music" but a *musical play*. True, the
singers were second or third division, and the orchestra was rough. But
the songs, for the first time, sounded like songs. Weill attended on the
opening night, and, possibly to his surprise, the audience loved the
piece.

That may have been the highlight of Weill's California stay, for
many movie projects were discussed only to dissolve at some later
point. Weill couldn't have picked a worse time to try to establish himself in the film business, for the biggest Broadway names had been
writing original scores for the movies since the first year of regular
sound production, 1929, and by now they were virtually colonizing
Hollywood. Irving Berlin's doing it, Jerome Kern's doing it, every-

body's doing it. Cole Porter even had a major hit, *Born To Dance* (1936), mixing his highbrow operetta style with dead-on classy pop and a ditzy waltz called "Hey, Babe, Hey" that uses little more than two chords.

How could the unsung Weill compete? "Opportunities in this place," he told Lenya, "are here one day and gone the next." The most promising idea was a movie to be based on a novel by Ilya Ehrenberg that G. W. Pabst had filmed silent in 1927 as *Die Liebe der Jeanne Ney* (The Love of Jeanne Ney). Clifford Odets was to write the script and Lewis Milestone to direct—but Walter Wanger, the producer, thought Weill too highbrow for movie scores. This despite the authority that the highbrow Erich Wolfgang Korngold was just then bringing to the very idea of the Hollywood soundtrack.

"I wish I could spit in the face of someone like that," Weill told Lenya. Wanger wanted to hear kitsch, not classical, and he cited a few of the German operetta songs then in vogue, the kind that Robert Stolz—another émigré—had made popular. Weill assured Wanger that he could write in that style. The same kind of songs, only better.

And Wanger replied, "To hell with better, I don't want better."

So Weill returned to New York with but one idea still firm: a movie musical with our old friend Fritz Lang, another of his American petty-crime romances. During Weill's California visit, Lenya enjoyed a new love affair with a certain Billy Jones, but she was back east in time to join Weill in a trip to Canada in August in order to re-enter the United States officially as a citizen-in-waiting. Europe was over.

The Weills now made their first serious stab at finding a place to live—their own place. They had been staying as sub-lessees in Cheryl Crawford's apartment, but now they moved to 231 East Sixty-Second Street, into a duplex with a terrace.

Good: stability. But Weill needed work, the art that defines one's place on earth. You can live anywhere—in a sublet, in Louveciennes, down the road in a tree. Can you work anywhere? Hollywood paid well, but you had to assert yourself aggressively simply to gain respect. It was a bit like the Berlin theatre scene, but that was the problem: Weill had noticed an essential difference between the old life and the new.

Back there, everyone raved at underlings and fawned upon superiors. Here, folks were friendly and open—like Johnny Johnson. Americans were modest about their heroism and inclined to help rather than hinder others. Hollywood was like Berlin: here be monsters. So Weill returned to New York.

Pursuing his intention to treat ultra-American subject matter, Weill teamed up with Hoffman Reynolds Hays (who preferred the byline H. R. Hays) in the first months of 1938 on *Davy Crockett*. The original title was *One Man From Tennessee*, and the Federal Theatre was to produce it, with Henry Fonda as the frontiersman of myth and history. Although the Federal Theatre's vast output ran from antique melodrama to children's shows, writers invariably focus on the agency's controversially leftist offerings, and *Davy Crockett* would undoubtedly have been one of them. As Hays saw it, Crockett's life was a struggle between America's natural man—Crockett himself—and a conscienceless capitalist, whom Hays named Job Spindle. According to David Drew, about forty-five minutes of music survives, "lacking in both vitality and conviction." Drew seems to feel that Hays didn't give Weill enough to work with, and we notice that most of the best music ended up in Weill's next few Broadway titles. Spindle's autobiographical number, "The Hand Is Quicker Than the Eye," employs a longish middle section that went just as it was (with new lyrics) into the title song of *One Touch of Venus*, and Drew hears in two other numbers bits of *Knickerbocker Holiday*. Unfortunately, Weill seems to have found no later place for *Davy Crockett*'s best number, the choral "Song of the Trees," in which nature cries out to the hero in haunting melody over a steady tom-tom beat.

Davy Crockett was never finished, for several reasons. The first was that Weill had to travel to Hollywood to complete work on his Fritz Lang film, entitled *You and Me*. George Raft and Sylvia Sidney played employees of a department store whose owner hires ex-convicts out of sheer generosity. The Raft-Sidney romance (actually, they get married early in the action) is threatened when some of their co-workers gang up to rob the store.

You and Me would have been Weill's first film musical, and he was aware of how crucially success in the form would affect his future earning power. Another difference between Europe and America: back there, one could be successful on sheer eminence, on the amount of intellectuals' conversation one's work generated. Over here, one had to achieve some measure of commercial success—especially in Hollywood. Complicating matters was the two-faced etiquette practiced by virtually everyone in the movie industry—the way executives lavished encouragement upon you the day before you were barred from the lot, the flattery of colleagues who were secretly engaged in a feud to the death with you, the fan dances and rope tricks and hide-and-seeks.

"I'm more disgusted with the place than ever," Weill told Lenya.

The worst of it was that, after Weill had helped Lang place *You and Me*'s music to emphasize the "money" theme that runs through the story—the grand emporium with its cackling cash registers, the lure of the merchandise that charms one poor soul into theft (Sidney catches her and lets her off)—the studio tore out almost all the songs. All that remained was the opening, "You Can't Get Something For Nothing," and a nightclub number, "The Right Guy For Me," along with a bizarre "percussion" sequence in which the gang recalls the knocking code they all used for communication in prison, banging on a table and calling out translations as Lang illustrates with expressionistic views of jail cells and corridors. Apparently Weill planned this as a full-scale musical scene, but it was filmed without accompaniment of any kind.

During Weill's time in Hollywood, Lenya got her first gig as a cabaret diseuse, at a new New York club called Le Ruban Bleu that specialized in booking European singers. Singing the obvious standalone pieces from Weill's German works, Lenya also plugged "The Right Guy For Me" and apparently included a new specialty written to order and capitalizing on her roughness in her new native language, "Few Little English." It was the work of Marc Blitzstein, a onetime Weill detractor enthusiastic about only the Brecht portion of Weill-Brecht. Perhaps exposure to Lenya turned him into an ally, for Blitzstein was to prove invaluable when his *Threepenny* translation initiated the Weill Renaissance in the 1950s.

Lenya's four weeks at Le Ruban Bleu were very successful, albeit only within the small purview of cabaret cognoscenti. Still, the celebrities of the columns paid their visit—even Cole Porter, though he was suffering from his horseback-riding accident of the year before, on crutches and in great pain. As Lenya happily told Weill, who was still in Hollywood, working on the dubbing of *You and Me*, Porter made a point of commending Lenya's diction. It was a Porter obsession, because, as a composer-lyricist, he knew that the melody always gets through if only because of the orchestra, while an inarticulate performance can kill your tastiest couplet. What mattered to Lenya, however, was the singularity of being invited to Porter's table: émigrés need all the help they can get. "Showing off to people," she reminded Weill, "is important."

Weill finally returned to New York, which brings us to another reason he never completed *Davy Crockett*: he had met up with a playwright who was to become the most constant collaborator of his American years as well as a close friend. He and Weill had embarked on a project early in 1937, and when Weill got back to New York he discovered that the book and lyrics of their musical were all but written and the opening set for the fall.

The playwright was Maxwell Anderson, and after so many playwrights who dallied, and went on vacations, and missed appointments, here was one who beat the clock as a rule. Weill was flabbergasted: an artist as productive as *he* was! The show these two put together offered one of Weill's best (and biggest) scores, again on a very American theme. It was also much closer to a standard Broadway musical than *Johnny Johnson* had been, though unconventional in its own way.

Then, too, this show came forth through what we might call an independent producing outfit (like *Johnny Johnson*'s Group Theatre). The Group broke away from the Theatre Guild because it wanted to experiment. The firm that Weill now joined up with also broke away from the Guild—but only because a number of Guild playwrights had sworn never again to work with its highfalutin, acrimonious, self-congratulatory six-person governing board.

Well, that was always happening. All the writers who worked with the Guild said as much.

This time they meant it.

11

There's Nowhere To Go But Up!

Of course, they never admitted this openly. Maxwell Anderson, S. N. Behrman, Sidney Howard, Elmer Rice, and Robert E. Sherwood offered the expected grand announcement about "making a center for ourselves within the theatre" and "setting a high standard of writing and production." But their program in fact was to rid themselves of the Theatre Guild's Gang of Six and its little coterie that controlled design and stage direction and even the Guild's acting troupe, though this did include those hit guarantors Alfred Lunt and Lynn Fontanne. The problem with the Guild's board above all was its determination to match each play to Guild style when it should have been the reverse. So now many of the Guild's most important American playwrights were to go free-lance.

They called themselves the Playwrights' Company, and their first offering, on October 15, 1938, was Sherwood's *Abe Lincoln in Illinois*, starring Raymond Massey and directed by Rice. Just four days later came the Weill-Anderson piece. It was billed as a "musical comedy," but as Anderson had never before written (or possibly even seen) one, the show was utterly unlike the Cole Porter and Rodgers and Hart titles that opened just after it, *Leave It To Me!* and *The Boys From Syracuse*. For one thing, Weill's star couldn't sing and, for another, Anderson was attacking F. D. R. and the New Deal.

An odd combination of social progressive and anarchist, Anderson nurtured a belief that professional politicians are not just corrupt but extremely dangerous. In an early play co-written with Harold Hickerson, *Gods of the Lightning* (1928), Anderson—for surely it was he and not the amiably unknown Hickerson—created a figure named Suvorin who sounds Anderson's own beliefs. "There is no government," Suvorin tells some fellow radicals, after having unmasked a federal spy in their midst. "There are only brigands in power who fight for more power . . . Till you die! Till we all die! Till there is no earth!"

One might fear for Weill, having escaped Bertolt Brecht, Helene Weigel, and Hitler only to land in the clutches of the raving Anderson. In fact, Anderson raved in print only; he was otherwise easy to get along with and became one of Weill's favorite people. The musical that the two unveiled, in October of 1938, was *Knickerbocker Holiday*. This is always said to be based on Washington Irving's *Diedrich Knickerbocker's History of New-York*. It isn't. The show is based, rather, on Irving himself, on his irreverent attitude toward history—and Irving serves as the work's *compère*, to set up the action and occasionally intrude on it to argue with the characters. This is one reason why *Knickerbocker Holiday* is different from the thirties version of musical comedy: at the time, book shows were realistic linear narratives. And here's an arresting coincidence: just like *Davy Crockett*, *Knickerbocker Holiday* juxtaposes a natural man against a conscienceless capitalist, the young and ardent Brom Broeck and the head of the city council of Nieuw Amsterdam (population: six hundred), Mynheer Tienhoven. And Tienhoven's daughter, Tina, is Brom's sweetheart. So there's the theme and the romance taken care of.

Perhaps Anderson had seen a musical after all—in his distant youth, when American theatre was overrun with the so-called "Dutch comic,* because all the council members were Dutch comics. So there was humor in the show, if of a quaint old-fashioned kind.

But Anderson had a villain far worse than the merely venal Tienhoven on exhibition: Franklin Roosevelt, in the form of the newly arrived governor of Nieuw Amsterdam, Pieter Stuyvesant, the one historical figure in the piece. (There is a Roosevelt ancestor as well, one of the council members.) In his three years in America, Weill had learned his national politics in the theatre community, which tacked to the left as a rule, and Weill would have had nothing but respect for F. D. R. Besides, like all émigrés from thirties Europe, Weill had had personal experience of evil government—and it wasn't anything like the New Deal.

Further, the rest of the Playwrights' Company, whatever they thought of Roosevelt, didn't see any future for a musical comedy sporting assaults on a popular president. Robert E. Sherwood, author of that Abe Lincoln play that the Playwrights' Company chose to inaugurate their venture, was one of Roosevelt's speechwriters. Wasn't his Lincoln meant at least in part as a portrait of the man who held the nation together in the hardest of hard times? Anderson compromised: he dropped some of the lines linking Stuyvesant to Roosevelt and added in a few—and, with Weill, one musical number, "All Hail, the Political Honeymoon"—whose wording cast Stuyvesant as an openly fascist tyrant of the European kind. "The Political Honeymoon" even invoked "an age of strength through joy," referring to the *Kraft Durch Freude* movement in the Nazis' German Labor Front. So the public generally took Stuyvesant to be a kind of Hitler.†

---

* "Dutch," a simplification of *deutsch* ("German"), referred to an outlandish use of a German or Jewish accent replete with malapropisms, as in this classic exchange of the two most popular Dutch comics, Joe Weber and Lew Fields:

WEBER: I am delightfulness to meet you.
FIELDS: Der disgust is all mine.

† So did Roosevelt, apparently. He attended *Knickerbocker Holiday* during its Washington, D. C. tryout, prominent in a box, and at every political jibe the audience looked up at the president to monitor his reaction before reacting themselves.

Anderson was known at the time for an apparently endless stream of verse plays, but he was a rather elastic writer, having co-authored (with Laurence Stallings) the scorching anti-war *What Price Glory?* (1924). Later, pursuing an interest in the influence of genetics on personality, he climaxed his career adapting William March's novel about a child serial killer in *The Bad Seed* (1954). However, Anderson was not elastic enough to turn into the writer of a typical musical-comedy book, and *Knickerbocker Holiday* is really a political argument in disguise:

> STUYVESANT: A government is a group of men organized to sell protection to the inhabitants of a limited area—at monopolistic prices.

complete with observations on how the powerful stay powerful:

> STUYVESANT: A short war with say—Connecticut, preferably victorious, would restore tone.

and what we might now call "beltway doubletalk":

> STUYVESANT: Under my system there is no such thing as ruin, and no such thing as bankruptcy; there is only a slight financial sophistication supported by unlimited government credit.

Anderson tucks in as well his support for the elemental American love of anarchy. Not of chaos or of a lack of law. Just of respect for each individual. There's a French term for this: *classe unique*, which means no first class, as opposed to second class, no front row center as opposed to balcony, no steerage. Every man and woman his or her own lord. The aforementioned "How Can You Tell an American?," a duet

---

Roosevelt was greatly enjoying himself (though he could not have missed Anderson's critique of Roosevelt's executive creativity), but the public was too distracted to enjoy the show.

for Brom and Washington Irving, is the score's key number. "It isn't that he's black or white" is one line, because being American is a matter of attitude, not of *völkisch* identity politics. It must have been exhilarating for Weill to collaborate on a show that—despite Anderson's antagonism toward Roosevelt—was formidably anti-Nazi in its worldview. It *isn't* that he's black or white—or that he conform to anyone else's view of how he should live. It's school without hall monitors.

Knickerbocker Holiday is nationalist art of a kind the Nazis never anticipated: it says you can choose your life, as Weill chose his. Other than in a few works like the tone poem after Rilke, Weill had never been attracted to nationalism as a theme; now he felt he must be. Before, he had been born into a nation. Now he had married a nation, and he needed to create within its borders. To paraphrase Trotsky, you may not be interested in history, ontology, and genocide, but history, ontology, and genocide are interested in you.

In self-definition, Weill is writing "American." Yet *Knickerbocker Holiday*'s score holds a passport to no known country. Of Weill's first American musicals, *Johnny Johnson* is the most "between" score; Weill even said that it conformed to the style of show he had been writing in Germany. But after that, Weill's sound emigrates just as Weill himself did. *Johnny Johnson* had its experiments in American pastiche. *Knickerbocker Holiday* goes American less in pastiche than in a bizarre and marvelous blend of what he was and what he has decided to be—and of course there is Lenya, many years later, telling us, "There is only one Weill." Not the German, nor the American: the man who chooses his liberty.

So, after a short prelude, *Knickerbocker Holiday*'s curtain rises on Washington Irving alone in his study, and a musical scene follows as he plans his next book: melodrama, rhythmic speech, dialogue without music . . . and then comes the show's first vocal period, beginning "I'll sing of a golden age in the history of New York," *Allegretto animato*, cued in by a flighty little tune on saxophone and violins over a 'cello bass and hiccupping woodwinds. It's fit for Broadway but new to Broadway. By the time Brom enters and sings his establishing number, "There's Nowhere To Go But Up!," Weill is working a standard

Broadway genre in music that Broadway had never heard before. It's that "Things couldn't be worse than this" idea, but Weill doesn't make Brom sound upbeat. He makes him sound big-shouldered and smart and as sexy as a porn star.

Stuyvesant's music is sly. Brom is anthems and ballads; Stuyvesant sings a grandly ironic habanera when he throws Brom into jail, though the Stuyvesant wasn't really a singer. When Anderson first planned the work, he didn't see the role as a star part. He wrote it too well, however, combining menace with a whimsical love of verbal duelling—and that seemed to point to Walter Huston, unchallenged in the line of charismatic rogues. Huston was a protean, to be sure: he, too, played Abraham Lincoln, in D. W. Griffith's first talkie, and Sinclair Lewis' *Dodsworth*, an Asian in *Dragon Seed*, Shakespeare's Othello . . . and later on Huston went completely seedy in an Old Prospector specialty in *The Treasure of the Sierra Madre*, complete with a Best Supporting Actor Oscar for his Old Prospector Crazy Dance.

So Anderson, Weill, and their director, Joshua Logan, went after Huston. Luckily, he made regular stops on Broadway; his Dodsworth was unveiled onstage before it was filmed, and his Othello had played the New Amsterdam Theatre (in its last legit booking for sixty years) just a year before. Huston liked the *Knickerbocker Holiday* script, and he was intrigued by the chance to play the peg-legged Stuyvesant in a trick costume, with his real-life right leg doubled back against his thigh, hidden in old Nieuw Amsterdam pantaloons. Weill concocted a kick-line dance for Stuyvesant and a line of Dutch girls in the mixed metre of $\frac{2}{4}$ and $\frac{3}{8}$ (to suggest Stuyvesant's awkward pounding), which was bound to bring the house down.

There was one problem: the role was too short. "Let me have something with the girl," Huston suggested. A romance? "Give me a song with her," he urged. Weill asked Huston about his singing range; Huston said he didn't have one. In a famous story, he promised to sing Weill something in a radio guest spot that was coming up, and, after hearing him, Weill said, "I'm going to write for Walter the most romantic song ever written": "September Song." Its vocal range isn't that narrow; it moves from middle C to the E flat a tenth above, and the latter is an important note. Still, the lyrics present a sweetly resigned air that supports a delicate delivery, and Huston made it memorable. This was the first genuine star show in Weill's entire career, and it gave him his second huge song hit (after *Threepenny Opera*'s Moritat).

Knickerbocker Holiday's casting was otherwise typical for 1938, with Richard Kollmar and Jeanne Madden as the lovers and Ray Middleton's Washington Irving bringing in some baritone swank. Still, the show was so atypical in its book and score that it had to be ecomically produced; Anderson wrote the continuity around a simple unit set of the city waterfront with two little inset pieces, for Irving's study and the town jail, all designed by Jo Mielziner. "How Can You Tell an American?" defines him as the guy who defies authority, but, in another answer, an American might be the guy who gets a show on Broadway, working with veteran pros and a classy show-biz star, because theatre is the place where the gifted tilt the room in the national culture.

Knickerbocker Holiday was but weeks from its New York premiere when Neville Chamberlain made the colossal blunder we generally refer to as "Munich," finalized on September 29, 1938. The Czechs were ready to fight and the German Army was ready to revolt against Hitler, but the French refused to act and the British ambassador to Berlin, Nevile Henderson, a Nazi enthusiast, actively sabotaged the *Reichswehr*'s plan to depose Hitler. Keith Feiling's Chamberlain biography quotes the British prime minister on Hitler: "I got the impression that here was a man who could be relied on." How can such an idiot function as a head of state? Winston Churchill, soon to succeed Chamberlain, stated the case against Munich in his famous speech in the House of Commons: "You were given the choice between war and dishonour. You chose dishonour and you will have war."

Weill must have been aware now, if not before, that America really was a world away from Europe: in temperament. The Civil War was ending its hiatus, and the "We are right and they are wrong" of the *Chanson de Roland* had moved from fighting invaders to liquidating citizen populations. The infamous *Reichskristallnacht* (The National Night of Broken Glass), Germany's statewide pogrom, occurred on

November 9, 1938, barely two weeks after *Knickerbocker Holiday* opened. Even in countries where rulers wished the whole Jewish thing would simply Go Away, there was fierce outrage that the very center of European civilzation had reverted to homicidal hysteria out of the middle ages. At least Weill's family was not in danger: his parents, brother Nathan, and sister Ruth had emigrated to Palestine, and Hans, Weill's closest family member, had brought his family to New York.

There was no American equivalent for the hatred that the Nazis breathed like air, not even symbolically, verbally. When *Knickerbocker Holiday* opened, no thugs sat in the house waiting to silence the piece, though it was overtly political. "Pedantic" was Brooks Atkinson's view, in the *New York Times*, of Anderson's dialectic: "He cannot trip it quite gayly enough for the [musical-comedy] company he is keeping." That, really, is the worst that happened, and the production had just made it into the black when it ended the New York run at 168 performances and started off on a tour.

Feeling triumphant, Weill and Anderson sought to continue their partnership. They found a likely subject in a bit of fiction by Harry Stillwell Edwards, *Eneas Africanus*. Published in 1919, the tale runs no more than twenty pages and was at one time a huge seller running into many editions. It's a novel of letters, set in 1874, when a former Civil War major, George E. Tommey, places ads in southern papers inquiring after his quondam slave Eneas. In 1864, to save the Tommey family valuables from marauding soldiers, Eneas rode off with a trunk containing the household silver and, above all, an heirloom known as the Bride's Cup, from which all Tommey daughters for many generations have sipped on their wedding day for good luck.

Unfortunately, Eneas has no sense of geography, and while trying to find his way back to the Tommeys he wanders all over the south for ten years. As letters answering Tommey's ad pour in, the reader pieces together the parts of Eneas' picaresque, as his mare foals, the resulting colt proves a racing champ, Eneas marries and sires children, and then takes up preaching. All this time he is desperately seeking the road homeward, but of course Eneas keeps asking folks to direct him to Tommeysville in a Georgian accent, which renders it as "Tomizville."

And of course there is a *Thomasville* in every county in the south: so Eneas keeps getting directed farther and farther afield. Edwards never mentions this confusion of town names specifically, assuming that his southern readership, at least, will make the connection, for the story is filled with authentic color. At one point, a woman answering Major Tommey's ad reveals that her son has married a northern girl: "Think of it Major! But she proved to be a noble-hearted woman and has influenced him to give up tobacco and stimulants in every form."

The final letter is actually a newspaper article, written by a guest at the wedding of Major Tommey's daughter—for, at the height of the festivities, poor old Eneas, complete with new family and race-horse, finally returns home. Hacking open the trunk that Eneas has so faithfully guarded, the major retrieves the Bride's Cup and hands it to his daughter as this endearing little sampler of a story ends.

One can see why Weill and Anderson wanted to adapt it. Musicals are about wanting—especially the musicals of the coming decade, with its Oklahomans eager for statehood, *Carousel*'s inarticulately infatuated Julie and Billy, *Brigadoon*'s alienated city boy who longs to live in a cathedral. No one wants more than Eneas—and isn't he, like Weill, an émigré looking for home? Changing the somewhat arcane (A)eneas to Ulysses, the authors had a truly classical hero, famed for his Odyssey. Tucking in, they wrote five marvelous numbers—"The Place I'm Referring To Is Home," "Forget," "Lover Man," "Lost in the Stars," and "Little Tin God." But they couldn't cast the lead to their satisfaction. Paul Robeson refused to play an Uncle Tom, and Bill Robinson wasn't free. They apparently didn't ask Todd Duncan (the original Porgy of *Porgy and Bess*) or Clarence Muse, the two other notable black singing actors of the day. It may be that they were unable to pin down the rights to Edwards' story. But it is worth noting that four of the five songs cited above, with "Thousands of Miles," form the core emotional numbers of Weill and Anderson's later show *Lost in the Stars*. "The Place I'm Referring To Is Home" became "Little Grey House," "Forget" became "Stay Well," and "Lover Man" became "Trouble Man." ("Little Tin God," which may have had different music in *Ulysses Africanus*, is not a "feeling" number, and was cut from *Lost in the Stars* before the opening.) As *Lost in the Stars* treats race relations realistically and Edwards' tale revives an antebellum idyll of little relevance to Weill and Anderson's day, they may have given up on the project because, for all its emotion, it lacked grip.

Still, Weill and Anderson wanted to work together again. *Knickerbocker Holiday* had not really proved a hit, but it turned a small profit and did at least fill out the fledgling Playwrights' Company's profile as—to all Broadway's merriment—the "Maxwell Anderson musical."* Yet it might have ended as a one-off but for how well Weill and Anderson worked together, especially as Anderson continued to prove almost fanatically industrious after the various layabouts and alibi Ikes Weill had encountered previously. The Weills became close to Anderson and his wife, Mab, and his children, Quentin and Hesper. Max and Mab may not have had the greatest marriage alive—and Mab, it appears, had psychological problems perhaps comparable to those of the wife in the modern musical *next to normal*: conforming to a received notion of homemaker while privately falling apart. Yet the Andersons appeared to create for themselves a dream existence in an enticing rural address in New City, in Rockland County, about twenty-five miles north of Forty-Second Street and Broadway.

The Weills had had virtually no experience of the American convention of the upper-middle-class rustic suburb. Kleinmachnow and Louveciennes, where they had owned or rented property, were townships sharing an identity with the proprietary metropolis, in a lower population density. They were adjuncts to Berlin and Paris. New City was country, a magic forest with, now and again, a house. There is no documentation for this, but the Weills might have seen in the whole Anderson family–New City idyll a paragon to emulate—a stability

---

* An irony: while the Group Theatre and the Playwrights' Company were both formed in opposition to aspects of the Theatre Guild, all three outfits had one eccentricity in common, an interest in offbeat musicals. The Group commissioned *Johnny Johnson*, the Playwrights offered two Weill-Anderson shows eleven years apart, and the Guild presented the quasi-amateur *Garrick Gaieties*, the Broadway opera *Porgy and Bess* (at a time when the notion of a Broadway opera did not exist), the radically leftist revue *Parade*, and the musical that all the smarties expected to become the flop of the century, *Oklahoma!*.

that the Kurt and Lotte union had never known, because it was based not on children and nature but on music. One thinks of that old magazine advertisement showing a male pianist and a female singer—or is she a violinist?—passionately kissing over the keyboard, swept away by their own art. That's the Weills. But there's no such analogy for the Andersons: they were real life, folk without a legend. Prosperous. Appealing. Next to normal. And Mab liked to play cards. She and Lenya gambled incessantly, bringing into their casino others of the art-and-acting demimonde who had settled near the Andersons in New City. Milton Caniff, the creator of the classic comic strips *Terry and the Pirates* and *Steve Canyon*, told Donald Spoto that "Lenya was the best card player I ever met . . . We taught her to play poker and she . . . usually took us to the cleaners." As always before, everyone found the Weills an odd couple, she so outgoing and curious and he so taciturn, as if he already knew everything worth knowing. Two such different people: yet so bonded. When Weill "wanted to leave a gathering, it was 'Lenya, ve go,'" Caniff recalled. "And dey vent."

Making himself useful to the Playwrights' organization, Weill contributed incidental music to two productions, Sidney Howard's *Madam, Will You Walk?* (1939) and Elmer Rice's *Two On an Island* (1940). The former closed out of town despite George M. Cohan's leading the cast, and the latter, an autobiographical look at the romance between a playwright and an actress (played by Betty Field, Rice's wife), was a respectable failure at three months. No matter: Weill had endeared himself to the organization, and he was invited to join when the original five playwrights expanded the letterhead, the only composer ever so honored. A good relationship with Rice was especially important to Weill, for he well recalled Rice's *Street Scene* in its Berlin production as *Die Strasse*, and Weill knew how strongly that drastic slice-of-life melodrama would take to music.

Determined to immerse himself in the marinade of *patria*—his new one—Weill all but gave up the speaking of German except, at moments, to Lenya. (A tireless correspondent, he continued to write in German when communicating with his parents in Palestine.) U. S. citizenship was of course his goal, but, more telling, he and Lenya wanted to move to New City, as if owning American land would reify their nationality. Apartment dwelling in the cultural capital, whether New York or Berlin, was so evanescent—so "émigré waiting for the nightmare to end." Ronald Sanders tells us that Weill "was often to remark that there was no spot back in Germany he had ever loved so much as he did the drugstore in New City, where he was always filled with admiration at the containers brimming with one of his favorite American discoveries, ice cream."

As we know, Weill was extremely contemptuous of Europeans who made no attempt to re-acculturate themselves on American lines. Commuting to Hollywood year after year in continued search for economic stability for Lenya and himself, Weill noted yet again how clannish and continental were the professional foreigners who saloned at Salka Viertel's. Wearing the old clothes, relishing the old feuds, and speaking the old language—German infused with Hungarian and Czech—they seemed unaware that their wonderful Europe had utterly cast them out. When Lenya's old mentor Richard Révy turned up in New York, Weill was polite but dubious. Jens Rosteck catches Weill making a judgment about how well Révy swims in the new stream: "The dotty old guy, Kurt thought, would never become a real American, even with his considerable abilities and his beautiful collection of paintings." Yet Révy countered in his journal, says Rosteck. It was after an evening at Ira Gershwin's, when Weill ran through the *Silver Lake* score on the piano. "Weill would be horrified," Révy observed, "if he ever realized how far from 'American' he really is."

Maybe it was the *Silver Lake* music that led Révy to this conclusion, with its echoes of that hopelessly bygone Weimar. They don't write music like that in America.

But Weill had embraced America far beyond its drug stores' ice cream. He was writing the music Americans wrote—for instance in the new genre that we might call the Patriotic Cantata With Resounding Narration. Related to the Lindbergh piece Weill had written with Brecht, this form flowered in the United States just before and during World War II. The pieces usually lasted about fifteen to thirty minutes, sometimes adding one or two vocal soloists to the narrator, and were essentially war-effort propaganda. Weill had already done something like this in an outdoor pageant for the 1939 World's Fair called *Railroads On Parade*. To the words of Charles Alan (who had written some of the lyrics for *The Eternal Road*), one hundred eighty actors, singers, dancers, and a few locomotives celebrated the previous century or so of the iron road in America. The huge stage was broken in half by a flight of steps, with a second flight all the way upstage, and the train cars pulled on thunderously at the far rear and the very front.

Some of the cantatas had their greatest impact when heard rather than seen, on radio. The most popular title in this line, Earl Robinson and John Latouche's *Ballad For Americans*, has no "action," though it was introduced in the theatre, as part of a musical revue, *Sing For Your Supper* (1939), listed in the program as "Ballad of Uncle Sam." The show failed, but the number took on a life of its own as a concert piece for a bass-baritone soloist serving also as the work's narrator, in conversation with the chorus. On a CBS radio broadcast, with Paul Robeson as the whimsically "unknown" *compère* who teases the chorus into guessing who he is (the spirit of America, it turns out), *Ballad For Americans* enjoyed a sensation, for it was ebullient and corny just when those qualities were what most Americans wanted from their popular arts.

There were also entries in a more classical and perhaps ponderously poetic vein, such as Marc Blitzstein's *Airborne Symphony*, so theatrical in flavor that when Victor recorded it under Leonard Bernstein, with Robert Shaw narrating, the label billed the 78 set as a "Recordrama." None of these patriotic cantatas was meant to outlast the war, but one did: Aaron Copland's *A Lincoln Portrait*, in which the president's own words are heard over Copland's characteristic Sweeping Yankee Panorama style. It's so grand and historic that recordings have assigned the narration to such Mount Rushmore magnificoes as Henry Fonda, Charlton Heston, Gregory Peck, Katharine Hepburn, James Earl Jones, Walter Cronkite, and even General H. Norman Schwarzkopf.

Weill wrote his patriotic cantata with Maxwell Anderson, for the same CBS show that had broadcast *Ballad For Americans*. Premiered on

February 4, 1940, *The Ballad of Magna Carta* gave Anderson another chance to take a poke at F. D. R. in the figure of a bygone despot, though, as with Pieter Stuyvesant, everyone reckoned that villainous King John was really Hitler. "Resistance unto Tyrants is obedience to God," cries the narrator—Burgess Meredith at the premiere, side by side with a baritone soloist, the Metropolitan Opera's Julius Huehn. Meredith had played *Winterset*, *High Tor*, and *The Star-Wagon* for Anderson, and he was eager to work with Weill as well, though something always seemed to get in the way.* *The Ballad of Magna Carta* is, typically for this genre, one of Weill's least-known major works. It is skillfully contrived, in a series of assertive melodic periods, angry and staccato except for one anthem-like theme that recurs with the expected arching grandeur at the end.

Weill was to contribute a great deal to the war effort, as we'll see; meanwhile, he was hunting for another idea in musical theatre. As so often before, he danced the Kurt Weill Tango with destiny, knowing exactly what he needed yet not knowing who could supply it. Happenstance would thrust some wonder worker into his path, and Weill would know him when he saw him.

What he saw was Moss Hart, one of the most imaginative and accomplished writer-directors of the day, though his directing career as such had hardly begun. Hart wrote fluff for the boulevard, yet it was fluff with substance, which explains why, for instance, *You Can't Take It With You* (1936), co-written with George S. Kaufman, lingers in the mind long after one has stopped laughing at the jokes about wastrels having more fun than workers. What *does* fulfill a life? One's music, of course, was Weill's answer; and Lenya comes right after.

But now, when Hart met Weill, he was fluffing up a substantial narrative about someone whose work is not fulfilling, and who turns to psychiatry—as Hart himself had done—for relief. Someone who needs not work but love. Shall we make it interesting? The story has a gay

---

* Meredith was in the cast of *Salute To France*, an Office of War Information propaganda film for which Weill composed the music, in 1944. Meredith later recorded the title role in the first *Johnny Johnson* recording, in 1956; most of my readers will no doubt recall him as the Penguin in the *Batman* television series.

coming-out subtext. Only the sophisticated would get it: a successful and creative member of New York's leadership class has neutralized sex in partnership with a beard, then is torn between a glamorous Hollywood hunk and a disturbingly masculine challenger, rough trade in a suit.

Is that the yarn that Hart is spinning, or is that the life that Hart is living? Because, on the surface of the script, everything has been heterosexualized. The protagonist is a woman whose "beard" is an unstimulating older man, and she dallies with the hunk only to submit to the bit of rough, her professional subordinate but, at the end, her light of love. And note how well Hart disguised himself, for his heroine, a cynosure in her fantasies, is in reality on the plain and dull side. Hart was anything but dull: affable and full of the latest stories, an honorable man in a world of cheaters, and the most connected person in show business. In fact, Moss Hart was exactly what destiny was shopping for in the next chapter of The Kurt Weill Story.

The two met at a party. They talked of how insubstantial the narrative component of musical comedy was at this time. They arranged to meet and talk more. And, somewhere in all this, Hart realized he had conceived the next great substantial musical while mistaking it for a play with a single song in it, a mystery melody serving as the objective-correlative of the heroine's neurosis. Yes, that part would be sung. But, otherwise, she would tell her analyst about her dreams—and now Hart must have smote his forehead. Of course! The dreams would be *shown*, not told: as mini-musicals, composed by Kurt Weill and with lyrics by . . .

Ira Gershwin. The best lyricists were generally attached to partners, but Ira had been so crushed by the untimely death of his brother George that he had folded into retirement in Los Angeles as the Widow Gershwin. Hart mustered his persuasive powers in a do-or-die phone call to Ira, who, as it happens, had just got bored with retirement. He could hardly get a word in while Hart pitched and cajoled.

"Moss," Ira finally said.

"No, don't answer till I'm through," Hart quickly replied. "These musical dreams will be innovative and fabulous!"

"Moss—"

"*No*, Ira, not yet, because you say no to everything, but when I tell you about the wild characters in—yes, and *Cornell* wants to do it. Of course, now that it's turned into a musical she'll have to—"

"Moss—"

"No, just listen, Ira, the *possibilities*! It's not a play. And it's not a musical. It's—"

"Moss, I'll do it."

"—something so unheard of that . . . You will?"

As the piece took shape, Hart realized that he had found his way into the most spectacular star vehicle in the musical's history, well beyond the gifts of Katharine Cornell—but a role with as much acting in it as singing. Shows of the day often seemed like top department-store window displays for an Ethel Merman or Bert Lahr; not till later would such artists be given roles with powerful character content. Hart's protagonist, Liza Elliott, is in effect two people, brisk and sexless by day and, in her dreams, the worship of the world. Both are having nervous breakdowns simultaneously, haunted by that mystery melody, an "unfinished" song from childhood that symbolizes a hurtful upbringing; through psychiatry, the hurt can be cured and the song finally sung to its last note. With so much to play—and the frisson of switching back and forth between the woman and the goddess—Liza Elliott would be the greatest song-and-dance role of all time.

So Hart and his producer, Sam H. Harris, would have to hire the greatest song-and-dance star of all time, and that would be Gertrude Lawrence. As historians love to observe, Lawrence was an iffy singer, an amateur dancer, and, as actress, given to indicating rather than coherent character composition. But she had, by all accounts, the most enchanting stage presence in the business. *Enchanting*: it's the word everybody uses to describe her. Not only was she perfect for the part: no one else would do.

"Gertie ought to pay you to play it," Noël Coward remarked after reading the script. Yet Lawrence didn't jump at it. Her habit was to say yes and then create a pile-on of impossible demands in an air of merry enthusiasm while her notoriously cutthroat lawyer, Fanny Holtzman, ate the producer for snacks. At one point, Hart (the real muscle in the show, far more than the aged Harris or the official director, Hassard Short) opened negotiations with Irene Dunne, and when Holtzman tried one last-minute stunt, Hart snapped and screamed over the phone at her that she had fifteen minutes to get a signed contract to him or Lawrence was out.*

Lawrence did make one demand that seemed sensible, asking for a title change so she could play a title role. She was used to it: in *Oh, Kay!*, *Treasure Girl*, *Nymph Errant*, *Susan and God*. Overjoyed about bringing his obsessive love of psychiatry to the stage, Hart had called his play *I Am Listening*—the words with which his medicine man always launched a session. The phrase took on an almost totemic significance as Weill and Gershwin developed the dreams, for the chorus emerged as a surrogate for Liza's doctor, inquiring and prodding. At one point, they cued in an important memory number, "The Princess of Pure Delight," with "We are listening": as if initiating analysis, linking Liza's fantasy world to her reality and thus indicating that she is making a breakthrough.

Then someone suggested they call it *Lady in the Dark*. It opened on January 23, 1941 as Weill's "security" piece. *Der Protagonist* was his herald. The first *Mahagonny* liberated his cabaret style. *Die Dreigroschenoper* was his international phenomenon. The second *Mahagonny* was his dangerous item, his blasphemy in the sacred halls of opera; it still shocks today. And *Knickerbocker Holiday* was his first star show.

But *Lady in the Dark* empowered Weill as a Broadway composer of gifts Broadway wasn't used to—literally hadn't heard before. Structurally, the dreams unfold in a kind of medley form, as descriptive music and ensemble scenes anchor self-contained vocal solos and duets.

---

* Bizarrely, the last demand was that the show must open at the Music Box Theatre. As Harris co-owned it (with Irving Berlin), this was feasible, though it might have inconvenienced him if the venue had prior commitments. However, Holtzman had won for her client a weekly percentage of the gross along with her salary. As the Music Box was one of Broadway's smaller houses, it would net Lawrence a share of a lower rather than a higher gross. In the end, the show opened at the Alvin Theatre, nearly half again as large as the Music Box.

These songs are very much in the Broadway manner, albeit in Weill's unique sound—but the way in which Weill expands the music around these songs into a driving narrative was new. The big first-act finales favored by musicals in the 1910s and 1920s or the musical scenes in the Gershwins' *Strike Up the Band* and *Of Thee I Sing* hark back to Gilbert and Sullivan in a studied, self-conscious way. *Lady in the Dark*'s dreams are like liquid music, flowing around the arias as the scene constantly changes—for instance from Park Avenue to Columbus Circle to the Club Seventh Heaven, where Liza's portrait is painted "for the new two cent stamp." Seeing it, she lets out a scream of terror and the dream rears up into nightmare.

Weill's expertise as an orchestrator enhanced the show's power, as in the many appearances of the unfinished melody, which at one point really does sound like Park Avenue at its most chic and, in another dream, when the chorus hums it over a thrumming in the strings, sounds like your parents saying, "I hate your face." There is this as well, though credit really belongs to Moss Hart: *Lady in the Dark* was literally the format between formats as neither straight play nor musical—nor yet a blend of the two—but rather the two genres taking turns.

The extremely profitable production gave Weill and Lenya, finally, relief from want. They bought a home from the former matinée idol Rollo Peters in New City, near the Andersons. At 100 South Mountain Road, the property was known as Brook House—because a stream ran through it—and this was the place that the Weills called home from then on. It was an innovation for them, as they had not only never lived in the country but had never owned *land*. Walking his devoted sheepdog, Wooly (or, in Weill's pronunciation, *Vu*-leee), Weill had time to collect his thoughts and plan the next realization of his talent. Lenya had time to enjoy a man on the side, in this case a young air force pilot named Howard Schwartz, whom she dubbed "Schwartzi."

And now Lenya's professional life took an interesting turn, for Maxwell Anderson's latest play, *Candle in the Wind*, was set in Europe and had a part for a housemaid from Vienna named Cissie. The role seemed not only designed for Lenya but based on her, as she explains to her mistress how to outwit the German army by wedging a chair against the doorknob of their hotel room:

CISSIE: A German soldier works by what is on his little card. He has orders on a little card. What to do with the proprietor, what to do with the guests. What to do when the door is open, and what to do when the door is locked. But what to do, when a chair is under the door, he does not have. Sometimes he goes away to find out.

HER MISTRESS: But he comes back.

CISSIE: Then you have time. You can get the hell out.

Cissie's mistress was played by Helen Hayes—unfortunately for Lenya, who found handsome young men in the cast to socialize with and the featured actress Evelyn Varden to confide in but could not harmonize with Hayes. Generally beloved by audiences, a devotee of quietly showy roles couched halfway between histrionics and naturalism, Hayes used a tiny frame and a sweet smile to hide the most notorious iron will on Broadway. Joan of Arc would give in before Hayes would.

But Hayes sold tickets. *Candle in the Wind*, in which Hayes made a heroic stand for freedom in Nazi-occupied France, was minor Anderson and lasted only three months in New York. It could count on a profitable tour, however, because of Hayes' appeal to what was then known as the "women's club" public: Hayes' fans. So off went Lenya to see America, just like the Anna that she had played in *The Seven Deadly Sins*.

Lenya didn't like it. Rochester, Buffalo, Indianapolis, St. Louis, Toledo, Cincinnati. As someone who had spent her days in cultural capitals, Lenya found these to be plain, flat, vacuous. She was now so at ease in English that she and Weill wrote to each other in that language—yet their America, really, was that of the New York theatre and music worlds, bohemian and educated, imaginative, stylish. Somehow, Lenya had not anticipated the sheer *Biedermeier* of America's midcountry. Pittsburgh she thought the worst—"ideal for a minstrel show," she wrote, to Weill. "You don't have to blaken [*sic*] your face, [the industrial air] does it automatically." With little to do between performances, some of the actors started playing cards with Lenya, which brightened her up considerably, especially when she blitzed the table and took in a tiny fortune.

At least Schwartzi could join her when he was on leave, or if nothing else telephone long-distance, which in those days was an unusual and cumbersome form of communication, a special event. At one of Lenya's stops, not knowing where she was staying, Schwartz told the operator, "Give me the best hotel in town." And there she was.

All this was going on in the spring of 1942, after the nation found itself divided between isolationists and interventionists or—as some saw it—between Nazi sympathizers and their stooges on one hand and anti-fascist democrats on the other. It must have seemed a bit like Weimar Germany to the Weills: another ferocious argument about the nature of Western values. An isolationist rally in New York's Madison Square Garden on May 23, 1941 acted at times like a Munich beer-hall hate pageant of the early 1920s.

Then came Charles Lindbergh's openly anti-Semitic radio address in Des Moines, on the following September 11. Lindbergh didn't scream like Hitler. Mooing like a contented cow, he threatened the Jews with punishment for supposedly dragging America into the European war. But then Pearl Harbor was attacked, and, four days later, on December 11, 1941, Hitler declared war on the United States. His treaty with the Japanese required him to open hostilities against any nation that attacked Japan, not the reverse. He could have remained neutral. And he had to have known that engaging with America risked his own annihilation.

Historians have puzzled over it ever since, because historians look for reason. But, as Henry Kissinger wrote in the *New York Times* in 2011, "Hitler [was] a romantic nihilist . . . [his essence] was the absence of measure and rejection of restraint."

Such reasonable assessment is inadequate in dealing with a figure as cartoonish yet millennial as Hitler. Say rather that Hitler was a raving genocidal loon who longed for Ragnarok, the mythological Nordic end of days. "If we cannot conquer the world," Hitler wrote in *Mein Kampf*, "we shall drag it into destruction with us."

And Weill, on his eternal road of escape from tyranny, went on writing music. It is as if there were two worlds, the one of war and peace and the other of humanist endeavor. When the two worlds collide, a generation of émigrés brings the edges of Western Civilization closer to its center. More art, more light.

12

How Can You Tell An American?

Devoting his gifts to the war effort, Weill produced pieces that by their propagandistic nature proved as ephemeral as minor works from his student days. There was a pageant put on for one night only in Madison Square Garden, *Fun To Be Free* (1941), written by onetime cutups Ben Hecht and Charles MacArthur and narrated by Tallulah Bankhead, Franchot Tone, Melvyn Douglas, and our Weill enthusiast Burgess Meredith. MacArthur was Hayes' husband, Lenya was touring in Hayes' play, and now Weill arranged "settings" of such tunes as "The Battle Hymn of the Republic" in an album of two twelve-inch 78s called *Mine Eyes Have Seen the Glory*. "America's Living Words of Faith," the album cover explained, "by the inspired voice of Helen Hayes."

It was as though the New York theatre world—far more than that of music—had become one great fraternity, less colleagues than siblings. It's bromidic to say so: but everyone suddenly seemed to know one another and want to work together. One of the recitations on Hayes' album was Walt Whitman's "Beat! Beat! Drums!," and, arranging the piece as a vocal solo, Weill added "Oh Captain! My Captain!" and "Dirge For Two Veterans" to complete *Three Walt Whitman Songs*, dedicated to Max and Mab Anderson. (A fourth poem setting, on

"Come Up From the Fields, Father," made the cycle a quartet in 1947.) More camaraderie: Oscar Hammerstein, Dorothy Fields, Howard Dietz, and Anderson were among Weill's lyricists for songs performed at the *Lunch Hour* (also called the *Lunchtime*) *Follies*, mini-revues staged for factory workers.

To take part was an honor. Harold Rome wrote a mini-show, with a boogie woogie, "Victory Symphony, Eight To the Bar"; a blues called "(I want a man who comes to work) On Time"; "On That Old Production Line"; "That's My Pop (there in the shop)"; and others such. Even Cole Porter chimed in, with "Sailors of the Sky."

One of Weill's Hammerstein lyrics, "(Hello there) Buddy on the Nightshift," a salute from the guy on the day schedule to the guy who relieves him at evening, has a confidential swing, a curious intimacy, even; and the Dietz contribution, "Schickelgruber," is a raucous mock-paean to Hitler. Both ceased to be heard after the war—indeed, were not even copyrighted—till Lenya entrusted them to Teresa Stratas for revival in 1981.

Weill even wrote a song with Archibald MacLeish, not only a noted poet but the Librarian of Congress. At one of their meetings, Weill played for MacLeish and his wife the Helen Hayes album, and, Weill wrote Lenya, "He raved about Helen, said that she spoke those words so completely american . . . that he could listen for hours and hours." When Lenya, still touring in *Candle in the Wind*, showed that section of the letter to Hayes ("The rest," Lenya admitted, "I covered"), the actress wept with pride. She even hoped to do more with Weill, because his careful handling of the arrangements for "Mine Eyes Have Seen the Glory" made Hayes feel she could actually find a place in the daunting world of music.

There's no American like a brand-new American. Weill even took up plane-spotting, with Maxwell Anderson, the two of them standing point in a watchtower to gaze through binoculars into the horizon in case the enemy should attack the homeland. This duty was known as "air observation," and Weill took it very seriously. But his sister-in-law Rita Weill shared with Ronald Sanders a family joke: after phoning an "all clear" to the local air force base, Weill heard someone on the other end tell a buddy, "Sounds like the Germans have arrived already."

In the spring of 1942, Weill's theatrical confraternity expanded yet further with the opportunity to make some truly unusual theatre history, the only kind he was interested in, anyway: a musical with the Lunts. The undisputed monarchs of non-singing Broadway, Alfred Lunt and Lynn Fontanne had become enamored of a play by the little-known Ludwig Fulda, *Die Seeräuber* (The Pirate, 1911). Weill's Playwrights' Company colleague S. N. Behrman was going to adapt it for Broadway, and while the Lunts weren't contemplating taking up singing, they felt the play's Caribbean setting and its strolling players (Lunt was to appear as the troupe's *capocomico*) cried out for music. Weill envisioned casting black singers and instrumentalists, all on stage, to haunt the piece with melody.

"It has to sound like improvisation," he wrote to the touring Lenya, "and I have to find a new style, half spanish half negro." He seems to have decided on fitting up a play with two intermingled casts—the principals, who speak; and the ensemble, who sing, play, and dance. Eagerly discussing the project with the Lunts, Weill threw out dozens of ideas, but he gradually realized that neither of the two stars was listening. S. N. Behrman was no help; Weill took to calling him *Dornröschen* (Sleeping Beauty), because whenever matters got thorny he would be unavailable.

Still, Weill continued to brainstorm *The Pirate*. This was partly because Behrman, when he troubled to show up, bribed Weill with talk of a musical they could write based on Max Beerbohm's wicked mock-epic novel *Zuleika Dobson*. The adventures of a lady magician who persuades a corps of Oxford undergraduates to kill themselves out of love for her, *Zuleika* was apparently intended to be Gertrude Lawrence's next vehicle.

Naturally, all Broadway was lining up to replicate the success of *Lady in the Dark*: not only because of its gross, but because Paramount paid $283,000 for the movie rights, far more than it took to mount the show in the first place and the largest amount Hollywood had ever laid out to film a play. But Lawrence was far too old in 1942 to embody Beerbohm's "lithe and radiant young creature" famed as "the toast of two hemispheres." Mary Martin would have been ideal—and Martin would star in Weill's next musical as the goddess of love. But Weill was not to work with the Lunts or with Behrman, all of whom disgusted him when it became clear that they refused to pay him for his work. Weill had in mind a percentage of the gross for a full-length score, but everyone else seemed fixed on a little tinkle here and there for . . . oh, a small flat fee, perhaps? It's such an honor to be associated with the Lunts, after all.

As loyal Lenya told Weill, "You're a little spooked by Max and Moss": because Anderson and Hart were reliable and appreciative. This new lot were at their best when exploiting talents for their own profit. "That's their mother milk," said Lenya.

Weill had sketched out some music for *The Pirate*, but in the end the show went up with accompaniment by one Herbert Kingsley. Some of Weill's ideas were used—the onstage playing ensemble, for instance, which included the later well-known jazz trombonist Wilbur De Paris. But it was another Broadway composer who finally turned *The Pirate* into a musical—Cole Porter, who wrote the songs for MGM's 1948 Gene Kelly–Judy Garland movie of the same title.

Speaking of exploiters, Brecht reappeared in Weill's life at this time, albeit from the other side of the country. Brecht's exile in, mostly, Scandinavia and subsequent trek to the United States had been a combination of indolent rural life, haggling with bureaucrats for papers to legalize his next address, and at last a turbulent railway trip across the length of Russia. Oddly, Brecht had visited the United States long before this, in 1935: he took the *Aquitania* to New York just about a month after Weill and Lenya sailed on the *Majestic*, to supervise the first English-language staging of *Die Mutter*, which was offered as, simply, *Mother*, without the article.* The most prominent communist

---

* Brecht's play is drawn from Maxim Gorky's 1907 novel entitled Мать meaning *The Mother*, the article being understood because Russian has no articles. Thus, the English for Мать is *The Mother*, though the novel appears in English translation as *Mother*, neat. This is, however, an affectation, perhaps accidentally (or even contractually) carried over when the play was set for Broadway.

thespian outfit, the Theatre Union, was producing; they never knew what hit them.

They expected to meet in Brecht not only a comrade but a visionary of radical theatre, but in interviews with Lee Baxandall some thirty years later, Theatre Union's officers all recalled an arrogant, contemptuous solipsist whom they eventually had to bar from the theatre. Albert Maltz and George Sklar, co-authors of the group's most interesting piece, *Merry-Go-Round* (1932), on the corruption of New York mayor Jimmy Walker's regime, were staggered by the sheer tyranny with which Brecht ran rehearsals. Maltz couldn't bear the stink of Brecht's unwashed body, and Sklar heard in Brecht "the same apoplectic indulgence, the same ranting and shrieking associated with [Hitler]." Nothing that Theatre Union had done for the play, from the translation to the acting style, pleased Brecht, though the organization spent a fortune putting it on and had marshalled a strong cast, including Lee J. Cobb and, in several small roles, television's future Aunt Bee on Andy Griffith's show, Frances Bavier.

Having destroyed his name on Broadway by his behavior—and *Mother* did not fare well commercially—Brecht returned to Europe till the outbreak of war forced him to take his family out of the Old World altogether. In California, he tried to get work writing screenplays, and 1942 found him collaborating on a film on the assassination of the Nazi Czech Gauleiter Reinhard Heydrich, *Hangmen Also Die*. Fritz Lang was directing, and Brecht's writing partner was John Wexley, a radical playwright who had achieved popular success. Hollywood loved Wexley, because a west coast production of Wexley's prison melodrama *The Last Mile* (1930) is where Clark Gable caught the attention of the studios. This is what the movie industry thought of as team playing. Wexley didn't team up with Brecht all that much, however, and got sole writing credit on the release print. The rest of the damage Brecht was able to do himself with his drama-queen personality, and there was no further work for him in Hollywood.

So he turned to his one sure thing, *The Threepenny Opera*, for production by the aforementioned Clarence Muse. Primarily a movie actor,

Muse specialized in glorified walk-on parts, but tragic ones: first he'd be established, do something touching, sing a spiritual, and then get killed by Indians. Now Muse had a notion to try an all-black *Three-penny* in his own English adaptation, and Brecht opened a correspondence with Weill about it. Despite *Threepenny*'s utter failure on Broadway in 1933, it was still a potential moneymaker, and Weill was not willing to entrust it to talents unknown to him. There was talk, too, of letting black musicians play the score in contemporary jazz: over Weill's dead body. "Could you come to Hollywood?" Brecht wired him; Weill was flabbergasted. Cross the country to talk to Brecht about a project Weill was totally wary of in the first place? Most offensive of all, poor old Muse wrote Weill that Brecht had said that Weill hadn't replied to Brecht's letter. On the contrary, Weill had indeed replied—and it was Brecht who was notorious for never answering letters unless he needed something from you.

"The good old swinish Brecht method," Weill called it.

"The hell with them," Lenya told him. "It's too much already."

And when Brecht's agent sent Weill a contract, he called it "exploitative as only contracts with communists can be."

So there was no all-black *Threepenny Opera*.* A year later, in 1943, Brecht made another overture to Weill, now for a new piece with a *Threepenny* feeling, as Weill-Brecht reconvene their Lenya cabaret on Broadway: *The Good Soldier Švejk* as a musical. Both authors had already used the material, Brecht in collaboration with others for Erwin Piscator's multimedia version in Berlin in 1928 (with scenic cartoons based on sketches by George Grosz) and Weill, at a remove, in *Johnny Johnson*. But Broadway would find the subject fresh and engaging—and, yes, there was a role for Lenya.

Of course, Brecht knew that, after *Lady in the Dark* and its Big Hollywood sale, Weill had become Important, while Brecht's theatre

---

* Coincidentally, there was a mixed-race adaptation of *The Beggar's Opera* on Broadway, in 1946, with a score by Duke Ellington and John Latouche, *Beggar's Holiday*. Alfred Drake played the Macheath and Zero Mostel the Peachum.

had, so to say, stood empty for ten years. He was so desperate that he had sent Weill a peace offering the year before, an ironic lyric entitled "Und Was Bekam des Soldaten Weib?" (And What Was the Soldier's Wife Given?). It's one of the best of the less-well-known Weill-Brecht songs, on a clomping march in b minor as the soldier's wife keeps getting apparel from different places—high-heeled shoes from Prague, a hat from Amsterdam—"and it fits her well, that nice Dutch hat." So it runs for six verses, till, *più tranquillo* and now in B Major, she gets her last gift, the widow's veil from Hitler's Russian campaign. The number was perfect for Lenya, Lotte in Weimar all over again with her two back-alley cavaliers by her side.

Brecht was struggling to seem tactful and pleasant—"and you know how long," says Lenya, "that will last." In fact, Brecht was double-dealing as always before, talking secretly with others (including Piscator himself, yet another in our catalogue of exiles) about the *Švejk* musical. It got serious enough for Brecht to travel to New York, and the Weills invited him up to Brook House to stay with them and meet their friends. What on earth were they thinking? Brecht and Maxwell Anderson, a hater of totalitarians? Elmer Rice, master of the psychological drama that Brecht execrated? John Fuegi puts it dryly: "He did not hit it off with either."

The notion of staging a Broadway musical with Brecht in the house was loony in the first place. A musical is a clockwork of intricately collaborative parts. To attempt to wind one up with Production Wrecker Brecht on hand was bribing failure. Ernst Josef Aufricht was also involved in these proceedings, and had actually raised the capital for a Weill-Brecht *Švejk* musical. Weill advised Aufricht to secure $85,000, Aufricht says, and he was able to do so, presumably on the strength of Weill's name alone. The figure is low for a Broadway musical of the early-middle forties; *Oklahoma!*, on an Uncle Scrooge budget, came in for only a bit less. But Aufricht knew the *Švejk* show was off when he saw Brecht's script, which updated Švejk's war from the First to the Second and ended in a scene between Švejk and Hitler in the snowy expanse of Russia. "Original in conception," Aufricht called it, but "in execution formless." Aufricht returned the $85,000 to his investors, and, in the end, it was left to Weill's *Eternal Road* partner Franz Werfel, adapted by S. N. Behrman, to create the Broadway *Švejk*. It was an original straight play called *Jacobowsky and the Colonel* (1944), in which the Švejk figure becomes a Jewish finagler considerably removed from the original.

At least Lenya got something out of all this, recording "Und Was Bekam" for the office of War Information for propaganda use in Europe. She recorded another side as well, "Wie Lange Noch?" (How Much Longer?), to the words of Walter Mehring (and reusing music Weill originally composed for Lys Gauty in Paris as "Je Ne T'aime Pas).* Meanwhile, for local consumption, Weill and Lenya made their only album together, for the BOST label: *Six Songs By Kurt Weill*, "interpreted by Lotte Lenya." There were two numbers each in English, French, and German, the first two from Weill's aborted *Ulysses Africanus* score with Maxwell Anderson. Lenya's range had lowered from her "squitchehdickeh" days, yet she had somehow retained the soprano's lightness, giving the concert an attractively fragile air. She is not yet the smoky-voiced diseuse with a thousand attitudes that she later became. For his part, Weill accompanies in a supplementary manner, throwing the act to Lenya in his typical approach: capable but completely lacking in flash.†

Pursuing his contribution to the war effort, Weill composed *We Will Never Die*, a "memorial" to Europe's Jewish dead with a text by Ben Hecht. Presented in concert style, the work nonetheless looked spectacular, with the chorus, mimes, and soloists ranged in groups against a backdrop of the two Ten Commandments tablets sixty feet

---

* Perhaps out of anger at Weill's lack of enthusiasm for restarting their collaboration, Brecht later "reassigned" the *Soldier's Wife* lament to his post-Weill house composers, Hanns Eisler and Paul Dessau—both of whom, to Lenya's ears, were raving Weill imitators. David Drew cites a fourth setting, by Mischa Spoliansky, one of our Weimar cabaret writers some chapters ago.

† The album does not identify the pianist, presumably because it was bound to be Weill. Moreover, the arrangements range freely from the published sheets: would a ringer dare? And would BOST have withheld the pianist's credit without some very good reason—such as the maestro himself enjoying a flourish of modesty?

high: not unlike *The Eternal Road* merged with *The Ballad of Magna Carta*. Staged on March 9, 1943 at Madison Square Garden with narrators Paul Muni, Edward G. Robinson, and Luther Adler (of the original *Johnny Johnson* ensemble) along with tenor Kurt Baum, *We Will Never Die* was heard also in Boston, Philadelphia, Washington, D. C., Chicago, and at the Hollywood Bowl, where it may have been seen by some 17,000 spectators, the arena's capacity. Further, each of the bookings was relayed on the radio, giving Weill stupendous exposure, albeit for what seems to have been little more than utility music, most of which is no longer extant.

The project originated with Hecht, who had approached some thirty Jewish Americans for help in publicizing Nazi genocide, albeit before the general public was aware of the actual death factories. Only two of the thirty offered their help: Weill and Moss Hart, who directed *We Will Never Die*. Obviously, the pageant was a huge success in terms of the crowds that it attracted, but Weill thought it a useless endeavor. "All we have done is make a lot of Jews cry," he told Hecht, "which is not a unique accomplishment."

Weill's real work, of course, was to realize his ideal of a musical theatre that would be more lyrical than theatre and more dynamic than opera. Yet here, in 1943, is where Weill wrote his least ambitious piece, *One Touch of Venus*. Based on an antique novella by one F. Anstey (pseudonym of Thomas Anstey Guthrie) entitled *The Tinted Venus*, the show was to have had a book by Sam and Bella Spewack and lyrics by Ogden Nash. As we already know, Cheryl Crawford was producing and Marlene Dietrich said yes and then refused; and the Spewack book pleased no one. The *New Yorker* humorist S. J. Perelman was brought in to write a new book with Nash, and Mary Martin, suddenly free because of the Boston closing of her Vernon Duke show, *Dancing in the Streets*, became the new Venus: a statue brought to life to turn New York upside down. At the end, she leaves her mortal likeness to pair off with the young man who has fallen in love with her.

The premise has a slight taste of Offenbach, but the show, a fast-moving and bawdy piece, was very much a Broadway musical

comedy of the wartime 1940s. Like others such—*Louisiana Purchase,
Panama Hattie, Let's Face It!, By Jupiter, Something For the Boys*—*Venus*
was built around a star personality. It virtually had to be, for the
public would have found it difficult to accept an unknown as the
ultimate love diva.

"Me in a part for Dietrich?" Martin cried, looking back years later.
"I couldn't believe it." Martin had achieved stardom as a hot little trick
performing a chaste striptease (outdoors, in Siberia!) in Cole Porter's
Leave It To Me! (1938), but workaday films at Paramount stalled her advance. She was attempting a Broadway comeback when the Duke show
fell apart and Venus was offered to her. What good luck!—even if Martin saw herself as a Texas tomboy, the hoyden she later trademarked in
the national company of *Annie Get Your Gun* and in *South Pacific* and
Peter Pan.

Enter then the celebrated couturier Mainbocher, back in his native
America after the troubles in Europe made Paris unhappy for him.
"Main," as they called him, had designed the gowns for Peggy Wood
and Leonora Corbett in the Broadway production of Noël Coward's
Blithe Spirit, in 1941, and was now to do the same for Martin, from an-
cient Grecian flowing white to name-in-the-columns nightclub black.★
This gave Martin the confidence to pose as the love of every man's life.
With Kenny Baker as the sweetheart and John Boles completing the
romantic triangle, the show had three Hollywood names and was thus
Weill's third star show in a row on Broadway.

★ In her memoirs, Martin claimed that Mainbocher "had never designed clothes
for a theatrical production," and writers have accepted her word on the matter, no
doubt because it was all but unthinkable for a nabob of *le chic* to mix with the jug-
glers and madcaps of the stage. (This is not to mention the bills a producer would
have to pay, for the star designer's work and the building of the outfits.) However, it
was a wonderful opportunity for Mainbocher to expand his business by addressing
the theatregoing lady with an evening-long commercial eight times a week, and
Main later dressed, among others, Tallulah Bankhead, Ethel Merman, Rosalind
Russell, and Lynn Fontanne in various Broadway outings. Martin used him repeatedly, even for *The Sound of Music*, though he must have been hampered by her role,
which took her from a holy order to a governess job and finally to membership in a
family singing group.

As director, Crawford hired Elia Kazan, one of her Group Theatre allies, though Kazan, like Strasberg on *Johnny Johnson*, had no understanding of how musicals work. He did make one contribution to the production, explaining to Martin that immortals dwell in time differently than humans. Venus is never going away, so she needn't cram her events into a lifetime: she moves in a stately manner, enjoying herself and taking in the sights of mankind. The choreographer, Agnes de Mille, laid out the first act's Big Ballet on this idea. Entitled "Forty Minutes For Lunch," it pictured Manhattan's office workers tearing about on a timeclock schedule while Venus ambled through the crowd at her own speed, pausing to bring a French sailor (Robert Pagent) and a secretary (Sono Osato) together for a tryst.

It appears that it was de Mille as much as—if not more than—Kazan who staged *Venus* (which would explain why Rodgers and Hammerstein asked her to direct and choreograph their third show, *Allegro*, at a time when the two jobs were almost never combined). Foster Hirsch tracked down some of the original *Venus* company for *Kurt Weill On Stage*, and none had anything positive to say about Kazan's contribution. Martin liked him, but then she had a one-man buffer zone in her manager husband, Richard Halliday. Paula Laurence, playing Boles' sardonic assistant (the Eve Arden role, so to say, and played by Arden in the film version), told Hirsch that Kazan "would let people move on laugh lines," which of course distracts the audience, who then miss the joke. "And he was asking me how to get laughs. He'd have me stand in the wings and take notes."

Kazan bristled at sharing the stage with the indomitable de Mille, but this was 1943, near the start of her reign, begun six months earlier, in *Oklahoma!*. That show's dances were regarded as elemental in its phenomenal success—and, Hirsch tells us, Weill wanted de Mille for *Venus* even before *Oklahoma!*. The two got along splendidly, and it would appear that de Mille's handling of the narrative drive in "Forty Minutes For Lunch" and the second-act Dream Ballet, "Venus in Ozone Heights" (in which the goddess vainly tries to fit in in suburbia), convinced Decca Records to include both dances on *Venus'* cast album, the first time such music joined the vocals in a prominent show recording.*

In truth, de Mille gave *Venus* prestige, because the songs themselves deliberately assumed standard musical-comedy positions. It was Weill's hat trick: to create a truly conventional forties Broadway sound. Weill was an American now in the legal sense, having taken the oath of citizenship (standing in the same room with fellow refugee Otto Preminger) on August 27, 1943, and with *Venus* he completed his assimilation. Not as the composer's composer, which he had long been: as the Broadwayite's Broadwayite. *Venus* actually starts with an old-fashioned "merry villagers" opening chorus of art students, and takes in a lovey-dovey list song ("That's How Much I Love You"), a Cole Porter Woman's Point of View number ("That's Him," with its cutting-to-the-heart-of-the-matter joy line "Overnight your hips grow slimmer"), a goof on country music ("Way Out West in New Jersey"), and even a comic barbershop quartet whose verse uses a melody first heard in both Germany (in *Happy End*) and France (in *Marie Galante*), here called "The Trouble With Women."

Further, *Venus* gave Weill his third all-time song hit, first published as "Speak Low (When You Speak, Love)." Nash borrowed the title from *Much Ado About Nothing*—Shakespeare's line is "Speak Low, if you speak love"—and an uncomprehending copy editor at Chappell and Co. added in an incorrect comma. "Love" is not an address in the vocative; it is the object of the verb. More important, the number shows how Weill could slip into the musical lingo of his wonderful accepting homeland while retaining his individuality. Simply to launch a show's primary ballad on a supertonic ninth chord, then to reach the subdominant minor sixth with a ninth in the melody suggests the Kurt Weill of Busoni's master class, fantasizing in the esoteric. Yet the result is any-

---

* It had happened once before, when Victor recorded *The Band Wagon*. But this was an experiment in the LP seventeen years before LPs were marketed, in 1948, and thus very little known. It was *Venus* that set the precedent: Victor's *On the Town* truly featured the dance music. Further, Decca's two-disc *Oklahoma!* appendix and Victor's *Brigadoon* both troubled to include the sound of the dances—again, music first invigorated by the work of de Mille.

thing but studied. The rich harmony is why the number is a showpiece in what they used to call "haunting."

Weill—and Nash as well—couldn't resist showing off in "Who Am I?," a hungover boogie-woogie playing with Nash's trademark chock-full run-on lines. The Weill musicologist Elmar Juchem says this was originally intended for a god in an episode set on Mount Olympus. The scene was cut (though the conflict between the immortal and human spheres over who gets Venus is still elemental in the finished show) and the song reassigned to John Boles' character. It suits him beautifully, its ratiocinating lyrics and mock low-down music perfect for the affected dandy that Boles played. But Boles apparently couldn't master the number's tricky rhythms, and it was finally cut altogether.

We don't want to read too much autobiography into every work of Weill's, but it is worth noting that *Venus* is essentially about a "poor schnook" type—"diffident, undistinguished, likable" is the script's delineation—who gets access to an enchantress:

> VENUS: All my other men have been such heroic figures. I want somebody nobody's ever heard of.

Granted, *Venus'* hero is a barber, not an artist like Weill. Still, it recalls Ernst Josef Aufricht's bemusement that "little Weill" had enthralled a femme fatale in Lotte Lenja. Yet, again, like Julien Sorel, Weill was remaking the logic of what was possible, sometimes without understanding why or how. As Venus tells the barber, after an imperious wave of her arm fells his impedient landlady:

> VENUS: Don't meddle with destiny, darling!

At 567 performances and a fine tour, *One Touch of Venus* strengthened Weill's position as a hitmaker. Now more than ever, he wanted to write a *Venus*, a *Lady in the Dark*, for Lenya. In fact, she needed something to do; with the closing of *Candle in the Wind*'s tour, she was back to her demoralized identity as a homemaker who found homemaking drab and ridiculous. Even playing Helen Hayes' maid was more fun—

and Hayes did come to realize what a genius Lenya's husband was when they worked on that album, which made the platonic concept of Helen Hayes much easier for Lenya to accept.

Lenya did get a little homework to occupy her—homework in the school sense, for she had to bone up on Americana in preparation for her citizenship hearing, joining Weill in getting her final papers, on May 5, 1944. The process involved a hearing before a judge, who usually sticks to Knowledge of American History questions, but has the power to inquire more personally. Weill's favorite conductor, Maurice Abravanel, recalled that Weill was alarmed by one question in particular: "If we were fighting Russia, would you take up arms against her?" Was this because of Weill's association with Brecht? Was this, even, the reason Weill, despite his interest in a *Švejk* musical, ultimately refused to team up with Brecht on it? Or had he simply had enough of Brecht's hypocritical love of The People and hatred of people? Lenya's hearing was less eventful, and when the judge asked her who was the first president of the United States she was thrilled, because that one she knew.

"Abraham Lincoln," she proudly replied.

"Congratulations," said the judge, perhaps a music lover. "You made it."

Donald Spoto has uncovered another of Lenya's love affairs occurring just about now, with Maxwell Anderson's son, Quentin. His marriage was failing, and, separated from his wife, Meg, Quentin found Lenya engaging and sympathetic. She was also, he discovered—as many had done before him—amazingly free of bourgeois cautions. "What Lenya wanted in the world," Quentin told Spoto, "she took and enjoyed."

This year, 1944, saw two of Weill's shows appear in film versions, *Knickerbocker Holiday* and *Lady in the Dark*. Both were debauched, Weill's scores used in tiny bits, with inferior numbers by others. *Knickerbocker Holiday* was at least well cast, with Nelson Eddy as the hero and Charles Coburn playing a deceptively mellow Stuyvesant. But the stage original was built on a star turn, and without Walter Huston's gamy bravado and Weill's music the material dissolves into that Hollywood cliché about the girl caught between the rich guy and the cute guy. It's a Joan Crawford picture in pantaloons.

Lady in the Dark is worse. Why did Paramount pay more than most movies cost just to get the rights to a musical and then crush the music? Screen technology could have toyed arrestingly with those dream sequences, but the director, Mitchell Leisen, just wanted to make a Mitchell Leisen romantic comedy—it was a genre then—instead of a fantasia about a woman having a nervous breakdown in the form of three operas. Worse yet, *One Touch of Venus* came off as a cheap piece of routine by Universal three years after this. It actually retained more of the stage score than the previous two films (five numbers, albeit with some new lyrics), but even with Dick Haymes and Olga San Juan in supplementary roles, the singing was uninteresting.

Hollywood really gave Weill only one opportunity in all his history with the film business, letting him and Ira Gershwin construct a score of their own design for an original title, *Where Do We Go From Here?* (1945). More important, this almost totally forgotten film marks the culmination of Weill's vast work for the war effort, after all the plane spotting and lunchbox propaganda songs. In Morrie Ryskind and Sig Herzig's scenario, Fred MacMurray, a frustrated 4-F reject from the services, finds a magic lamp and awakens a genie (Gene Sheldon). Impishly incompetent, the genie grants MacMurray's wishes to serve—but always in the wrong era. The army: so MacMurray finds himself back in 1776. The navy: now he's on one of Columbus' ships, in 1492. A third such sequence places him in old Nieuw Amsterdam, facing down a rascally town council very reminiscent of the one in *Knickerbocker Holiday*. (Instead of "Dutch comic" accents, this crew simply inverts the wording of sentences, as in "The bill of sale signed you haven't.") Throughout, MacMurray keeps meeting versions of his co-stars, sweetheart Joan Leslie and vamp June Haver. Finally, MacMurray gets his uniform and Leslie. Even the genie joins up. Ironically, MacMurray was to marry not Leslie but Haver: in real life, almost a decade later.

What makes *Where Do We Go From Here?* an anti-fascist piece specifically of its time—it was filmed in mid-1944—is a big chunk in the center of the running time that moves from a jesting assault on Nazi arrogance to a valentine to America. It starts in the Revolutionary War episode. Spying on Hessian mercenaries for General Washington, MacMurray, in a three-cornered hat with a long-stemmed pipe, finds his loyalties challenged by the Hessians. He responds with a harangue. "Von day, Chermany vill lick de whole world!" he begins. "Ve get our place in de sun! Und after ve take over de sun, ve take over de moon! Und de stars! Den ve go after de Poles! Ve take over de North Pole!" And so on up to "Den ve are ready for de big game— Notre Dame! *Sieg heil!*"

Then, to sabotage the Hessians' battle plans, MacMurray suggests double-crossing General William Howe, the British commander-in-chief:

HESSIAN OFFICER: But General Howe is mit uns. An ally!
MACMURRAY: So vat? If you don't double-cross an ally, who you
    going to double-cross?

Unmasked, MacMurray is to be shot, and he envisions a loony tombstone: "Born 1910. Died 1776."

Just before the firing squad pulls its triggers, MacMurray is transported to Columbus' ship. A mutiny is under way; Weill and Gershwin conceived it as a vast musical scene lasting nearly ten minutes. One would have to go back to early talkies to find the like—the Al Jolson vehicle *Hallelujah, I'm a Bum*, much of which is through-sung conversation; or *The Gay Divorce*'s "Continental" production number, which is mostly dance. The Columbus sequence, however, isn't merely long: it is overtly operatic, featuring a head mutineer (Carlos Ramirez) with a blazing tenor, a baritone Columbus (Fortunio Bonanova), and a rousing male chorus. As the film was shot in Technicolor, the ocean waves breaking against the ship's hull and the resulting spray take us far from Twentieth Century–Fox's sound stages, though the musical heat cools when MacMurray joins in for a solo hymning the pleasures of the America yet to be discovered—really, the pleasures of democracy. This section of the music, published as "The Nina, the Pinta, the Santa Maria," sails over a driving beat as if mesmerized by the wonders of modern American life, but MacMurray's voice sounds flimsy after the Verdian booming of the previous seven minutes.

Weill had feared that the film's director, Gregory Ratoff (who was more usually a character actor), would eviscerate the score. However, this time a Hollywood producer, William Perlberg, was thrilled with Weill's work, and the lengthy number remained intact in the release print, along with a few conventional ballads, "Song of the Rhineland" for the Hessians, and a snazzy march setting up a big dance number for canteen girls and servicemen, the madly festive "Morale (is the gal that you're fond of)."★

Weill's only full-scale movie musical, *Where Do We Go From Here?* confirmed his belief in America as more than a refuge: a home. During the summer of 1944, still in Hollywood for post-production work on the scoring, he was amazed that, even now, some of "those" Germans who had been relieved to emigrate to the United States were "still living in Europe." As Weill was talking to Walter Slezak about taking part in Weill's next show, Weill was included in a Slezak dinner party—"a German language evening of the worst kind," he told Lenya. In fact, it was worse than German: "that awful mixture of Hungarian and Viennese" popular among the artistic set in Lenya's hometown and an affectation of theatre-world Berliners. The guests themselves were even more objectionable. The Werfels were there—still one of Weill's least favorite couples, though at least Alma liked *Lady in the Dark*—and also a screenwriter named Walter Reisch. As always when speaking to Lenya, Weill got right to the point: Reisch "ought to be shot right after Hitler."

And Hitler, indeed, was finished. By the time *Where Do We Go From Here?* was released, in the spring of 1945, moviegoers were tired of war films as they were tired of war, and the picture did not live up to the studio's expectations. Perlberg's enthusiasm had led Fox into excessive

---

★ Joan Leslie had a solo called "It Could Have Happened To Anyone," a sort of "Bill" without the wit. The tune is draggy, too. Worse, it contradicts Leslie's genuine love for MacMurray, who plays his role as a combination of stumblebum and live wire. Presumably written before the authors fully understood the characters, the number was dropped before filming.

capitalization, and Weill himself felt that, for once, Hollywood had well-nigh coddled him. He actually watched an orchestra of fifty waiting—on salary, of course—while it took forever to work out exactly how to play a particular melodic line.

The war's end had been in sight for some time. Certain historians, cutting through complicating detail with Occam's razor, point to Hitler's attack on Stalin's Russia after the two years of the Nazi-Soviet Pact—in Niall Ferguson's words "the bloodiest divorce in history"—as the act that inevitably terminated the Third Reich. More precisely, there were three turning points in that direction: the German defeat at Stalingrad (which proved that the unstoppble Hitler could lose) at the start of 1943; the tank battle at the Kursk salient (which proved that Hitler probably would lose) in July of 1933; and the D-Day landings on June 6, 1944, which proved that Hitler had lost. His last gamble, the so-called Battle of the Bulge, launched at the end of 1944, was no more than a desperation ploy, to dishearten the allies and try to break apart their unnatural bond of democrats and communists. Could it be this simple? The inconclusive conclusion of the war about nothing—World War I—provokes the war of barbarians—World War II—which ends when the barbarian chief is dead.

Writing to his parents in Palestine, Weill noted the "courage and pride" that Nazi victims showed, compared to "the cowardice, the degradation, the sickening rage of self-destruction which the so-called master race" was showing. It was Ragnarok, the great Nordic suicide, as Nazis, raving at the demolition of their vast temple of murder, killed themselves or other Germans, and as Hitler, at the very end, ordered that nothing be left for the German people, who had dared to lose his war. Stendahl's Julien Sorel changed his social class; Weill and Lenya changed the address of their civilization.

And Weill said, "It was so totally a war of good against evil."

13

Nel Mezzo Del
Cammin Di Nostra Vita

In one way, Kurt Weill had been spoiled since he had arrived in New York, because casting his shows had been easy. For *Johnny Johnson*, the Group Theatre came with a prefabricated ensemble. It was like a furnished bungalow: one simply moved in. *The Eternal Road* had no star parts, and the Depression's contraction of thespian opportunity threw a lot of gifted performers into Reinhardt's auditions in any case. Then came three star shows in a row—*Knickerbocker Holiday*, *Lady in the Dark*, and *One Touch of Venus*.

But now Weill hit a snag. The Depression was over, and the need for escapist entertainment had swelled the theatre. In 1944 alone, four of the houses on the fringes of Broadway—the old Majestic in Columbus Circle, the Ziegfeld, Jolson's Fifty-Ninth Street, and the Craig, some bearing newer names—were reclaimed from disuse or the cinema to ease a booking jam. Most were refurbished; all but the Ziegfeld were christened yet again. And all four were musical houses: which meant that everyone worth hiring not under contract to the movies might be otherwise engaged.

And this was when Weill came up with a stunner of a casting problem: a show with four leading roles of more or less equal importance.

None of these parts was big enough to attract a star, yet the usual Broadway journeymen working "in support" would not be sharp enough. The work was *The Firebrand of Florence*, drawn from Edwin Justus Mayer's 1924 comedy-drama *The Firebrand*, on the adventures of the artist-adventurer Benvenuto Cellini. "Eddie" Mayer was adapting his play, and Weill was working (for the last time) with Ira Gershwin. Having written variations on musical comedy—and, in *Venus*, one conventional musical comedy—Weill was eager to try something more expansive. "A vast and unexploited field lay between opera and musical comedy," he was to write a bit later. But "such development could only take place on Broadway[,] the living theatre in this country." What Weill had in mind for this risqué costume drama about a lover who is also a fighter was an operetta, but a dramatic one with hotrodding music of power and sexy fun. Not your father's operetta, like *The Student Prince*. Not corny. But an intense Big Sing piece. Almost a Broadway opera.

Weill would get to that Broadway opera in time, but *The Firebrand of Florence* was something different, comic and crazy but also passionate, with exhibitionistic solos and grand choruses in big blocks of harmony. In a vaguely Medicean Florence, the court swirls with intrigue as Cellini confronts a hateful personal enemy, romances a beauty, tries to stay on the Duke's good side, and fends off the advances of the randy Duchess.

Cellini: dashing yet poetic, an opera-weight baritone. Alfred Drake (the original Curly in *Oklahoma!*) was ideal, or perhaps Wilbur Evans (of *Mexican Hayride*) or Bill Johnson (of *Something For the Boys*). They all had the voice and style for the part. More strictly "operetta" baritones would have been too stodgy. John Raitt hadn't been discovered yet, as he was the understudy and then replacement Curly in Chicago, unknown to Weill. Keith Andes, who was later to take over for Alfred Drake in *Kiss Me, Kate*, had been lost in *Winged Victory*'s huge cast, and Ray Middleton—whom Weill of course knew from *Knickerbocker Holiday*—lacked devilry. Cellini is a firecracker.

Straight actors of this type are already rare: and Weill needed one who could ring the playhouse with song. Unfortunately, Alfred

Drake wasn't available. When he left *Oklahoma!*, he stayed with its management team at the Theatre Guild for *Sing Out, Sweet Land* (1944). Wilbur Evans, under contract to the producer Mike Todd, was still in *Mexican Hayride* while *Firebrand* was casting, and was headed for Todd's next show, *Up in Central Park* (1945), in any case. For some unknown reason, Bill Johnson did not work out, and Weill toyed with the notion of Don Ameche, a wonderful performer who would have been miscast as the sensualist scapegrace Cellini.

By now, Weill had exhausted all the singing actors and acting singers and was considering just plain singers, especially those of operatic weight—Nelson Eddy, Lawrence Tibbett (who actually was celebrated for thespian intensity), even the tenor James Melton. Weill spent much of 1944 in Southern California, not only because of his film at Fox but to collaborate on *The Firebrand* with Ira Gershwin, who no longer cared to spend time in New York. Perhaps, like so many, he reveled in the easy-living semi-retirement he had discovered in Los Angeles: he could always work for the studios if he wanted occupation. Weill referred to him sarcastically as "His Highness" and to Ira's favorite easy chair as if it were the throne of a dozing pasha. It is also possible that Ira had left New York because so many of its places reminded him of his late brother and of the days when they were young and taking the town with their songs.

Then, too, as Ira pointed out, he had had to come to New York to work on *Lady in the Dark*—and, anyway, their current librettist, Eddie Mayer, was in Los Angeles himself, writing for the screen. So Weill became a temporary Angeleno, impatient as always with his partner's dilatory attitude. When working, Weill was obsessed, determined, fast: because he fell in love with each new project. Their very novelty mesmerized him, as if they were mystery tales and he was dying to see how they would come out.

Too few of his collaborators were as intent on this sublime act of creation, this purely human mark of greatness, this contradiction of the devil's "No!" It was what ennobles mankind; it was why Weill and Lenya left Europe. It was freedom—doesn't everyone want to be free? Eddie Mayer was so lazy that when Weill insisted Mayer write that damn scene already, Mayer simply typed out lines from the original play. Look what I wrote! Scolding him, Weill ordered Mayer to go back and *create* something; Weill even began to wonder if he should chuck Mayer out and write the script himself. In fact, like many composers—Verdi instantly comes to mind—Weill often planned each work from a musico-dramatic viewpoint himself. He didn't merely set the poet's verses: he told the poet what to write.

It may be that Weill was *The Firebrand*'s auteur in the cinematic sense, for the music is not only the work's heart but its very body. No wonder he considered casting from the opera world. In Los Angeles he took in a local *La Traviata* just to hear the Germont, Met baritone Alexander Sved—a robust performer but too long in the tooth for Cellini. The Violetta that evening was Norina Greco, also of the Met (Weill somehow got her name wrong, as "Irina") and not a bad choice for Cellini's love, Angela. One wonders if Weill was running through the catalogue of lyric sopranos, for he definitely wanted to cast Susanna Foster, who had abandoned opera for the movies and was tied to a contract with Universal.*

In the end, Weill had to open his show with a Cellini and Angela who were frankly unsuitable. Earl Wrightson was young and cute, but he was what was known then as a "radio singer": nice to hear but not a stage animal. The Angela, Beverly Tyler, was pretty but couldn't put her music over. At least Weill had no problem deciding on the Duchess: *finally* he had a great part for Lenya. And opposite her would be the perfect European counterpart in Walter Slezak, who could actually sing—the juvenile lead in Jerome Kern's *Music in the Air*, Slezak introduced "I've Told Every Little Star." This is a crucial point, for Weill had composed wonderful music for this essentially *buffo* character.

---

* By an odd coincidence, two of Weill's first choices for the leads, Foster and the aforementioned Wilbur Evans, were married, in 1948. Foster is another forties celebrity now forgot, though she deserves mention especially because she originated a line Bette Davis is famous for. Eight years before Davis, in a film called *There's Magic in Music*, Foster entered a cabin at Interlochen Music Camp, looked around, and observed, "What a dump!" Davis echoed the line in *Beyond the Forest*, in 1949.

Alas, like so many others, Slezak turned out to be unavailable, and the Duke was assigned to Melville Cooper. He would have been right for the part in a revival of the original play, but not for a singing role; when Cooper appeared in the Hugh Martin musical *Make a Wish* (1951), second-billed after the star, Nanette Fabray, he wasn't in a single number.

Of course, Weill was not solely in charge of *The Firebrand of Florence*, which was why the show flopped with one of the best scores of the decade: too many incompetents had power. The producer, Max Gordon, had put on a lot of hits, but he was now one year short of retirement and too exhausted to troubleshoot. The director was John Murray Anderson, famous for spectacle and piquant musical staging details but utterly uninterested in working with actors on characterization and the like. The worst of the lot was the author, Mayer, because his script was clumsy and tedious. Historians point to the incoherent casting, and that did hurt the show. But the out-of-town title, *Much Ado About Love*, suggests a poetic romance, something almost Shakespearean, and Mayer never aspired above mirthless jokes and dreary plotting.

The book that Mayer should have written existed—by implication only—in Weill and Gershwin's score. They wrote to match a libretto rich in irony: the artist as criminal, the law as whim, love as danger, violence as an intoxication of the senses. What Mayer never gave them they had to put into the music, for instance in what critics today point to as a dazzling tour de force, the nineteen-minute opening, a musical scene built around the scheduled (and then aborted, by a pardon) hanging of Cellini.

This is literally gallows humor, for at first everyone is in a merry mood, like an audience gathering for the latest hit, complete with an opportunist selling the souvenir book. This builds into a swirling chorus in praise of Florence, Gershwin waxing rambunctious with his rhymes ("statue" and "[looking] at you"), making music out of sheer joy of life. What a contrast, then, with Cellini's entrance and his putative last words, "There was life, there was love, there was laughter," as rueful as the previous musical period was festive. Weill builds Cellini's solo into an ensemble of luscious power, a kind of glorification of life-loving regret and, yes, Shakespearean in its richness. Had Mayer been able to create a book for the show that Weill had in mind, *The Firebrand of Florence* would have been one of the classic musicals of the 1940s.

Immersed in a dispirited tryout, Weill probably took little notice of the war in Europe, driving to its end as Nazi fanatics fought to the last victim. General Alfred Jodl was to surrender on May 7, 1945, just two weeks after *The Firebrand*'s New York opening, at the Alvin. It was Weill's worst failure since *Happy End*, and the critics felt entitled to a pile-on. They were especially hard on Lenya. It was her accent; her arch line-readings contradicting her no-nonsense plastique; her relationship to the composer. George Jean Nathan, always extreme in his ridicule of anything he disdained, blasted everything in sight. "The ladies of the ensemble," he wrote, "resemble Mr. David O. Selznick, and many of the males would provide perfect illustrations for the tales of the Brothers Grimm."

Lenya was devastated (though she did console herself with an affair with one of the lads in the ensemble). She even determined to quit the stage, *futsch!* Weill, however, had seen one of his most ambitious scores disposed of. Only four numbers were published, there was very little radio play, and no cast album was made, though this essential piece of theatre infrastructure had become the delivery platform for shows from *This Is the Army* and *Oklahoma!* to *Carmen Jones* and *Song of Norway*. Infuriated, Weill then saw *Carousel* open a month after *The Firebrand* to critical celebration. Even George Jean Nathan behaved himself, though he couldn't resist freaking out over "the protrusion of [John Raitt's] sweatered chest."

The worst of it was that Richard Rodgers was the only composer with whom Weill was holding a hard-on contest, and it was especially frustrating because Weill himself had initiated several negotiations with the Theatre Guild for the rights to musicalize Ferenc Molnár's *Liliom*: the source of *Carousel*. Weill had been certain that this achingly wistful and brutal play could inspire the Broadway opera that Weill desperately needed to create. But Molnár said no. He'd been saying it for years—to Puccini as well. No music for *Liliom*. Then came *Okla-*

homa!, a triumph not only in itself but in the possibilities it revealed. So Molnár said yes to Rodgers and Hammerstein, and *Liliom* became *Carousel*.

It was a terrible time for both Weills, for Lenya now learned that her aviator lover Howard Schwartz had been killed in a plane crash. To Lenya, a refugee from fascism, American servicemen seemed like protectors, warriors in this crucible of Western resolve. It had all started as the war about nothing and then was reinstituted as the war to define what "Christian Civilization" means, and Lenya found herself, once again, playing a role in it as much because of the friends she made as because of her beliefs. Weill was the one who pursued a program. Lenya was the one who turned around and said hello to the next fascinating event. One day, you collect little potted cactuses; another day, you're a symbol of anti-fascist survival, you know?

But now Weill got the chance to create his Broadway opera. Ferenc Molnár said no, but Elmer Rice said yes, to a plan Weill had made some twenty years before this. His source for the opera was *Die Strasse*, the play that so stimulated him back in Weimar Berlin: Rice's *Street Scene*. And it may be that Rice would have resisted a musical adaptation—but authors of straight plays were aware of the recent "artification" of the musical. After all, Molnár had said yes to *Carousel*. Further, Weill was now a member of the Playwrights' Company, the only composer thus elected. Rice would have seemed churlish to turn down his fellow Playwright.

Again, doesn't it appear that Weill is shaping his life step by step—even in ways he presumably could not have foreseen? Meeting Maxwell Anderson, collaborating with him on the Company's second entry, a successful one, writing incidental music for one of Rice's plays, being taken into the Company as an equal among creators of theatre . . . doesn't all this invent Elmer Rice's willingness to let *Street Scene* achieve completion as an opera?

Street Scene: a melodrama about a husband so protective of his marriage that when it is threatened by an adulterous interloper, he goes berserk and murders the man.

Actually, no: that's *Tiefland*, the opera that impressed the young

Weill many pages ago. But Weill *was* the protective husband. And though *Street Scene*'s husband is a brusque, intolerant thug clearly denoted as the villain of the piece—he murders not only the interloper but his own wife as well—he is perhaps driven mad by the apparent loss of his marriage.

One wonders if Weill and Lenya ever talked about this aspect of the piece, perhaps his most self-defining work: because in it he finally executed his ideal of an opera for the theatre. A mixed cast of opera singers, trained singers who had gone "popular," Broadway voices, actors, and two specialty dancers for a boogie-woogie raveup, "Moon-Faced, Starry-Eyed," interlocked with one another just as Weill's use of every practice in the musical-theatre manual created a blend that amounts to a new genre. It's hard to know what to call it. If it's an opera, why is so much of it spoken? Yet what are its impassioned solos and ensembles but opera? The adulterous wife, Anna Maurrant, has a long establishing solo, "Somehow I Never Could Believe," composed of some five sections, ranging from autobiography to lament to optimism, the different periods bound by use of leitmotifs. Interestingly, the words are deliberately prosaic, to catch a working-class woman's feelings just as she might express them. The music, however, soars with the wonder of looking into the human spirit. By the number's end, Mrs. Maurrant has been utterly revealed to us. This happens very rarely in the musical. (Buffs will instantly cite such exceptions as *Carousel*'s "Soliloquy" and *Gypsy*'s "Rose's Turn.") But it is the business model in the writing of opera.

For the lyrics, Weill turned to the black poet Langston Hughes, presumably because so much of his verse is devoted to characterizing through the use of dialect, in the manner of the "folk" art so popular in America from the 1930s on. Naturally, *Street Scene*'s book was by Elmer Rice, hewing closely to his play—too closely. Every time Weill or Hughes wanted to cut dialogue, Rice would cry, "But that was a sensation in 1929!" or "No, no, the audience went all a-hush when those words were uttered!" Even Hughes' lyrics had to conform to the phrasing in the 1929 script, so much so that the published vocal score credits fully half of the musical numbers to Hughes *and* Rice, and one number, the "Lullaby" of two nursemaids couched in the language of the scandal tabloid, is credited to Rice alone. (It is derived directly from a scene in the play, but with mostly new words.)

Step by step, then, and more or less over Rice's dead body, Weill and Hughes made their way through this saga of twenty-four hours in the life of a Manhattan apartment house. There is no protagonist, but two families interest us: the Maurrants and the Kaplans. The former are, of course, the troubled family, with the hateful husband and the unfaithful wife. Their daughter, Rose, is in love with the Kaplan son, Sam. With the Met singers Norman Cordon and Polyna Stoska as the senior Maurrants, operetta soubrette Anne Jeffreys as Rose, and Met tenor Brian Sullivan as Sam, *Street Scene* acknowledges an operatic basis. Yet many secondary principals have to "pop" their way through their roles—the "Moon-Faced, Starry-Eyed" duo, or Rose's boss, who tries to lure her into show biz (and his bed) in a jazzy strut.

Thus, *Street Scene*'s score blends vocal types just as apartment living blends personalities. Weill wasn't really writing an opera. He was writing a form he invented: theatre opera, or actors' opera, with the art of music but the bitter kick of life. Interestingly, Mrs. Maurrant's affair hangs over the entire action like oracular advice in a Greek drama, constantly mentioned, almost making the murders necessary. Yet Mrs. Maurrant's adulterous partner, Sankey, is hardly in the show at all and doesn't sing a note—just as, in life, the invasive third party in a marriage is so often a figure of small acquaintance. The two are together when Mr. Maurrant shoots them only because Mrs. Maurrant asked Sankey to meet her—to say goodbye, the critic Ken Mandelbaum believes. What makes Mrs. Maurrant's tale so moving is that she entered into the affair out of not lust but a need for shelter from her stormy marriage, and that she is ending the affair when she is killed. Unlike *Street Scene*'s other wives, Mrs. Maurrant seeks an emotional freedom from the narrow culture of working-class wedlock, where everything not compulsory is forbidden. This is what we hear in "Somehow I Never Could Believe," making it more than a character number: a thematic explanation for the entire work.

Because Rice's play was a melodrama, the killer goes on the

run—hard to do in a single-set play showing the front door of your address. When he is caught, Mr. Maurrant duets with Rose against choral backup that Weill builds into a searing ensemble, "I Loved Her, Too." Notably, Weill quotes *Tiefland*'s *Wolfserzählung* theme on the number's four title words. One of the pitches is different, and the harmony, too, is skewed from D'Albert's score. But the quarter-note triplet dropping to a half note is unmistakable—as, of course, is the subject matter. "I couldn't stand to see nobody takin' her away from me," Mr. Maurrant tells his daughter: just like the hero of *Tiefland*, who similarly cries out, "It drove me into violence!" Three men defending their home: *Tiefland*'s Pedro, *Street Scene*'s Frank Maurrant . . . and Kurt Weill, husband to one of the planet's most irresistible women? If only he had had the power to give her his music as he did his love—for Lenya sang relatively little Weill in his lifetime: the first, short *Mahagonny* and of course *The Threepenny Opera*, "arrangements" of the *Mahagonny* opera that weren't the real thing, *The Seven Deadly Sins*, *The Firebrand of Florence*, a few concerts, and the BOST album. Ironically, Lenya as the ultimate Weill stylist was an invention dating from after his death, and the inventor was yet another third party in the Weill-Lenya household, as we'll see.

Opening on January 9, 1947 at the Adelphi Theatre, *Street Scene* was billed as a "dramatic musical" but identified as "an American opera" in the vocal score. It had suffered a calamitous tryout in Philadelphia; for three weeks, the company played to a sprinkling of ticketbuyers while everyone waited for a play called *Lovely Me*, co-written by Jacqueline Susann, to vacate the Adelphi in New York after blistering reviews. (George Jean Nathan's blurb was ready: "a turkey raffle.") In order for *Street Scene* to come in, Dwight Deere Wiman, co-producing with the Playwrights' Company, had to pay expenses out of pocket—but the New York reception was invigorating. Except for the *Post*, the critics admired or even loved the show. The *Daily News*' John Chapman, who generally responded to works with "extra" music, called *Street Scene* "a moving, remarkable opera," and the *Times*' Brooks Atkinson, who took his music in small helpings, nevertheless thought the show "a musical play of magnificence and glory" and Weill "the foremost music maker in the American theatre." Attendance was good, and Weill now troubled to visit his brother Nathan and his parents in Naharia, Palestine. He dropped in also on London, Paris, and Geneva. He did not visit Germany or Austria.

Street Scene lasted 148 performances—not enough to pay off but an impressive run for an opera on Broadway. Other such attempts tended to fail at that time, including works by Benjamin Britten and Marc Blitzstein, though by the 1950s Gian Carlo Menotti had some success and Frank Loesser, using Weill's format of a short book cut into a program of song, recitative, and underscored dialogue, had a triumph with *The Most Happy Fella* (1956).

Especially gratifying to Weill was Columbia Records' Goddard Lieberson's decision to give *Street Scene* a cast recording—Weill's second in America (after *One Touch of Venus*), and, on six twelve-inch 78s, one of the longest Broadway albums of the decade. All the same, as staging or recording, *Street Scene* was a "prestige success" rather than a commercial property. "Prestige successes?" Lenya once cried. "You can starve on them!" In fact, Columbia's *Street Scene* proved a steady if modest seller, and has never been out of print since its initial release.

The foremost music maker in the American theatre. That's quite an encomium from a critic who turned to stone at the mere whisper of the word *operetta*. The other half of the old Weill-Brecht outfit was doing much less well. Though he failed to get any movie work beyond his uncredited collaboration on *Hangmen Also Die*, Brecht had remained in California. His *Katzenjammer* charm still viable, Brecht enchanted Charles Laughton and worked with him on a translation of one of the scripts that had come to life during Brecht's exile, *Galileo*. As *Leben des Galilei*, the work had been staged at Zurich's Schauspielhaus in 1943. But a Hollywood production (at a small theatre, the Coronet) with a Hollywood star under Brecht's supervision (though nominally directed by Joseph Losey) promised to revive not only the Brecht byline but the Brecht *presence* on the world stage. Better yet, the producer, T. Edward Hambleton, planned to take the production to New York.

Brecht does not appear to have invited Weill to compose the incidental score, for he had selected his next Weill in Hanns Eisler.

Otherwise, it was the same old Brecht, perhaps a little less abusive of the actors. They tended to drive him crazy with their nuanced characterizations, for by 1947 the tenets of what we loosely call Method acting—the Stanislafskyan realism that was the opposite of the impersonally reportorial delivery that Brecht demanded—had permeated the profession in America. True, some rejected it, some absorbed bits of it, and some thought it fascinating but exotic, like living in an igloo or getting lost in the Hindu Kush. Brecht's *Galileo* cast seemed—at least to Brecht—to be full of it. Yet even if he forbore screaming at them, he was as dictatorial as ever, changing everything—the text, the costumes, the most minor props—till the first week of the four-week run had to be cancelled. James K. Lyon gives us a list of the celebrities who graced media reports on the first night: Charlie Chaplin, Charles Boyer, Ingrid Bergman, Anthony Quinn, Van Heflin (whose sister Frances was in the cast), John Garfield, Gene Kelly, Sidney Greenstreet, Frank Lloyd Wright, and others. The short run sold out, and Hambleton did indeed move the show to Broadway, opening at the end of the year at Maxine Elliott's Theatre, with Laughton repeating his Galileo and the Broadway dancer Joan McCracken taking over Heflin's role as Galileo's daughter.

Just as with the Broadway *Threepenny* and *(The) Mother*, it was still too early for mainstream theatregoing to absorb Brechtian art. Brecht himself was not around to see it, as he had fled the country after answering a subpoena from the House Un-American Activities Committee, appearing on October 30, 1947. Though not an actor, Brecht gave a superb performance that was totally out of his usual manner except for the inevitable cigar. He was well-dressed and mild-mannered, and in the footage of the hearing, says John Fuegi, "He does not look like a revolutionary. He has an air of benign cooperation about him that is signal contrast to the embattled truculence" of the "unfriendly" witness. Virtually every writer offers the same analogy in analyzing Brecht's response to the committee's questions: he is the Good Soldier Švejk, so helpful yet somehow never quite getting to the point, using minutiae, doubletalk, and, in areas unfamiliar to his interrogators, outright lying to defeat all attempts to learn the truth. Though Brecht was by now fluent in not only the reading but the speaking of English, he faked a need for a translator, and someone was brought over from the Library of Congress. But this man had such a heavy accent that he only thickened the haze behind which Brecht was hiding. At one point, the Committee Chairman, the infamous J. Parnell Thomas, remarked, "I cannot understand the interpreter any more than I can the witness."

Finally, the committee reached the era's *Gretchenfrage*, "Are you now or have you ever been a member of the Communist Party?" To ask this of Brecht shows how worthless a question it was, because Brecht never did join the Party. Yet if Brecht wasn't a communist then neither were Lenin, Stalin, and Trotsky. "No, no, no, no, no, never," Brecht answered. Then he was dismissed with thanks, went back to New York, and left for Europe the next day, never to return.

At the same time, Weill was having a fight with his publisher, Max Dreyfus of Chappell, who had handled every one of Weill's American stage works from *Johnny Johnson* and *The Eternal Road* on. The most powerful music publishers maintained connections with impresarios of the opera, concert, and theatre worlds, and even back in Germany, in his dialogues with Universal, Weill made it clear that he expected his publisher to promote his work and arrange for its performance. Having launched *Street Scene* theatrically rather than operatically, Weill nevertheless wanted Chappell to interest opera companies in mounting it. *Street Scene* did, decades later, become an opera-house staple, but it made very slow headway, despite Columbia's cast album and a concert at the Hollywood Bowl in 1949 that was broadcast. Weill was hoping for a Covent Garden *Street Scene*—and, indeed, the fitful history of English opera was just then exploding into its golden age, with an audience interested in, if not hungry for, new work in its own language. The fall of 1947 was a bit early, perhaps—but then Weill learned that Chappell was negotiating with Gian Carlo Menotti's publisher, G. Schirmer, to handle British stage rights to Menotti's operas, which were in English and somewhat popular in style, like *Street Scene*.

Weill was irritated enough to inform Dreyfus that Weill now felt "completely free with regard to the publication of my next show and any future works."

He meant it. Weill's next work, an expanded version of his short radio opera *Down in the Valley* (1945), was published by G. Schirmer, not Chappell. Little more than half an hour in its revision, this very simple and tragic tale has the feeling of a folk ballad in its narrative of sweethearts parted because he is hanged for murder (in self-defense). With a libretto by Arnold Sundgaard, the piece was intended for amateur and college groups, and was premiered in its completed form on July 15, 1948 at Bloomington, Indiana.

All the same, when Weill returned to Broadway that same year, he also returned to Chappell (even after hearing that, indeed, Menotti's *The Medium* was to be produced in London, at the Aldwych Theatre, in 1948). It should have been *Street Scene*, Weill thought. But Chappell had a virtual monopoly on the publication of Broadway musicals. G. Schirmer was fine for a fiddly little folk piece meant for voice majors, but only Chappell understood the big time. Weill had nowhere else to go in any real sense.

The same was true of Lenya in a different way: her notices on *The Firebrand of Florence* had killed her career and even her wish to reimpose it as, say, a cabaret singer. But then, she didn't think of herself that way. She was a dancer, once; then, for much longer, an actress. She had played classics and the headline-making moderns as dutiful daughters, revolutionaries, whores. She created character, lived on the stage like a sage on a mountain peak, made them ask, "Who was she?" the next day. *This* was Lenya, she felt—not Kate Smith or Dinah Shore. So the late 1940s were the emptiest years of her life, the ones without a shred of professional promise, of vocation beyond card-playing and commiserating with Weill over the latest acts of ingratitude by his collaborators. And this while being isolated in a rural retreat well under the tempo of life that she had been used to in the addresses that had been hers since birth: Vienna, Zurich, Berlin, Paris, New York. Once she was the talk of the Weimar arts scene. Now her audience was trout swimming through the stream in the backyard. As

Weill's biographer David Farneth puts it, "She tried to find happiness keeping house and acceptance in a gossipy social circle of women married to creative men."

Weill's next show was arguably the most imaginative of his life. By a strange irony it was the direct precursor of Lenya's first Broadway musical after *The Firebrand*, *Cabaret*—for *A Dish For the Gods*, the working title, was the first song-and-dance show to intersperse full-scale commentative numbers between the story scenes. "That's progress," a suave male octet blithely intones, to a soft-shoe accompaniment when an increasingly industrialized economy ruins the artisan's livelihood; a hobo sings the wistful "Love Song" when romance is taking a hit. "A vaudeville" was the billing that Weill and his new partner, Alan Jay Lerner, settled on for—as they eventually called it—*Love Life*. Cheryl Crawford was again Weill's producer, and she again hired Elia Kazan to direct.

That last bit is strange: haven't we established that Kazan had no ability in this realm? Lerner was fresh from one of 1947's two smash-hit fantasies, *Brigadoon*, and *Love Life*'s choreographer, Michael Kidd, had created the musical staging for the other smash-hit fantasy, *Finian's Rainbow*. And Ray Middleton (most recently Frank Butler to Ethel Merman's Annie Oakley in *Annie Get Your Gun*) and Nanette Fabray (who won a big career boost taking over for Celeste Holm for most of the run of *Bloomer Girl*) had the leads in what is essentially a two-person-plus-ensemble show, among the biggest roles of the decade. These are the makings of a hit.

But Kazan? What does this master of Group Theatre naturalism know about the structure of a musical—especially one that keeps bumping up the narrative with showy numbers that have to land precisely, to keep the action and its decoration in balance? Anton Chekhof directs *Show Boat*.

Further, even when *Love Life* was realistic it was crazy, for it moved from 1791 to 1948 as Middleton and Fabray agelessly survived sociopolitical changes in American life. Weill and Lerner thus wrote two separate scores, one for the leads' marriage and the other for everyone else. There was a great deal of the latter, for the vaudeville kept popping up and then, in the show's climax, wholly took over the continuity for a minstrel revue. So, again: with so much "musicalness" to be juggled, why did Crawford think Kazan a smart choice? For that matter, how did Weill regard the hiring of Kazan?

We do know that Weill got on very well with Alan Jay Lerner—and this, too, is odd, because nothing irritated Weill more than a collaborator who wouldn't collaborate because he was dependent on helpers or out playing golf or just lazy. Lerner was notoriously the slowest worker in the business; the reason he was free to work with Weill after *Brigadoon* is that *Brigadoon*'s composer, Frederick Loewe, had broken up the partnership out of exasperation. (They would get back together and break up several times more.) But Lerner was as well very smart about how a musical is put together, not just as author but as general factotum, with savvy counsel about design, performers, advertising. Weill could appreciate that: he also had opinions about how musicals prosper that surpassed the standard composer's understanding.

Lenya liked Lerner, too, though later on it irked her that, whenever somebody expressed an interest in staging *Love Life*, Lerner would refuse to allow it. "I've turned into everything I satirized in that show," he explained, presumably referring to his inability to make a marriage work. (He ended up with eight wives.) However, when Lenya was enjoying the film of *Gigi* (1958), she suddenly heard a number lifted from *Love Life*, "I Remember It Well." Lerner had changed the words and Loewe set them to new music, but the song remained what it had been when Lerner wrote it with Weill: a slow waltz between the man hazy on details and the woman clear on them. And Lenya suddenly realized the real reason Lerner had never allowed a revival of *Love Life*: because he had planned all along to use that number again. "But what can you do?" Lenya said. "That's Alan."

Weill reused a bit of his own music in *Love Life*, as he had in *Street Scene* and virtually all his shows before. As originally composed, *Love Life* was the most American of his Broadway titles, with a sweeping look at national styles in music. But a hectic tryout in the usual not-enough-time schedule demanded field expedients. The crumbling of Sam and Susan's marriage found voice in his and her solos, "Is It Him

Or Is It Me" for Susan and "This Is the Life" for Sam. So far, so good. But the two were separated by a vaudeville set in that manly preserve the locker room, filled with strutting hunks bragging about their conquests. They hated it in Boston, so Michael Kidd had to throw together a Big Ballet, "Punch and Judy Get a Divorce."

So here is more autobiography. Like *Street Scene*, *Love Life* is about a marriage in trouble. The earlier show ends in murder, but *Love Life* doesn't end: we last see Sam and Susan at opposite ends of a tightrope, unsure of reaching the Happy Ending. Yet doesn't Weill assure us in his music that these two will end in each other's arms? For the last thing *Love Life*'s public hears is the coda to Sam and Susan's love song, "Here I'll Stay": it's Weill's way of telling us that this couple will soothe their differences and make the most of what they share.

But Punch and Judy *did* get a divorce—and, anyway, if Weill could confer with Kidd on what music he needed for the ballet, Weill didn't have the time to compose and orchestrate the piece himself. He mapped it out and handed it over to an assistant, Irving Schlein, to execute. All the ideas are Weill's, not least the bizarre re-use of Act One's "Green-Up Time," a lively gavotte, as an eerie dirge with the melody played by the violins in harmonics. To start the music up, Weill even retrieved a bit of *Die Bürgschaft,* the *Barbarischer Marsch* near the beginning of the opera's third act (at the words *"Tag und Nacht marschiert der Armee"*). Out of context, it has a gleeful, mischievous air.

It was often said then, and in decades after, that Weill was notable for writing his own orchestrations. None of the other familiar Broadway composers did. But the classically trained who found their way to Broadway often did some or all of their own scoring, from Reginald De Koven, John Philip Sousa, and Victor Herbert on. To these musicians—and especially to Weill—the melody and its instrumentation were not divisible elements but the music itself, *their* music. The historian Steven Suskin tells us that Ted Royal had to step in to orchestrate *Street Scene*'s two pop numbers, "Wrapped in a Ribbon" and "Moon-Faced, Starry-Eyed." Was this because they were added to the show in Philadelphia and Weill lacked the time, or because Weill thought Royal could better tap into the needed Hit Parade sound?

Certainly, Weill was pushing himself too hard in these years. Hypertension ran in the family, and its treatment and pharmacology were woefully inadequate at the time. Hans Weill, Kurt's favorite sibling, had died of it just the year before, aged forty-eight.

Further, Weill was faced with an extracurricular duty during *Love Life*'s tryout, for Lenya's mother suddenly decided to visit her daughter, taking Lenya's sister, Maria, along. (Lenya's step-father, Ernst Hainisch, stayed in Vienna.) It had been some sixteen years since Lenya had seen her mother, but it must have seemed longer, considering the upheaval they had lived through, with its diaspora of refugees followed by the war. Frau Hainisch was eighty but in good shape, though when Lenya noted that one lens of her eyeglasses was missing her mother waved it away as trivia.

"Leave it as it is," she said. "I've seen enough of the world."

Lenya's people arrived in the middle of *Love Life*'s Boston run, one week before the New York premiere—and yet, Lenya says, Weill came down for the event. He even accompanied Lenya to pick up *Mutter und Tochter* at the airport.* Johanna and Maria stayed for six weeks, time enough to see the sights, do the tiniest bit of shopping, and satisfy Lenya's mother that her daughter had risen in the world. Did she attend a performance of *Love Life*? Did she hear the BOST album? Did she comprehend what a unique and imperishable gift she had bestowed upon the Western world? "Thank you, Herr Weill," she says, shaking his hand and then marching off to the car for the ride back to the airport. "Modest in her wants, envying no one," Lenya observes, "she was delighted to have all her children [out of the house] and to be alone with her second husband." And back went *Mutti* to Vienna, never to see her daughter again. Be smart, Linnerl, and, if you can manage it, don't come back.

---

* Lenya recalled it as La Guardia, but that very year, 1948, saw New York International Airport, Alexander E. Anderson Field (popularly known as Idlewild, its original name, and now of course called John F. Kennedy International Airport) take over global traffic from La Guardia. It is possible that there was some overlap between the two airfields until La Guardia was settled as the domestic caravanserai and Kennedy as the international one.

Opening on October 7, 1948 at the Forty-Sixth Street Theatre (today the Richard Rodgers), *Love Life* got very mixed reviews, from Brooks Atkinson's grumping at "the lugubrious train of the story" to Robert Coleman's tribute to its "great heart, soaring imagination, welcome novelty, and keen observation." It lasted eight months, and while the two stars' big performances, the elaborate production, and the temporary popularity of "Here I'll Stay" and "Green-Up Time" made it seem like a hit, it probably lost money. And it did recede instantly into that paradoxical twilight of forgotten shows with famous titles.

In the ten years since *Knickerbocker Holiday*, Weill and Maxwell Anderson had always hoped to re-establish their partnership. It was not just that they liked each other; to Weill, Anderson was like Brecht without tears, imaginative yet professional. Every so often, Broadway tattle had it that Weill and Anderson were working on a musical version of Anderson's *High Tor* (1937), one of those three Anderson plays that Burgess Meredith had appeared in. Indeed, sometimes the scuttlebutt revealed that Meredith was urging them on, hoping to reclaim his old role of the misanthrope whose nature is changed after a night spent on his own private mountain, in the company of crooked realtors and the ghostly crew of a lost Dutch ship. Meredith was not the only one who heard *High Tor*'s secret music: the Williams College student Stephen Sondheim wrote to Anderson for permission to adapt it, too. Anderson said no.

There is no record of Weill's actual participation in this project— Anderson later wrote a *High Tor* musical for television with the composer Arthur Schwartz, starring Bing Crosby and Julie Andrews—but Weill and Anderson did write another show. According to Ronald Sanders, it was Oscar Hammerstein's wife, Dorothy, who gave a copy of Alan Paton's *Cry, the Beloved Country* to Anderson. It may sound grandiose to say so, but her thinking apparently was not that Paton's novel would make a good musical but rather that postwar reconfirmation of Western humanist values after the defeat of the barbarian seemed to call for music theatre on the theme of brotherhood and tolerance. And Paton's poetic storytelling, on race relations in South Africa, seemed ideal as a source. Anderson thought so, too.

What he might also have been thinking was: At last Weill and I can place the songs we wrote for *Ulysses Africanus*. The earlier project was not about race relations; on the contrary, it's essentially a comedy about a simpleton who can't find his way home. That wouldn't have given the hero much to sing about, so the *Ulysses* songs appear to have expanded the character symbolically, lost not just geographically but spiritually. That precisely matched the dilemma of Paton's protagonist, Reverend Stephen Kumalo. He, too, is on a quest: searching for his son who has gone to the devil in the big city and taken part in a robbery that ends in murder. In the show's last minute, he is executed. "O Tixo, Tixo, Help Me," Kumalo's great soliloquy, reveals how far Weill and Anderson's Ulysses had journeyed: from a loyal old family retainer to a man of God so lost in moral quandary that he prays to a heathen diety.

Leery of the high capitalization that musicals demanded—a good-sized show of the late 1940s generally cost around $225,000—the Playwrights' Company insisted on a spare staging. George Jenkins designed what amounted virtually to a unit set, so that the nineteen different locations called for in the script could be effected through the use of backdrops and small side pieces. Only the courtroom in which the young Kumalo's doom is pronounced seemed to change the view completely, hogging the stage with the appearance of great weight overseen by a huge stone archway: as befits the place of state power in this saga of individuals crushed by events beyond their control. Even Weill's orchestra was half the normal size, just twelve players including three utility reeds (covering ten instruments) and five strings but only one of the brass family, a trumpet.

The small pit must have thrilled Maxwell Anderson, for, in those days before comprehensive miking, lyrics were routinely drowned by the brass. A real act of display for Weill, the scoring gains in atmosphere what it loses in volume, as in the transition from the first scene, in Kumalo's home, to a railroad station and a song called "Train To Johannesburg": pounding piano in g minor under staccato pointings in the woodwinds, then the melody, a keening on the accordion (with flute and oboe) as the Station Master calls out the next arrival and the chorus cuts in with frantic cries of "Johannesburg" in discordant intervals. Because the black man who gets on that train never returns to his people.

The choice of director fit the budget, for Rouben Mamoulian had staged *Oklahoma!* with great artistry around a comparably tight allowance. *Lost in the Stars* came in at a trim $90,000, and those who saw it long recalled a beautiful production, almost a concert version of a musical, with picturesque use of the chorus and scene melting into scene at the changes. Todd Duncan (the original Porgy in *Porgy and Bess*, also directed by Mamoulian) was Kumalo, opposite Leslie Banks as the father of the man Kumalo's son has killed; Weill and Anderson saw them as antagonists in a morality play on the nature of justice. There was a love plot as well, though only the girl (Inez Matthews) sang; the boy was Kumalo's son (Julian Mayfield). At that, only one number could be called a romantic ballad in any sense, "Stay Well" ("Forget" in its original form in *Ulysses Africanus*), which Weill set to an accompaniment of pizzicato strings with the cello outlining the melody; in the second chorus, a clarinet plays against the voice in descant.

So *Lost in the Stars* typifies Weill's lifelong attraction to large ideas with sociopolitical writers like Anderson (and Brecht, Kaiser, and Green) and novelties with everyone else. A timely work, *Lost in the Stars* was art of the postwar period, requesting of the survivors a more humanist survey of society and its laws. Despite some glowing reviews and an eight-and-half-month run (with bookings in California but no tour), the show lost the Playwrights half their investment.

And then Kurt Weill died. He and Anderson had already begun work on what might have been Weill's most American piece yet, an adaptation of *Huckleberry Finn*. The five songs they wrote show the pair in fine fettle, especially in "River Chanty," an intimate "Ol' Man River" with a tidy panorama all its own. However, while playing tennis with Alan Jay Lerner on a hot day, Weill virtually collapsed. He insisted that he would recover—and no one tell Lenya! Then, on March 16, 1950, two weeks after his fiftieth birthday, Weill suffered a terrible night of chest pains and eventually had to seek treatment, at Flower Fifth Avenue Hospital. In critical condition at first, he began to improve and before long was sitting up in bed, watching television, reading *The New Yorker*, and correcting the galleys of the piano-vocal score of *Lost in the Stars*. At first hesitant to encourage visitors, Lenya now felt she could invite them—Lehman Engel, for instance. "Call tomorrow," she told him, "and if things are all right, come pay us a visit."

That afternoon, however—on April 3—Weill's condition took a worrisome turn, and Lenya called the Andersons. When they arrived, they saw, says Ronald Sanders, "a group of doctors who were in a commotion over something; they sensed it to be Kurt."

"I think this the end," Lenya told them.

Within an hour Kurt Weill was dead. "Any life," George Orwell wrote, "is simply a series of defeats." Weill's might well have seemed so in 1950, with so many of his German scores utterly unknown; the relative failure of *Street Scene*, the work that commanded the center of his aesthetic; his lack of success in Hollywood; even *Oklahoma!* and *Carousel*'s having overshadowed *Lady in the Dark* in the forties revolution in American music theatre. Weill may have died disappointed, but only because he had no idea that his music was headed for a revival comparable to that of only one other twentieth-century composer, Gustav Mahler. This time, destiny was going to handle the job all on its own, while Julien Sorel slept.

Lenya, however, had a feeling that her Kurt couldn't possibly delegate authority in something so important as posterity. She buried him in business casual: a pair of slacks and his favorite white turtleneck.

"He's going to be very busy up there," she explained, "and I want him to be comfortable, you know?"

14

Pirate Jenny

W hen he died," she said, "I wanted to crawl into a hole and never come out." It wasn't just that the music was over. Lenya and Weill had crossed through history together, lived in the very meaning of the terrifying twentieth century. "How she grieved!" Hesper Anderson told Donald Spoto. "She just couldn't be left alone . . . And she cried, night after night after night. She just did not want to live."

The music wasn't over, of course. Three months after Weill's death, he got an evening at Lewisohn Stadium, New York's equivalent of the Hollywood Bowl. In the first part of the program, Alan Jay Lerner narrated a concert version of *Lost in the Stars* led by Todd Duncan; the second part offered a semi-staged *Down in the Valley* followed by "September Song," "Speak Low," and the two hits from *Love Life*: the latest Weill and a bit of the classic Weill, all-American. Then, in February of 1951, Ernst Josef Aufricht reappeared in Lenya's life. He was not the man who brought Weill and Brecht togther; they did that themselves. And he was not the man who cast Lenya as the first Jenny; Weill did that. But Aufricht did put on that first *Threepenny* production, the event that turned the eyes of the West upon the music of Weill and the power of Lenya.

An old friend, Aufricht—and he owed even more to Weill and Lenya than they owed to him. Aufricht now proposed a "Kurt Weill Memorial" in Town Hall, and he knew exactly what music he wanted everyone to hear: songs in German, French, and English, performed by Grete Mosheim and Inez Matthews (of *Lost in the Stars*) in the first part, followed by the New York premiere of *Die Dreigroschenoper's* score in German, with narration in English and, front and center, Frau Weill.

"It was hard," Aufricht later wrote, "to persuade her to come out of the hiding place she had crawled into after [Weill's] death. In her grief, it was shocking to her to sing Weill's music."

But she did say yes, submitting to a rigorous rehearsal schedule, for Aufricht did not want simply to throw the evening onto the stage. Had he perhaps realized that Weill's death made necessary a Weill Renaissance? Or was Aufricht just very, very proud of the one work that distinguished his producing career—this *Threepenny* that gave liftoff to so many careers over the decades?

And then "Lenya telephoned me in tears on the morning of the concert, demanding that the evening be cancelled lest I make her and Kurt ridiculous." Aufricht doesn't say how he managed it, but she went on that night, the sold-out event was a great success, and it had to be repeated. ("Many times," according to Aufricht.) The producer noted also that among the well-wishers after the show was George Davis, "a plump little man . . . with a child's face and dreaming eyes."

Davis was far more than an enthusiast storming the green room, for he had known Lenya since her stint at Le Ruban Bleu in 1938. A gay man, Davis served as Lenya's escort when Weill was busy or uninterested. Further, Davis was appreciative of the special sound Weill had been bringing to Broadway; nothing endeared one to Lenya like respect for Weill.

George Davis was a prime example of the sort of homosexual common to the great cities of Western society for the last several centuries: intelligent, cultured, refined, "amusing," and usually creative but in a general rather than obsessive way. They often fall into one of the literary trades. In money trouble, they can fill in at the piano keyboard or take on the perilously amorphous responsibilities of what is now known as the "personal assistant." They obtain reviewing gigs to get onto the free list and rush the great and near-great till one encounters them at every fashionable premiere or at the *most* dinner parties yet never knows what they do for a living. They charm for a living; they know the famous for a living; they gossip for a living. At some point they may have acted or published a novel or co-managed a chic club till . . . oh, I won't bore you with the savage details, but everyone knew his so-called partner was the greatest swindler since . . . freshen your drink?

At their luckiest, they end up as Jean Cocteau. At their saddest, they end up like the character Bob Stillman played in the musical *Grey Gardens* (2006), the merry vocal accompanist who closes out his story "in a two-bit fleabag, a suicide." Davis, at first, appeared to be hitting a stride somewhere between these two paradigms, for he got good editing jobs at *Vanity Fair* and then *Harper's Bazaar.* Later, Davis got to *Mademoiselle* and then *Flair* till it folded. He was a good editor, and good editors have, above all, perspective. Artists are fixed in their personal vision; the editor comprehends the context.

Above all, everyone who knew George Davis and Lenya agrees that it was Davis who saw that Weill's music had not yet resonated with the public in all its detail, because it was too . . . interesting. And Lenya had had no chance at all because she was too interesting as well. Davis the editor, seeing more broadly than Lenya the artist, realized that resuscitating her career as the voice of Weill would restart the entire Kurt Weill and Lotte Lenya Story—which is why these gay pets of the cultural capitals have always had far more influence than we know of. Because the arts world seldom gives out a concept credit of this kind. It's Lotte Lenya Sings Kurt Weill, and that's all we know.

So Davis' appearance backstage at Aufricht's Kurt Weill Memorial marks the first moment of the Kurt Weill Renaissance. And then, on July 7, 1951, Lenya took Davis as her second husband.

Why?

Because, first of all, Lenya was unable to function well on her own. Alone in a strange city touring with that untrustworthy but at least she liked my husband Helen Hayes: fine. Alone during Weill's many Hollywood sojourns: fine. Because the union was secure, and sooner or later she would nest herself within it once more. But alone without an abiding partnership was alone in its truest sense: without being held and loved ever again. A friend is a bit of this and that. A husband is The Story of You.

And now comes another happy event. As before, with *Candle in the Wind*, Maxwell Anderson, a genuine friend of the Weills, wrote a play with a great role for Lenya. *Barefoot in Athens* recounted the last days of Socrates, and Lenya was to play Xantippe, Socrates' wife. Legend tells that she was a shrew, and Anderson had to honor that, but in the event, the characterization suited her beautifully: she got most of the good lines in a very talky show. Barry Jones played Socrates in a vast white beard, and—again honoring legend—Anderson gave him too much to say in endless speeches that made audiences fidgety. Still, we hear in Lenya and Jones' scenes a tribute to the Weills. Lenya was no shrew and Weill no orator, yet aren't these lines for the Weills?:

XANTIPPE: You've never loved me!
SOCRATES: Xantippe, you come right after Athens—next to the
   city of Athens I love you best . . .

But, Lenya, you know you come right after my music! Above all, Anderson wrote of the Cold War that had succeeded the Great European Civil War, for democratic Athens is occupied by totalitarian Sparta much as the eastern half of Europe was occupied by the Soviets, and as the rest of Europe, in 1951, was living under the menace of Soviet expansion all over the continent. "Sparta," Anderson wrote in the preface to *Barefoot in Athens'* published script, "was a complete, thorough and conscious communist society . . . in a closed, hard, grim slave state . . . Sparta had neither commerce nor art." Whereas Athens "invented democracy . . . and turned loose a flood of creative work in every field that has set the pace for western civilization ever since."

The destructive evil of oligarchical state power was Anderson's favorite topic, as we know. What is remarkable here is that he saw his friends the Weills historically, as foes of the police state. With the Spar-

tan king, Pausanias, Socrates patiently "dialogues" on their respective
political systems:

> PAUSANIAS: Democracy is an ugly and disorderly form of govern-
> ment. The people . . . do what they please and say what they like
> and they actually charge a profit for supplying each other with the
> necessities of life!

To which Socrates eventually replies:

> SOCRATES: Then what you have is a governing class of freebooters
> and murderers, holding the population down by terror and strict
> controls?

Xantippe, too, is leery of this head commissar and is quite willing to
say so:

> XANTIPPE: If [Pausanias] knows any good of me, that's more than I
> can say for him.

Anderson was so often critical of his home government that it's a
relief to find him railing at the fascists for a change, but *Barefoot in Athens* was a failure. (Donald Spoto even tells us that during the Philadelphia tryout, Lenya was replaced by an actress with a more indigenous
accent, then rehired.) The show lasted but a month in New York, and is
not among Anderson's better-remembered plays—if, by now, any of
his plays can be called remembered. Still, the piece did put Lenya back
on the acting stage for the first time since *The Firebrand of Florence*, an
important step in George Davis' agenda.

The next step was taken on June 14, 1952 at Brandeis University,
where Leonard Bernstein conducted a concert of *The Threepenny Opera*
with Lenya as Jenny, in a new English translation by Marc Blitzstein,
who served as narrator. We've already met Blitzstein: a curious amal-
gam of Weill and Brecht as the sole author of biting musical-theatre
pieces. But Blitzstein lacked Weill's melodic gift and Brecht's sleazy

charm, even if Blitzstein's best-known work, *The Cradle Will Rock* (1937), is thought by some to be an American *Threepenny*. Ironically, Blitzstein's translation of *Threepenny* proved his most enduring work, for the Brandeis concert led to the off-Broadway *Threepenny* revival that most truly instated the Weill revival. Opening March 10, 1954 at the Theatre De Lys on Christopher Street and Eighth Avenue—a very central point in Greenwich Village—this production became, in a way, the most famous thing that ever happened to Weill and Lenya.

Of course, she at first refused: too old for Jenny, too unsure of the public. And of course Davis coaxed and soothed. Maybe he had to get intense about it, giving her neurotic lack of confidence a slap. However it was managed, Davis got Lenya onstage, with Scott Merrill as Macheath, Jo Sullivan as Polly, and Beatrice Arthur, a raw young Maude, as Lucy. The reception was so welcoming that the producers, Carmen Capalbo (who also directed) and Stanley Chase, had a number of offers to transfer the show to Broadway. They must have been tempted, for another production had booked the De Lys before their *Threepenny* opened, forcing it to close while it was selling out. Instead, they put the entire kit on warehouse hiatus, waited till the De Lys was free, and reopened, making New York theatre history with a combined-tally run of 2,706 performances.

Over the years, such luminaries-to-be, names to cheer the aficionado, or just actors known mainly to playbill typesetters went into and out of rotation, from James Mitchell, Nancy Andrews, Jane Connell, Jerry Orbach, Georgia Brown, and Estelle Parsons to David Atkinson, Pert Kelton, Edward Asner, and the Carmen Mathews of off-Broadway, Jenny Lou Law. During that hiatus, which lasted eighteen months, Brooks Atkinson famously kept ending reviews with "Bring back *The Threepenny Opera*." Yet his opening-night notice had been rather measured in its praise. He called the piece "one of the authentic contemporary masterpieces," but his assessment of the cast stood at "satisfactory" and complained of "inexperience." Of Lenya, all he could come up with was "delivers her role with the necessary strength and authority."

Others were more enthusiastic from the start. Upon the De Lys reopening, Jerry Talmer in the *Village Voice* singled out Lenya's very first notes of "Pirate Jenny" as conjuring up "Hogarth and Gay, Goya and Lautrec, Koestler, Malraux, Traven, and even such as Remarque and George Grosz—all of it, all of them, and a hundred others, are packed into this one hot hellish instant." Artists and writers of social commentary, pacifists like Erich Maria Remarque and former communists turned anti-communist like Arthur Koestler: it was all the humanism of the West ranged against "the smoke still rising from the crematories and Bert Brecht's old friend Uncle Joe Stalin."

Note that Tallmer separates Lenya from Brecht, *Threepenny* (as art) from what Brecht loved (the slave empire of communism). Brecht himself, back in Europe, married his love by settling in East Berlin to run his own company, the Berliner Ensemble (though nominal directorship was assigned to Helene Weigel). What Brecht probably wanted was a kingly position in the theatre scene of a cultural capital, a seat among the satraps, playing to a stimulated public and discussed in think-pieces in the journals of the West.

That scene would have been in Paris or London. East Berlin was a backwater. "An etching by Churchill from an idea of Hitler's," Brecht called it when he arrived, in 1948, noting how wrecked the place looked. Much of the rubble had been cleared away, but even the ruins were ruined. The Allies had pounded the city, but it was the Soviets, in the Battle of Berlin at the very end of the European war, who finished it off. An etching by Churchill? "To survive indefinitely in a communist state," Ronald Hayman wrote, "an intellectual needs to be an opportunist." That is, wiping off the euphemisms: one stooges for the commissars against The People one pretends to care about. Or they kill you.

Brecht, who screamed at helpless thespians like the Second Coming, was now helpless himself. While he applied for and received an Austrian passport and banked his money in Switzerland, Brecht chose to resettle in police-state Berlin, and he avidly stooged. Still, what makes a monster feel more empowered than to be relatively exempt from victimization in a society of aggressors and prey? Brecht got into trouble even so, perhaps most notably for his *Lukullus* opera, written with Paul Dessau. Originally a radio play entitled *Das Verhör des Lukullus* (The Trial of Lucullus), the piece relates the hearing of a Roman general after his death, as a soviet of abrasive zombies judges whether he is to enjoy an afterlife or be transmitted *ins nichts* (into nothingness). They decide on the latter.

The liquidation of a Western warmaker would seem to be ideal communist propaganda, but North Korea's invasion of South Korea on June 25, 1950 put pacifism on the Russians' Index of Forbidden Concepts. Even so, the work could not be banned straight out, for the Staatsoper* had given it a big production with much attendant publicity. Brecht's biographer Martin Esslin reports that the East Berlin government decided to allow just three performances of the opera, "before a strictly controlled, hand-picked audience of party stalwarts and members of the [communist] youth organization." They would reject the work, it would "fail," and it could then be taken off through the apparent lack of public interest.

However, the kids of East Berlin were eternally at war with the authorities, whom they saw as vicious killjoys. Party stalwarts could be counted on to show up and register disapproval, yes—but the kids black-marketed their tickets to opera buffs, intellectuals, Brechtians, and the usual whatnots keen on an Event. *Lukullus'* premiere, on March 17, 1951, resounded with cheers, for, despite the relentless self-righteous partylining of the protagonist's judges, the opera is entertaining and very imaginatively scored.

Enraged, the state cancelled the remaining two performances and called Brecht and Dessau into an all-day sweat session. To Dessau's horror, Brecht made no attempt to defend either libretto or music, even when Dessau was accused of anti-socialist tendencies for using a big percussion section but no violins. When he and Brecht finally emerged from their own trial of Lucullus, Brecht famously said, "Where else in

---

* This was in fact the Staatsoper *company*, playing in an alternative house, the Admiralspalast, because of bombing damage to the Staatsoper building itself on Unter den Linden. Note that the first of Berlin's three opera houses lay in the Russians' eastern sector: all of what had been central Berlin stood east of the Brandenburg Gate, the doorway between free West Berlin and the Berlin of the German "Democratic" Republic.

the world can you find a government that shows such interest in, and pays attention to, artists?" John Fuegi has the answer: "the Soviet Union," East Germany's owner, "where this kind of 'attention' from Stalin often meant death."

Brecht gave the most authentic demonstration of his politics when the workers of East Berlin (and elsewhere in East Germany) rose up against the tyrannical regime, in June of 1953. Brecht sided with the tyrants, of course: he had migrated from democracy into tyranny, after all, navigating in the opposite direction from that taken by Weill and Lenya. Indeed, Brecht is their opposite in every respect imaginable, and not least because, once he made his way into his new home, he never again wrote anything of interest. Weill, by contrast, expanded as an artist; Brecht was reduced to renovating old plays by other writers, as if admitting that anything original would be condemned by his masters. There is no art under tyranny: *art* is another word for liberty.

Brecht was finished, anyway; he died in 1956, at the age of fifty-eight. He did see Lenya again, though, for she now began making annual trips to Germany to set down the sound of Weill in recordings for the American Columbia label, with participation by Philips, based in the Netherlands. In April of 1955, Mr. and Mrs. George Davis traveled to Germany: and Lenya saw Berlin. Even then, much of it was gone without replacement, with block after block of the empty survival of pebbles; some of London, too, looked like that in the 1950s. "It was like walking through Pompeii," Lenya observed. But "you can't find a single Nazi in Germany; nobody was one. It was all a dream."

The reunion of Lenya and Brecht was momentous for them both. George Davis, who came along on one of these visits, likened Brecht and Weigel to "a pair of shrewd and hard-bitten peasants . . . or two shady con artists." Despite all the cheating and exploiting Brecht was guilty of, Davis thought Weigel "the really dangerous member of the team." He liked the way Lenya stood up to her—but Lenya always spoke of the encounter with Brecht himself in quite touching terms. Hearing that she was about to record classic Weill-Brecht, he told her, "I hardly remember some of those songs." He asked for "*Surabaya-Johnny*"—a cappella, for there was no piano, and, partway through,

Lenya stopped, asking if Brecht's epic theatre demanded a less overtly emotional reading.

Touching her cheek, he said, "Lenya, darling, whatever you do is epic enough for me."

A moving encounter, then: but it gives no hint of the distress that Weigel and others in the Brecht camp were to give Lenya for the rest of her life over legalities involving productions of the Weill-Brecht works.

While in Germany, Lenya advertised for help in locating Weill's missing scores, and something extraordinary happened. All this time, it was thought that Weill had composed a single symphony, the one begun in Berlin in 1933 and finished in Paris in 1934. However, in response to Lenya's notice, an academic presented her with the autograph partitur of that earlier Weill symphony that was written for Busoni's master class. Kim Kowalke tells us that this academic was a Professor Herbert Fleischer, who was planning to write a biography of Weill before the Nazi *Machtergreifung*. Weill had entrusted some of his manuscripts to Fleischer for research, but when Fleischer sent them back (addressed to Universal, in Vienna), the Symphony ended up in a different package, of Fleischer's personal papers. This package spent the war in the safety of an Italian convent. Interestingly, someone in the convent had apparently destroyed the Symphony's title page—as if protecting the work from possible destruction if the wrong party happened to catch sight of it and recognize Weill's name. Weill's known symphony automatically became Symphony Number Two and this newly rediscovered work Symphony Number One. An intense, slashing work in Weill's early atonal style, it was first heard in 1957, on Northwest German Radio, conducted by Wilhelm Schüchter.

The Weill Renaissance was advancing, based on Lenya's Columbia discs, now made in Hamburg with the conductor Wilhelm Brückner-Rüggeberg. The *Mahagonny* opera, not the most popular but the central work of the Weill-Brecht canon, received its first-ever complete recording thus, and *Die Sieben Todsünden*, *Die Dreigroschenoper*, and *Happy End* followed, all in German. There was a disc of Weill's American show music as well, made at home, in English.

Otherwise, the rediscovery of Weill consisted of the De Lys *Three-penny Opera*, famous even to many who never saw it. As it continued its for the time phenomenal run through the 1950s, recordings of "The Ballad of Mack the Knife" in the Blitzstein translation proliferated. Bobby Darin's, in 1959, was the most popular, with a mention of Lenya herself in the list of Macheath's doxies forming a line on the right. At the second mention, Darin piled Ossa upon frolic with "Look out, Miss Lotte Lenya!" In fact, Lenya's name had been added to the lyric four years earlier in Louis Armstrong's version; by the time Darin cut his single the interpolation was all but traditional, showing how powerfully "Lotte Lenya" had become the summoning term for the world of Kurt Weill.

Still, that world was opening up all too slowly. During the 1950s, there were important redisclosures: American television broadcast *Lady in the Dark* (with Ann Sothern, Shepperd Strudwick, and Carleton Carpenter) and *One Touch of Venus* (with Janet Blair and Russell Nype). The New York City Ballet revived *The Seven Deadly Sins* in new Balanchine choreography (with Lenya reprising her old role, opposite Allegra Kent). *Die Bürgschaft* was revived in Germany for the first time since 1932, unfortunately riddled with fastidious little cuts that made the action even harder to follow than originally. Still, by something like 1960, to the general public, Kurt Weill was not much more than a song by Bobby Darin.

Meanwhile, George Davis had suffered a heart attack in 1956 and died a year later, at the age of fifty-one. It is astonishing how influential Davis was in the saga of Kurt and his Jenny, for unlike Ferruccio Busoni, George Kaiser, Bertolt Brecht, Maxwell Anderson, and Moss Hart, Davis had no impact whatsoever on Weill's creativity during his life. Nor did Davis wield the kind of artistic authority that molds a performer; Lenya needed no styling, in any case. And yet, just as if destiny once more gamed with Julien Sorel, Davis seemed to have been put on earth for the purpose of producing The Kurt and Lotte Show. Make no mistake: Davis *drove* Lenya into her role, for even after *Threepenny*'s imposing comeback, Lenya overflowed with excuses and rationalizations. Too old, too strange, too worried. Besides being gay,

Davis was one of those who cruised the dangerous margins of the parish in search of sex with the ruthless—a bizarre prelude to our modern age of marriage and adoption. Davis was Old Gay, the very opposite of the men today who paint their own watercolor of the cottage small by a waterfall. Who would have thought that this reckless bon vivant would more or less singlehandedly get Weill's music into the jukebox and put Lenya back on the varsity squad with a letter in Sardonic?

Devastated once again at the loss of a spouse, Lenya did at least accede to Davis' late insistence that she rejoin the great world: she took an apartment at 404 East Fifty-Fifth Street that would keep her close to the show-biz circuits. She maintained the residence at Brook House—and there had been Manhattan addresses in the past, to be sure. Still, now Lenya was serious about fixing the new place up a bit and letting everyone know where to find her. Brook House was a twilight home, fit for the desolate widow. Lenya was now back in circulation in every respect.

It was excellent timing, for this was when Lenya got one of the best parts of her life, as the Contessa Terribili-Gonzales in the movie version of Tennessee Williams' 1950 novella *The Roman Spring of Mrs. Stone*. The eponymous protagonist is an attractive widow who, she says, is helplessly "drifting" through life. She takes up residence in Rome, where a procuress—the Contessa—sets her up with an Italian gigolo. All the while, a homeless young man, the corrupt but perhaps more honest version of the world of the paid escort, stalks her. At the end, having lost all connection to respectability, Mrs. Stone throws her apartment key down to that waiting stranger. As he makes his way to her, to debauch or even kill her, she revels in her own destruction: "Look! I've stopped the drift!"

José Quintero, celebrated for his stagings of Eugene O'Neill (including not only the off-Broadway revival of *The Iceman Cometh* that reclaimed the work's vexed reputation but the Broadway premiere of *Long Day's Journey Into Night*), was to direct the movie. His producer saw the Contessa as a show-off part for a Hollywood dragon—Barbara Stanwyck, for example. But the project already had a Hollywood imprint, with Vivien Leigh and Warren Beatty set for the leads. As Quintero saw it, someone in the movie was going to have to be European—not English, like Leigh, but continental, local to the dolce vita where money marries beauty. Quintero telephoned Lenya to offer her the role: a bolt from the blue, as they say. Her first film in thirty years! A tip-top Hollywood production with all the trimmings! No audition, no screen test! Just: will you do it?

Lotte Lenya to the core, she immediately said yes, and off she went to London for the shoot. Though the Contessa is a supporting role, it is the third-biggest part, and the unique one. Any number of grandes dames could have graced the role of Karen Stone, if not with Leigh's wonderful light touch in what is essentially a tragic part. And there were many jeunes premiers loitering around Los Angeles who, like Beatty, had just Arrived in a film or two and could have justified Paolo, the Contessa's prize stallion.

Lenya, however, brings an almost insane brilliance to her portrayal. When Beatty tells her that Leigh is a "great lady" and Lenya—in a statement from Williams' original—replies that "Great ladies do not occur in a nation less than two hundred years old," she gets so much sheer European Civilization into her line reading that we believe her. The Contessa is one of the cinema's great Survivor parts, but it isn't only the woman who has survived. It is a way of life, a society, a culture. We don't know her backstory: is she indeed a penniless aristocrat, as she claims, or simply an opportunist? Certainly, she represents that enlightened aspect of Old World mores that knows what varied forms the human appetite may take. It regales her; she is tolerant.

Thus Lenya and the Contessa are a perfect fit. It was 1960 when she began filming *The Roman Spring*, and she was ahead of the decade's love of the independent being without "hangups": liberal in a world bound by phobias and protocols. Lenya created her life as she went along, which is one reason everyone liked her. She was easy in the best sense, above resentful judgments about her associates and nourishing a curiosity about everything. Above all, she was a fearless actress, without a shred of vanity, eager to show an ugly side if it helped identify her character. Her costumes looked like finery bought at the last garage sale of Grendel's Dam, and her delivery of certain lines was deliberately ugly, reflecting the anger of the cultured poor at the parvenu rich. At a noontime party sequence, we find Lenya alongside Leigh at the buffet. Leigh takes a bit of this and that, but Lenya, feeling the hunger of all the odd-jobbing women of doubtful caste in Rome's thousands of years, heaps her plate. "Delicious *lobster!*" she caws, taking one as if she may never eat again. She even relishes shockingly autobiographical lines. Clutching her ratty fox fur, she brings Beatty and us back to 1950, when the house of Weill-Lenya was cut asunder:

LENYA: I remember, Paolo, when my first husband died. I retired like Signora Stone. I had to be forced back to life.

Lenya also brings much-needed comedy to the film, as when arranging last-minute escort gigs in her apartment. A waiting woman is given her instructions on where to meet her beau—"Ten o'clock, Caffè Minerva." Then Lenya turns to a distinguished old man. "For you, Barone," she purrs, her smile ironically amused, "I need a little bit more time."

Quintero, too, was fearless, for his depiction of the way gay life operates in the midst of everything is surprisingly explicit. When Beatty gets a haircut, his barber is clearly besotted, gazing worshipfully down at him and—a marvelous touch—even stooging Beatty's cigarette for him, depositing it in his mouth for Beatty to inhale and then removing it.

Lenya got a Supporting Actress Oscar nomination for the Contessa, competing with a very strange slate—Judy Garland; the forgotten Warner Bros. cutup Una Merkel; the even never remembered Fay Bainter. Garland was cited for her dire cameo in *Judgment at Nuremberg*, Merkel for a showy bit in *Summer and Smoke*, and Bainter for *The Children's Hour*. Everybody lost, to Rita Moreno for *West Side Story*. *The Roman Spring* got just that one nomination, and it is a further testament to Lenya's performance that even Anne Bancroft, in a television remake in 2003, could not challenge her.

Further, Lenya was becoming essential to the rediscovery of not only Weill but Brecht. To set a group of actors on an empty stage to run through excerpts from Brecht's writing was a fine idea, despite the odd assortment of Viveca Lindfors, George Voskovec, Dane Clark, Anne Jackson, and Michael Wager. Still, it would have been all but unthinkable without Lenya, to sing the expected Weill but also some Eisler and Dessau. As *Brecht On Brecht* (1962), arranged by George Tabori and directed by Gene Frankel, the event began as a special matinee one-off, then launched an open run at, inevitably, as it were, the Theatre De Lys. Weill-Brecht had become Weill-Brecht-Lenya—but it limited her to an extent. Her movie roles varied from James Bond to a Burt Reynolds sports comedy. Elsewhere, however, Lenya was hemmed in by the brand. There were exceptions—an old Elisabeth Bergner role in *The Two Mrs. Carrolls* in summer stock, a shortened version of Tennessee Williams' *Camino Real* on television, readings of Kafka and German poets from Goethe to Rilke on spoken-word recordings. Beyond these, Lenya appeared only in Weill, in Brecht, or in something related to their Berlin, as in the musical *Cabaret*.

Lenya played *Brecht On Brecht* in London as well, amplifying her profile as the central figure in one of Europe's most definitive placetimes, between-the-wars Berlin. But it was less her backstory than her style that specified her thus. She always enjoyed telling how athletic the Americans in the cast were—"with them swinging their heads and their legs and God knows what else." Lenya, the true Brechtian, just stood and recited, and Lee Strasberg told her, "I learned something." *Brecht On Brecht*'s New York production billed the six players aphabetically in equal-size type. But in London, at the Royal Court Theatre, the marquee lights spelled out "Lotte Lenya in *Brecht On Brecht*."

Then, alas, the Weill revival was staggered by a ghastly remake of *The Threepenny Opera*, an "international" production that ended up, in its American release, with Sammy Davis Jr. as the Street Singer, his scenes cut into the original print on a soundstage set having no visual relationship to the rest of the film. Worse, the movie's credits are confusing, because the English-language soundtrack album was released with most of the leads dubbed even though all of them—including the Germans—did their own singing in the English-language print. Yet, on the disc, the Macheath, Curd Jürgens, suddenly turned into George S. Irving; the Jenny, Hildegard Knef, became Martha Schlamme (who has a completely different voice in the soprano range while Knef is virtually a bass); and even June Ritchie, the Polly, a natural-born singer who would play Scarlett O'Hara in Harold Rome's *Gone With the Wind* musical in London, was re-sung, by Jo Wilder.

Further confusing the issue, the movie credits Eric Bentley as translator of the lyrics while the soundtrack album credits Marc Blitzstein. Because "The Ballad of Mack the Knife" had become so well known in Blitzstein's rendering, the film gave him separate billing for that number—yet his lyrics are heard elsewhere in the film, as in the Second Finale, which Davis, taking another of his "beamed in from another planet" solos, caps with a ringing high G. Yet more confusion: though spliced into the American release only, Davis was nonetheless billed in a *European* release of the *American* version, complete with the silly respelling of the leads' names as "Curt Jurgens" and "Hildegarde Neff."

With helter-skelter characterizations and a ditzed-up playing of the music, the film was a disaster—though not as ill-intentioned as a Berliner Ensemble concoction that toured Europe in the invented title of *Das Kleine Mahagonny*. It took three "editors" to concoct this arrogant destruction of the opera's music, with a stormload of spoken Brecht and some cawing of the dribbles of Weill that these editors allowed. This was one of many instances of the trouble that Brecht's heirs—those of both blood and spiritual affinity—gave Lenya as she struggled to keep the Weill-Brecht repertory in fair order while they kept cheating, stealing, and "editing." A typical line in a letter from Lenya to almost anyone at this time is "New difficulties with Brecht's heirs are approaching": because at any interest in staging or recording Brecht-Weill, including even Lenya's historic Columbia series, the Weigel camp would create a disturbance that could only be soothed with a payoff.

So Lenya decided to take a break from all this vexation and marry another gay man. This one, it seems, she genuinely loved. His name was one of those doomed to be routinely misspelled: Russell Detwiler. A painter with a heavy drinking problem, Detwiler was thirty-seven when he and Lenya met (to her sixty-four), in November of 1962; the difference in age flattered her vanity, often a singular Lenya soft spot in times of stress. As many have said, there was something of Peter Pan in her, and being with the young made her glow with youth herself. And as Lys Symonette told Donald Spoto, "She had an incurable need to care for a man . . . Weill she could not baby, so he wasn't the perfect mate. But Russell Detwiler was."

Lenya was aware of this herself. She told one friend, "I've married a child," and she wasn't gloating. Perhaps she had taken Russell to be one of those creators who seizes the world in a few brushstrokes but can never find his housekeys: silly-helpless. Detwiler was in fact addictive-helpless, the sort of person who cannot be helped: the classic drinker who hides his bottles in places so exotic they really do evade detection, and who, when confronted, half-smiles with a tiny wave of careless despair. Unlike Lenya's marriage to George Davis, so productive in its emphasis on Lenya and music, the marriage to Russell Detwiler was, even by Lenya's tolerant standards, a failure. It lasted seven years, ending only when he took a fall in the Brook House driveway and cracked his skull.

That was in 1969, a dividing-line year for Lenya in that she began to cut way back on her performing schedule; till then, the 1960s proved her second-greatest decade in public life, behind only the 1950s, when she implanted herself as the Voice of Weill. After *The Roman Spring of Mrs. Stone* came her diabolical (if secretly comic) Rosa Klebb, James Bond's nemesis in *From Russia With Love* (1963). Perhaps the most memorable moment in Sean Connery's entire run of Bond films is his frantic attempt to get Gert Fröbe to untie him as the laser beam nears Bond's genitals in *Goldfinger*—but surely Lenya's last scene in *From Russia* takes second place. Disguised as a hotel chambermaid, she provokes gasps from the audience, who recognize her—as Bond does not—as the villain of the piece. And then, of course, the blade comes slicing out of her shoe so she can kick at Connery in a furious deathmatch.

On stage, Lenya attempted Mother Courage, in 1965, at Reckling-hausen, a smallish city far to Germany's west in the Rhineland. It must have seemed like natural casting: the survivor as survivor. In fact, the role can defeat even the most gifted actresses—Anne Bancroft again, in a Broadway production directed by Jerome Robbins in 1963. Brecht's camp follower who drives hard bargains even for the life of her own child presents a soul beyond cold, beyond dead: inhuman. The vivacious, like Bancroft and Lenya, can't find their place in her.

But Lenya was what *Cabaret* required, at the height of her last great decade, in 1966. Though she was one of five leads, with promi-nent but not star billing, she lent authenticity to this Return To Wei-mar. That same year, Lenya appeared on WNET (the forerunner of Public Television) in *The World of Kurt Weill,* running chronologically through the songbook with the assistance, in the spoken intros, of her *Brecht On Brecht* colleague George Voskovec. From "Alabama Song" to "Lost in the Stars," Lenya once again justified the material till one couldn't tell where Weill ended and Lenya took over: love songs. It is almost as if *Cabaret*'s authors saw the show and said, "Let's get a musical out of that."

"We had heard all the Kurt Weill music, all the Lotte Lenya rec-ords," the show's bookwriter, Joe Masteroff, later said. "And some-how in the back of our heads that is how we wanted it to sound." True enough: the John Kander–Fred Ebb score never retrieves even a note of that old cabaret style, yet it has the feeling. "The flavor," said the com-poser, Kander, "had soaked in just enough"—in the "Willkommen" vamp, a tidily anarchic little strut on the tonic $\frac{6}{2}$ chord, or in the am-bivalence of Lenya's establishing song, "So What?," frivolous lyrics set to a momentous tune. It's in the air.

Lenya's character, the boardinghouse proprietor Fräulein Schneider, originated in *Cabaret*'s source material, billed, through poor contract writing, as "the play by John Van Druten and stories by Christopher Isherwood." The stories are, of course, the aforementioned *Mr. Norris Changes Trains* and *Goodbye To Berlin,* and the unnamed play is *I Am a*

Camera (1951), in which Julie Harris explored her versatility, after her vulnerably wishful Frankie in *The Member of the Wedding*, with a portrait of an erotic gadabout, silk at the surface and nails below. *Cabaret* could not ask Lenya to play Isherwood and Van Druten's Schneider, a bustling autocrat of conservative social values who welcomes the rise of the Nazis. No, Lenya had become so identified with resistance to fascism that Schneider was reset to halfway between the appearance of respectability and the *Realpolitik* of the sensual, and her light of love was a Jewish fruitgrocer, played by Jack Gilford. All that was left of Van Druten's Schneider was a speech about her late partner, "a man for bosoms," that was slipped, with some editing, into "So What?," and a chance remark that "a pineapple [is] her idea of luxury," which furnished the objective-correlative for Lenya's comic duet with Gilford, "It Couldn't Please Me More."

As youthfully eager as when she was a dancer arriving in Berlin from Zurich, Lenya enjoyed rehearsing and performing *Cabaret*. The play was wonderful and the company adorable, with no Helen Hayesing from anyone. Coincidentally, the work that first put Lenya over, *The Threepenny Opera*, and this work, *Cabaret*, are in their vastly different ways two of the most influential pieces of twentieth-century theatre. It's nice to have a hit, but it's thrilling to board a future classic for a ride in history. Better yet, *Cabaret*'s Fräulein Schneider was really *Cabaret*'s Lenya: "full of vitality," as the stage directions read, "interested in everything, probably indestructible." In "a flowered dressing gown and carpet slippers," she erupted onto the stage, after the opening "Willkommen" and the book scene that brings Isherwood's alter ego to Berlin, showing him a room to rent:

SCHNEIDER: You see! All comforts! And with breakfast only one
hundred marks!

Lenya played everything in the part—wistful and a bit cagey in her romance (and bed-hopping) with Gilford, exuberantly life-loving in "So What?," and at last so crestfallen when they must part (because of Nazi race mania), yet still the survivor, pragmatic in her sorrow in

"What Would You Do?." And there was Lenya the comic as well, as in this exchange with her bête noire, the tenant and prostitute Fräulein Kost (Peg Murray), who intrudes on Schneider's engagement party:

KOST: Fräulein Schneider—I am welcome?

SCHNEIDER: . . . Forgive me! I did not invite you. But only because I know you work in the evening.

KOST: Tonight I am free.

SCHNEIDER: (aside) I should live that long.

Fräulein Kost brought her "cousins from Hamburg," three sailors, one of whom gave Lenya the opportunity to dance once again, a uniquely beguiling moment. In all, Lenya graced *Cabaret* with such theatre-filling power that Alan Jay Lerner offered the title role in *Coco* (1969) to her before he made the deal with Katharine Hepburn.

Lenya had said no, for she was indeed slowing down. In November of 1969, a benefit concert at Philharmonic Hall offered a Weill sing-off by Richard Kiley, Mabel Mercer, Nancy Dussault, Danny Meehan, and others and then, after the intermission, a concert staging of *Lady in the Dark*'s three dreams with Angela Lansbury. Lenya took part in the first half, but she sang only one number, one of the Weill-Brecht classics. The audience demanded an encore, and Lenya went over to confer with the pianist, presumably to find out if they could wing it through some other song. But they could not proceed; if only Lenya had brought some of the music with her! Yet why would she have done, after forty years of intimate acquaintance? So Lenya had to leave after a single number, frustrating her public. Surely an evening of Weill should have paired a Lenya half with Lansbury's Lady. Did anyone really need to hear Danny Meehan's Weill?

She did make one last movie, *The Appointment* (1969), an interesting attempt by Sidney Lumet to make a European New Wave film. Omar Sharif played a lawyer so obsessed with his wife, Anouk Aimee, that he tries to lock her away from the world; Lenya appeared as another version of her Mrs. Stone agent of the sensual. Watching the film without knowing who had directed it, one might guess

Antonioni, not least for the grand-opera pacing. The American distributor dumped it in a hasty release, and today it is seldom seen in any venue.

By now, Lenya was, professionally, the Widow Weill, administering rather than embodying the legacy. When the co-producer of the De Lys *Threepenny*, Carmen Capalbo, decided to give New York its first experience of the *Mahagonny* opera, aficionados readied themselves for an Event. Though Capalbo was again staging Weill on off-Broadway, it was in the building once used by the Phoenix Theatre, a Broadway-sized house. The *Threepenny* music director, Samuel Matlowsky, was again conducting.

Lenya took no role in the preparations, though Stefan Brecht, as much a nuisance as his father loved to be, made so much trouble that New York theatre people passed around a choice Lenya quotation: "Someone should tell Stefan Brecht to shut his mouth."

But Brecht had reason to complain. Following the trendy idiot's belief that The Musical Must Change With the Times—even if the musical be an opera—Capalbo had someone "arrange" Weill's score into sleazy pop-rock. Nor did Capalbo cast the show sensibly, using pop musicians in some of the roles and, as the leading man, Mort Shuman, possibly because he had been particularly Trendy in the off-Broadway revue *Jacques Brel Is Alive and Well and Living in Paris*. Shuman was replaced during previews by an operetta tenor, Frank Poretta, who played oddly with Barbara Harris and Estelle Parsons in the other two leads. When Lenya finally saw the show (at a dress rehearsal or the first preview, in different versions of the tale), she was flabbergasted by the debauch of what might be Weill's unique masterpiece. Yet it was this same Capalbo who had put Weill's theatre back onto the New York stage sixteen years before at the De Lys. Caught between her survivor's shrug and genuine outrage, she was helpless. Much of the "arranging" was cleaned up during a protracted preview period, but bad word of mouth devastated *Mahagonny*—so it was billed, in a single word—and when it finally opened, on April 28, 1970, it had only a week to run.

Lenya did perform now and again, taking part in a *Silbersee* in the

Netherlands and even trying Mother Courage again, at the University of California Irvine, both in 1971. One wonders, though, what she thought of *Berlin To Broadway With Kurt Weill* (1972), a "musical voyage" directed by Donald Saddler at Weill-Brecht Central, otherwise known as the Theatre De Lys. With a narrator and four young Americans singing through Weill's core catalogue in costume changes and juggling the odd prop—Mack the Knife brandished one—the revue accidentally emphasized how centrally Weill stood in Western culture. The merrily all-American cast sounded naive in the German half and too comfortably slick in the American half, unworldly, untraveled. Weill is European-American in an almost historical sense, all-Western, too large a figure for this notion of a "Berlin" Weill, a "Broadway" Weill.

"There is only one Weill," Lenya often told us: but also only one Lenya. Her flavorful accent places that musical voyage, because we hear the trip they took in the way she spoke. "You can scream if you want," she tells the football player Burt Reynolds in the movie *Semi-Tough* (1977), as the comically sadistic masseuse Clara Pelf, of the Institute of Muscular Harmony. Sixth-billed but with no more than three minutes of the running time, Lenya celebrates her identity as a citizen of the greater West, with a European's perspective but an American's address:

LENYA: (working on Reynolds) You have sexual problems?
REYNOLDS: No.
LENYA: You are resisting. All American men have sexual problems.

In a way, Lenya, now seventy-nine, was confounding the typical three-step show-biz paradigm of "Get me Lotte Lenya," then "Get me a Lotte Lenya type," followed by "Who's Lotte Lenya?" She never let them take her past Step One, because there was no Lotte Lenya type. There was only one Lotte Lenya.

Mahagonny, finally, was redeemed by a production at the Metropolitan Opera, in 1979. The conservative Met public disdained it, despite a vivacious staging that ended with the Mahagonny picket line stalking right into the auditorium, a thrilling violation of Metropolitan respectability. Of course, this was an authentic *Aufstieg und Fall der Stadt Mahagonny*, with no "arranging." Further, Lenya found in the Jenny, Teresa Stratas, a kind of daughter in art, and she regenerated the Weill Renaissance, passing the crown of Chief Diseuse to Stratas, along with the manuscripts of songs unknown to the public.

Stratas now began recording Weill, marking a break in stylistic tradition. There was by this time an either-or in the Weill Cabaret. Either one sang in the Lenya manner, more or less, or one devised a variation on it. Stratas debuted with a third option, using her opera-soprano weight to rearticulate the music and her opera-house intensity to enlarge it. Authoritative yet newly minted, the Stratas style presented an alternative diagram of Weill's characteristic joining of opera and theatre, a street-scene Aida.

Survivors deceive us with their ageless vitality, but Lenya was eighty-one now, finally exhausted by her vicious father; the Great Inflation; Nazi assaults on democracy; her guilt over divorcing Kurt and her greater guilt at how gently he drew her back into his heart; her helpless inability to re-establish her career till George Davis *made* her the Voice of Weill; and the incessant battles with Weigel that became known to those in the Weill and Brecht business as "the widows' wars." All this: no wonder Lenya was tired—indomitable, yes, but bewildered and, at times, confused. She even contracted for a fourth marriage, unwisely, with a man she hardly knew; many of her friends learned nothing of it, and it was soon ended.

She still had to monitor the state of the Weill revival, as when Hal Prince created a version of *Der Silbersee* for the New York City Opera in 1980. Though a major talent in the making of musicals, Prince did not understand crazy European sophistication, with its anarchical tone and bubble-wrap divertissements. So Prince "integrated" the piece, fleshing out Kaiser's bony parable with explanations, reassigning numbers from one character to another, adding in the "Muschel von Margate" song from *Konjunktur*, introducing one of his typical spotlit symbolic figures—representing Hunger—and casting Joel Grey as Olim. Hugh Wheeler, a veteran of the Sondheim-Prince shows, made the English adaptation, cutting and changing Kaiser till Wheeler got the worst reviews of his life. But it was not Wheeler who failed: it was Prince, who couldn't deal with the use of the cabaret insert in Weimar music theatre. Prince gave Fennimore's "Ballad of Caesar's Death" to Frau Luber, because its tone is vicious and so is Frau Luber. But "Caesar's Death" isn't a character song. It's a song, period. And it's exactly what Brecht would have given to Fennimore if he had written the play himself.

Now it was The Ballad of Lenya's Death. Increasingly enfeebled, she began to move away from many of her closest friends, and on November 27, 1981, having recently turned eighty-three, she died of cancer. She lies next to Weill in Mount Repose Cemetery, not far from Brook House. Weill's stone bears his name, years of life, and the music and lyrics of the last four phrases of "A Bird of Passage," from *Lost in the Stars*. Lenya's reads "Lotte Lenya Weill Detweiller," not only misspelling Russell Detwiler's surname but, questionably, omitting George Davis.

Theodor Adorno famously said that "to write poetry after Auschwitz is barbaric." He later changed his mind; indeed, it could be argued that art is how democrats defy fascists, as the highest expression of the human zeal for liberty. Why else do totalitarians ban art or exercise devouring control over it? The human spirit survives in art, even when threatened by the fascism of psychopaths, whether Nazis, communists, or Islamists. As long as there is civilization, The Beast must try to destroy it, for nothing enrages the savages of nihilism like ideals of freedom, beauty, inquiry.

And here's an irony: nowhere on earth are Weill's stage works more frequently performed than in Germany. Even his three one-acts, the least sexy of all his theatre pieces, are becoming almost common, lifting the heavy diet of *Mahagonny*s and *Street Scene*s. In 1948, as Weill was writing *Love Life*, Traute von Witt of Universal wrote Weill, "The *Dreigroschenoper* songs, during the Nazi era, formed in certain secret communities a kind of hymn and served to refresh the spirit of many oppressed people! You cannot imagine how loved and honored you were."

It sounds political. Yet all Weill sought was the right to make his bargains with destiny without having to throw off a *Berliner Blick*— the typical glance over the shoulder to see who might overhear and denounce one to a security service. The right to pursue an ideal of music theatre. The right to buy a used Buick.

Weill couldn't do that in Germany, or anywhere in Europe. The open culture that officially prefers mass production but keeps making room for the unique is in the America of Johnny Johnson's Love Life. If there ever were two Kurt Weills, it was only because one was trapped and one was freed.

"The moment I landed here," he said, "I felt as though I'd come home."

Sources and Further Reading

The first biography of either Weill or Lenya was Ronald Sanders'
The Days Grow Short: The Life and Music Of Kurt Weill (Holt, Rine-
hart and Winston, 1980). As the subtitle suggests, Sanders emphasized
Weill's writing as much as his comings and goings, even unto detailed
synopses of the stage works. Working within thirty years of Weill's
death, Sanders was able to interview many who knew him, from Weill's
contact at Universal, Hans Heinsheimer, to Weill's "house" conductor,
Maurice Abravanel. George Balanchine and Rouben Mamoulian also
shared recollections, as did no fewer than five major participants in the
original production of *Johnny Johnson*. Interestingly, Lenya refused to
participate but for a single interview. A great deal of what we might call
common knowledge in the Kurt Weill Saga originated in Sanders'
book.

Yet another Ronald came forth with the second English biography,
Kurt Weill: Composer in a Divided World (Northeastern, 1992). The author, Ronald Taylor, stresses the perception—as undying as it is
incorrect—that there is, first, the mordant, elite German Weill and,
second, the soft and popular American Weill. As I've explained in the
preceding pages, this ignores the questing nature of Weill's oeuvre, his

obsession with innovating. The German works aren't different from the American ones: the German works are different from each other just as the American ones are. There are not two but twenty Weills. Taylor ultimately leaves it to the reader to make up his mind on the matter while discovering the music itself in greater detail than Sanders.

There are a number of German books on Weill; to my knowledge, only Jürgen Schebera's has been translated (by Caroline Murphy), as *Kurt Weill: An Illustrated Life* (Yale, 1995). The abundant pictorial material takes in first-night programs (including a choice Weill-Lenya curiosity, the cast page of the original *Threepenny Opera* with the slip crediting Lenya's Jenny appended at the bottom), stage shots, posters, record labels, vacation snapshots, Weill's naturalization certificate, and even a look at Brian Morgan, grinning with gigantic, blinding white teeth, as Johnny Johnson in the little-known Federal Theatre production that Weill caught in Los Angeles in 1937. Still, the book is as much written as decorated, and Schebera, like Sanders and Taylor, includes information lacking in other books.

Kurt Weill: A Life in Pictures and Documents (Overlook Press, 2000), put together by David Farneth with Elmar Juchem and Dave Stein, is a remarkable compendium of illustrations and letters, time-charts, music scores, and articles that amounts to biography by other means. The wealth of detail is uncanny. Many Weill writers note that the "Afrikanischer Shimmy" called "Komm Nach Mahagonne" may have inspired Brecht's use of the word as a place-name. But this volume alone reproduces two braces of the actual song sheet to show how Brecht appropriated the song's piquant "Zi-zi-zi-zi Ziehharmonika" for *Mahagonny*'s "Zi-zi-zi-zi-Zivilis." Comparably, a map of Weill's hometown is keyed to show the seven most important locations in Weill's youth. Or the Weill family tree is produced, to show that Kurt's cantor father was descended from an ancient line of rabbis, incidentally giving proof that Kurt's favorite sibling's name was spelled Hans, not—as often seen—Hanns. The illustrations favor the unusual, for example with two shots of *Johnny Johnson* appearing in a book for the first time. A few pages later we get another view of Brian Morgan's Los Angeles Johnny in Paul Green's most unnerving scene. Surrounded by corpses on the battlefield, Johnny comforts a German soldier also named Johnny (in German: Johann), who, perhaps unknown to Johnny, is dead. Typical of this book's completeness is a page of the knocking sequence from the movie *You and Me*, showing how Weill "scored" the voices in precise rhythm. The accompanying still from the scene fails to caption him, but a young Robert Cummings is one of the gang, second from right. In all, the book is indispensable for Weill buffs.

Similarly indispensable is Foster Hirsch's *Kurt Weill On Stage* (Knopf, 2002). Exhaustive research and interviewing along with his own insights make this a reading adventure for even the confirmed aficionado. Just for example, the pages on *Street Scene* rediscover the work for us, as we learn about casting; about how Weill redefines the relationship between dialogue and song with underscoring; about the work's hit-parade pastiche number, "Moon-Faced, Starry-Eyed," from the two dancers who performed it, Danny Daniels and Sheila Bond; about how Weill sneakily broke down the barrier between opera and musical with this score in particular. And there's loyal Lenya, of course, outraged that during *Street Scene*'s ill-attended Philadelphia tryout, "some stupid show" (*Finian's Rainbow*, actually) was packing them in nearby. The book is generously illustrated, sometimes with familiar shots, though the one of *The Eternal Road* on page 155 reveals how astonishing that production must have been, not only in its size but in the innovative use of lighting to help Reinhardt place his mythology as a kind of fantasy-history.

Donald Spoto's *Lenya: A Life* (Little, Brown, 1989), her only biography per se, is rich in report from her intimates. Though a wonderfully gaudy presence in all Weill books, she comes alive most successfully here: in all her contradictions. Lenya the Survivor seems so single-minded as she marches arm in arm with Weill through the battlefields of ism politics into the welcome of a loving democracy. But Spoto shows us the fussy, parsimonious, and vain old biddy that Lenya became, breaking with one of her oldest friends, Georg Kaiser's wife, Margarethe, because she sent some of Lenya's old clothes to the poor without asking, or even seeking cosmetic surgery for her breasts.

Still, the fun-filled Lenya is available under separate cover, in her many articles and interviews, retelling the familiar stories but always slipping in a new nugget or two. In *Theatre Arts* magazine, early in *The Threepenny Opera*'s second run at the De Lys (the piece was signed by Lenya but presumably written by George Davis), Lenya revealed who had taught her how to get through the English of the *"Alabama-Song"*: Greta Keller. Talking to Neal Weaver in *After Dark* in 1969, Lenya reveals that among those under consideration to play Jenny in the upcoming New York premiere of *Mahagonny* is . . . Cher! At about the same time, Lenya tells Rex Reed that she likes only two singers—Barbra Streisand and Judy Garland. And two years before her death, she tells *Vogue* that her famous energy is a myth: it's just that everyone else is lazy.

David Farneth created a book for Lenya rather different from the one for Weill: a compendium not of pictures and documents but of pictures and reminiscences—Lenya's own, which Farneth assembled into a coherent narrative. The illustrations—photographs, for the most part—present the public Lenya. The narrative presents . . . well, the same public Lenya, for she was as much the artist in her autobiography as in her performances, and why not? She kept a little privacy, so to say, to herself. Wasn't she public enough in her career, with all that exposure to so many storied talents, from Kaiser and Brecht to Warren Beatty and Helen Hayes? "Possessing only an eighth-grade education," Farneth notes in his introduction, Lenya "took unstated but evident pride in moving comfortably among some of the brightest creative minds of the century." Because it isn't the education they give you that matters: it's the education you give yourself. All her life, Lenya sought to expose herself to the best in art, and she returned the favor. I quote from her very last statement in the book: "If you become a legend you must have made your point somewhere."

Yet more Weill and Lenya is revealed in their letters to each other, in *Speak Low (When You Speak Love): The Letters of Kurt Weill and Lotte*

Lenya, edited and translated by Lys Symonette and Kim Kowalke. (University of California, 1996). It's a fascinating view through the keyhole, and, amusingly, they are filled with contempt for many of those they encounter. Still, look at whom they're dealing with: the megalomaniac Brecht, the usual Hollywood hypocrites, the frantically unreliable Lunts, or even good old Helen Hayes, dragging everyone on the *Candle in the Wind* tour to local zoos. But they did like Moss Hart, as did everyone else in the theatre.

Only one Weill-Lenya biography precedes mine, Jens Rosteck's *Zwei Auf Einer Insel* (Propyläen, 1999), the title drawn from Elmer Rice's *Two On an Island*. Never put into English, Rosteck's book differs from the others on Weill in its greater interest in the man than in the work, and from others on Lenya in more emphasis on events mentioned in her letters. Thus, Rosteck narrates an arresting episode in the mutual infidelities of the two Weills (which I haven't seen in any other book or document), taken from a letter Lenya wrote to Hans Weill's wife, Rita. As Rosteck tells it, Weill had got involved with a young Swiss woman in Hollywood, and the affair grew so heavy "that Lenya felt compelled to take immediate action and herself journeyed to Los Angeles." Using an idiom common to German and English alike, Lenya "lays the cards on the table" to Rita about "the Swiss maiden, whom you already know of." Confrontation: Lenya "speaks *ein Machtwort* [a command]" to Weill, "bearing in mind her own missteps." It's a delicate operation, requiring "much diplomacy" but also "enough fingerpointing to send a signal." Rosteck philosophizes: "She is smart enough to know how easily porcelain breaks and how long it can take to put the pieces back together." Finally, Rosteck quotes from Lenya's letter to Rita itself: "Don't worry, my love. You won't lose your sister-in-law after all."

On Weill's music, the basic work is David Drew's *catalogue raisonné*, *Kurt Weill: A Handbook* (University of California, 1987), nearly five hundred pages of detail on works large and small, from drafts to scores, on publications and performances. Drew befriended Lenya in the early 1950s, hoping to write the first Weill biography. Instead, he ended as Weill's first musicologist. Nothing is left out, not even the unfinished (and, says Drew, lost) musical that Weill was writing in 1937 with E. Y. Harburg and Samuel and Bella Spewack, a very strange project about German émigrés putting on an operetta whose key melody escapes them until . . . As Drew points out, it's like a conflation of Weill's own story and *Lady in the Dark*. Drew doesn't develop a psychological interpretation of Weill's choice of subject matter, but one can argue that Johnny Johnson's ultimate alienation from his background and people, *Knickerbocker Holiday*'s anti-fascism, *The Firebrand of Florence*'s artist-as-enemy-of-the-state, and *Street Scene*'s and *Love Life*'s troubled marriages were autobiographically chosen.

Kim Kowalke, who heads the Kurt Weill Foundation,* gave his subject a thorough academic analysis in *Kurt Weill in Europe* (UMI Research Press, 1979). Then, editing *A New Orpheus: Essays On Kurt Weill* (Yale, 1986), Kowalke collected seventeen inquiries into the German and American work. The essays take in Christopher Hailey's look at Weill's relationship with his Austrian publisher, Universal; David Drew on *Der Kuhhandel*; Douglas Jarmann on how Berg's *Lulu* owes to Weill a sneaky use of the orchestra to cut into or question the vocal activity in the narrative; John Graziano's "Musical Dialects in *Down in the Valley*." This is one of the richest texts on Weill, a sturdy defense of his innovations but also a tour through the bizarre little details of a life conducted in feverish creativity. One footnote alone, in Kowalke's introductory essay, tells the story of how Weill's First Symphony was saved from extinction by accident. Or Ronald K. Shull explains—finally!—why *The Seven Deadly Sins* has an alternate "spurious, extended title," going on to *Of the Petit Bourgeois*. Or John Rockwell invokes the poisonous atmosphere of the Weimar arts scene, picturing the fascists' being "gleefully appalled" by experimental opera production. Or Ian Kemp notes that *Der Silbersee*'s succession of at times unre-

---

* The foundation, dedicated to the preservation and dissemination of Weill's music, publishes a magazine-style newsletter twice a year, as a kind of diary of the Weill Renaissance. This includes sizable articles on works undergoing reinvestigation. Subscriptions are apparently free upon emailing one's name and address to kwfinfo@kwf.org.

lated scenes "is entirely appropriate to a fairy-tale . . . Characters come and go with the logic of a dream."

On European history generally—or, specifically in the context of this book, events leading up to Western Civilization's Great Civil War—two weighty and well-regarded works came out in the same year, 1996: Norman Davies' *Europe: A History* (Oxford) and J. M. Roberts' *A History of Europe* (Allen Lane, American edition, 1997). Both are masterly. Davies is a bit eccentric in the use of three hundred "capsule" essays designed to bring together themes separated by space and time, as well as to "illustrate all the curiosities, whimsies, and inconsequential sidestreams" often disregarded. "Utopia" is one, "Hatred" another, along with "Romany," "Baletto," "Nibelung," "Oedipus," "Brie."

That lover of controversy A. J. P. Taylor offers a pictures-and-text in *The First World War* (Putnam, 1966), and the reliable Margaret McMillan follows up with a superb but also delightful reading of the peace in *Paris 1919* (Random House, 2002), thoroughly researched to clear out the cobwebs of myth. In the interval before the second war, Olivier Bernier gives us *Fireworks at Dusk: Paris in the Thirties* (Little, Brown, 1993), which tells us why Weill would have found Max Reinhardt's invitation to come to America one of those *Godfather*esque offers one couldn't refuse. Then, in summation, Niall Ferguson is not less than magnificent in *The War of the World: Twentieth-Century Conflict and the Descent of the West* (Penguin, 2006), which sees a "fundamental reorientation of the world" as the "underlying trend" of the epoch of the Civil War. "A hundred years ago, the frontier between West and East was located somewhere in the neighbourhood of Bosnia-Herzegovina": the fault line in the quake of aggressive Islam. "Now it runs through every European city."

On German history, Hagen Schulze's *Germany: A New History* (translated by Deborah Lucas; Harvard, 1998) is an ideal one-volume traversal, concise and wonderfully expanded by profuse pictorial display. David Clay Large's *Where Ghosts Walked: Munich's Road to the Third Reich* (Norton, 1997) explores the concept of a cultural capital whose culture is, increasingly, barbarian fascism. Scholarly but lively, like

Schulze. In the vast field of Hitler bios, I go with Joachim Fest's *Hitler* (translated by Richard and Clara Winston; Harcourt Brace Jovanovich, 1974), dry but authoritative. On the other hand, John Lukacs' *The Hitler of History* (Random House, 1997) is liquid with passion in its review of historians' treatment of Hitler. Seldom is so short a book so filled with stimulating insights. Lukacs likes Fest, but is scathing about some of the other major names in the Hitler business.

On Berlin, Alexandra Richie's enticingly named *Faust's Metropolis* (Carroll & Graf, 1998), a vast tome, offers a somewhat personalized view of chronicle, especially in what she sees as the American enabling of the Russian enslavement of "East Berlin," not to mention a third of Germany and Eastern Europe. Richie explores a great deal more of Berlin's early history than her colleagues, yet, after three hundred fifty pages on all the years before the Nazi *Machtergreifung* of 1933, she devotes five hundred pages to just the fifty years that followed. Roosevelt's failure to stop Stalin from devouring half a continent is, to Richie, "criminally stupid," but she also notes 304,000 Russian casualties in the Battle of Berlin—casualties the Allies would have suffered if we and not they had taken the city. And what if these two gigantic armies had faced each other at the ruins of Hitler's capital? Would a new hot war have broken out, instead of the Cold one?

Giles MacDonough's *Berlin* (St. Martin's, 1997) is a historical guide to the identity of Berlin rather than a chronological saga. The book ranges all over the subject in beguiling anecdotal detail, some of it quite loony, as befits this eccentric town. Speaking of the "turnip winter" of World War I, when even basic foods became rare, through the British naval blockade, MacDonough explains that even *Ersatz* (fake coffee) was now being faked, as *Ersatzersatz*. Meanwhile, on her Silesian estate, Evelyn, Princess von Blücher, fights starvation by eating a kangaroo. (The estate's holdings included a private zoo.)

Gerhard Masur's *Imperial Berlin* (Basic, 1970) looks at how a backwater became "a city of destiny" through sheer historical necessity, and Suzanne Everett's *Lost Berlin* (Contemporary, 1979) is the photo album, in which a very rhetoric of imperial architecture tries to ignore the touts and floozies and artists and Nazis of the 1920s. Some of the photographs are familiar, such as that eloquent shot of an alley between two tenements during a rent strike, in which Nazi and communist flags stare each other down over a graffito reading, "*Erst Essen—dann Miete*" (First food, then rent), strongly related to a much-quoted *Threepenny* line, "*Erst kommt das Fressen, dann kommt die Moral.*" Most of the shots are novelties, and there are even some unusual views of the original *Threepenny* production along with the standard view of Macheath merrily posing on the gallows in the finale, here incorrectly identified as "The opening." This Berlin was lost through bombing but also because the battle between liberty and homicidal fascist control ended when Hitler started the war to decide which energy defined the concept of "Europe."

Now Weimar itself. Two useful introductions are Walter Laqueur's (Weidenfeld & Nicolson, 1974) and Eric D. Weitz's (Princeton, 2007). Weitz's, more political, is marred by a coddling of the communists, who were just as instrumental in destroying democracy as the fascists were. And on Weill, Weitz adheres to the standard nonsense that Weill's German shows are more "innovative" than his "sentimental" American ones, making him, says Weitz, "something like Paul McCartney without John Lennon."

Weitz says also, "Weimar was Berlin, Berlin Weimar," so Otto Friedrich's *Before the Deluge: A Portrait of Berlin in the 1920's* (Harper & Row, 1972) is apropos here. Separating books about Berlin from books about Weimar is like breaking up Lenya and Weill. Moving year by year through the era, Friedrich depends more on anecdotal report than hard data. So Salka Viertel mocks Ernst Josef Aufricht ("the pretty son of a very rich man . . . but he was pleasant and amusing") and Lenya puts in a few words and Stefan Brecht tries to doubletalk his way around the facts when Friedrich asks why his father settled in the communist Berlin instead of the free one. A very lively read.

The Brecht specialist John Willett offers *Art and Politics in the Weimar Period* (Pantheon, 1978), with a subtitle bearing his own translation of *Die Neue Sachlichkeit*: The New Sobriety. A load of worthy illustrations includes a great shot of what is either the last moment or the curtain call of Křenek's crazy jazzopera *Jonny Spielt Auf* (on page

166). Photographs and Weimar are another inseparable duo, as in Bärbel Schrader and Jürgen Schebara's *The "Golden" Twenties* (Yale, 1988). See also *The Weimar Republic: Through the Lens of the Press* (Könemann, 2000), which seems to have been assembled by a committee. The tenant's strike photo with the opposing flags is here, too, now with its address: 34–35 Köpenicker-Strasse.

Peter Jelavich's *Berlin Cabaret* (Harvard, 1993) is a merry look at a form that Berlin made its own, and one that strongly influenced Weill and Brecht. As Jelavich reveals, cabaret satire was much less political than one might think, but it was subversive all the same. Jelavich's cover shows Margo Lion and Marlene Dietrich singing *"Wenn die Beste Freundin"* in *Es Liegt in der Luft*: bosom buddies, one might say, encoded enough to regale the sophisticated and baffle the police spies.

Now John Willett is back, with *The Theatre of the Weimar Republic* (Holmes & Meier, 1988), an essential work for anyone interested in European drama. Was this the most productive era in stage history? Somehow or other, Willett put together an appendix listing all the major productions (in German-speaking lands) from 1916 to 1945. It's worth noting that George Bernard Shaw was happy to do business with the Nazis during the war years, right up to the closing of the theatres, in 1944.

For the underside of the age, see Maria Tatar's *Lustmord: Sexual Murder in Weimar Germany* (Princeton, 1995) and a spectacular picture book, Mel Gordon's *Voluptuous Panic: The Erotic World of Weimar Berlin* (Feral House; second edition, 2006), a guilty pleasure if there ever was one. A tablet of "Berlin Lesbian Types" gives us the *Fächer* of the species, from the *Bubi* (butch) and the *Mädi* (femme) to the *Dodo* ("tuxedoed . . . serious and ironic") and the *Gamine* ("pert" and "saucy"). We learn even where to go to find these players, such as Cafe Dorian Gray and Cafe Olala. Gay men will seek out the Zauberflöte or the Cozy Corner— note, once again, the Berlin love of things English. The Nazis had their own clubs, of course: the Cafe Aryan and the Pension Schmidt. Gordon records also a Rio Rita Bar—not, as one might guess, from the reference to a Flo Ziegfeld title, a show-tune piano bar but one of Berlin's spots for men seeking young women.

"Die Strafe beginnt" (The punishment begins) is how Alfred Döblin treats the moment when Franz Biberkopf walks out of prison, a free man, in *Berlin Alexanderplatz*, a novel of 1929. It is Weimar's *Ulysses*. Frederick Ungar has reprinted Eugene Jolas' translation of 1931 for the Viking Press, and some may want to screen Rainer Werner Fassbinder's fifteen-hour film version. Criterion's DVD box includes an earlier movie of the material, by Phil Jutzi, one of Germany's first talkies. As the novel ends, Döblin predicts the marching of men and the coming of war to the sound of drums, the end of Weimar, *widebum, widebum*.

On the émigré's perspective, try Joseph Horowitz's *Artists in Exile* (HarperCollins, 2008), written to show how the European diaspora enriched American culture beyond measure. Balanchine and Stravinsky, Rouben Mamoulian, Salka Viertel again, Fritz Lang, and many others are here, as of course is Weill, unfortunately with that nonsense about Weill's abandoning art when he abandoned Brecht. Horowitz does quote a balance of contradicting writers, even that tarantula of a music critic and sometime lady composer Virgil Thomson, who at first attacked Weill as having "a great facility for writing banal music" and then, on Weill's death, said, "Everything he wrote became in one way or another historic . . . He was probably the most original single workman in the whole musical theatre . . . during the last quarter-century."

Among biographies, Mary Martin and Cheryl Crawford present their own, as *My Heart Belongs* (William Morrow, 1977) and *One Naked Individual* (Bobbs-Merrill, 1977), respectively. Ernst Josef Aufricht's *Erzähle Damit Du Dein Recht Erweist* (roughly: You Have a Right To Tell Your Own Story, Propyläen, 1966) is certainly useful, though the absence of an index irritates in a work virtually made for the archivist's dig. Kitty Carlisle refused to assist Steven Bach when he wrote *Dazzler: The Life and Times of Moss Hart* (Knopf, 2001). I don't know why, because it's very appreciative of her late husband as artist, man about town, and friend to all the gifted. Besides being a great read, the book is rich in arresting tidbits. Did Weill and Lenya really denigrate Carlisle's talent out of fear that she would be cast in "Lenya's role" in *The Firebrand of Florence*? Carlisle was by that time the most accomplished operetta diva on Broadway, and would have been superb in the part. And did Gertrude Lawrence really try to get Hart to cut "The Saga of Jenny" when she first heard it, as something fit for Ethel Merman? Hart ordered her to sing it, anyway, and, in Moss' words, "She just says, 'Yah, yah, yah, yah, mumble.' " Overall, I can't imagine a better monument to Hart, one of the best-liked honchos of The Street. Still, Kitty's friends all knew never to mention the book to her.

Now to Brecht bios and studies. Frederick Ewen's (Citadel, 1967) is too forgiving of Brecht and propagandistically defensive of communism. Of June 17, 1953, Ewen claims, "The workers' protest was directed . . . not against socialization . . . There was no clamor for the removal of the Soviet forces." The workers were protesting the enslavement of their country by the Soviets, you vile idiot. Ronald Hayman (Oxford, 1983) offers nothing original, but is an acceptable starting place on the life itself. Martin Esslin (Doubleday, 1960) breaks his study into a short bio, thinkpieces on Brecht's art and politics, a chronology, and entries on each of the plays. Eric Bentley (PAJ Publications, 1985) offers an intimate reminiscence of "the most fascinating man I have ever met. There were times when I hated him, but there were no times when I did not love him." The big Brecht bio is John Fuegi's, pointedly entitled *Brecht & Co.* (Grove, 1994), an irritant to idolaters for its honest look at literature's greatest crook. All Brecht writers report on the man's personal magnetism; Fuegi reveals an army of worshipers. Yet his subject was not just an apologist for Stalin's murder of twenty million but an enthusiast. "The more innocent they are," he famously said, "the more they deserve to die."

Meanwhile, James K. Lyon's *Bertolt Brecht in America* (Princeton, 1980) is very useful, with many a telling detail not available elsewhere. Let me offer one example. I have tried to emphasize how consistent Weill was, throughout his life and no matter where he was living, in pursuing an ideal of very theatrical yet no less musical music theatre. *Street Scene* is the work in which he finally executed his ideal; this is not only my belief but Weill's. Once more, the notion of the "two Weills" is absurd—but there is one telling difference between Weill's German and American stage works. His most important German scores were all written with Brecht or (in the case of *Der Silbersee*) with Georg Kaiser in a Brechtian vein. And that format does not integrate all songs but leaves room for party pieces inserted into the action for no apparent reason. After leaving Europe, Weill employs this very elastic view of the use of song spots only once more, in *Johnny Johnson*. In his next musical, *Knickerbocker Holiday*—and from then on—the numbers submit to plot and character continuity as a rule.

So this is the one identifying feature that divides Weill into a Before and After—and Lyon's book highlights it in a conversation between Brecht and Abe Burrows, which is a bit like citing a conversation between Jane Austen and Lady Gaga. The two men came together at the time of the California staging of *Galileo* with Charles Laughton; scene nine of the play is given over to a Ballad Singer performing for a crowd rather like the one in the first scene of *The Threepenny Opera*, and Brecht wanted Burrows to write the lyrics, whose subject is Galileo himself. Later famous for writing, directing, and doctoring musical comedies, Burrows was then busy creating radio scripts, but he was also known for offbeat ditties such as "The Girl With the Three Blue Eyes." Reconstructing the duologue for Lyon, Burrows recalled asking Brecht about the singer's attitude. Is he praising Galileo? Brecht said no.

Is he attacking him? Brecht said no.

"What do the pamphlets that he's selling say about Galileo?" Burrows went on.

And Brecht replied, "They just tell about him."

Well, okay, but "Are they for him or against him?"

And Brecht said, "It doesn't matter."

Of course, having been raised in America, Burrows was used to the American plan: the song describes the position of the person who is singing. Songs don't "just tell about" something. They have an opinion, like "Can't Help Lovin' Dat Man" or, from the first musical that Burrows was to write himself, "Adelaide's Lament."

So Burrows asked why the Ballad Singer is singing a song in the first place.

And Brecht answered, "Because I want him to."

Discography

This is a selective, not a complete, catalogue, to isolate the elements of the Weill-Lenya style. The classic exhibition piece is the 1930 Ultraphon 78 set of *Die Dreigroschenoper*, for these discs gave the cognoscenti their first taste of both our subjects. Lenya sings not only her opening-night role of Jenny but also Polly and Lucy (and even gets a crack at the Moritat). The discs feature only one other player from the premiere, Kurt Gerron, though Willy Trenk-Trebitsch (Macheath), Erich Ponto (Peachum), and Erika Helmke (sneaking around in various parts) all played the show during its original run. Most listeners learned these readings from reissues by Telefunken on 78 and LP, and they sing today on countless CD labels.

The classic postwar exhibition piece is 1955's *Lotte Lenya Sings Berlin Theatre Songs By Kurt Weill*, which initiated Columbia Records' program to bring the major Weill material back into Western cultural rotation. Issued with an elaborate pictures-and-text insert, the LP was framed by, on the front, Saul Bolanski's painting of Lenya as Jenny and, on the back, S. Neil Fujita's famous photo of her in the same costume, right arm thrust outward, her features scathing as she tosses off some Brechtian irony. Twelve cuts cued up the Weill-Brecht jukebox, along with two by Kaiser; today on CD, paired with Lenya's *Seven Deadly Sins*, it remains one of the phonograph's glories. Note, though, how much less combative Lenya sounds than many Weill interpreters who followed her. "*Surabaja-Johnny*" is plangent, not angry, and in "*Matrosen-Tango*," on the repeated line "*Da wird eben auf alles _____*," which ends now with "pissing" and now with "shitting," it is the fashion today to hurl the words into the public's face. Lenya is discreet. It's intense already: Why intensify it?

"All of the music preserved here is, of course, heard in Kurt Weill's original orchestrations," stated the unsigned liner notes on *Berlin Theatre Songs*. Yes, of course. But then why did Columbia record Lenya's American theatre songs, entitled *September Song*, in studio arrangements? They aren't offensive, simply inauthentic. Lenya is more nuanced here than in Berlin. For many years, the cut from *The Firebrand of Florence*, "Sing Me Not a Ballad," was the only sample of this marvelous score on disc, and Lenya's delivery of the lyric's double meanings is the acme of innuendo. Especially amusing is her pronunciation of the verb in "Please don't vocalize" as "vocolize"—as if she had just invented a new way to be erotic. The CD reissue is a gold mine of Weill-Lenya style, for while using the original stereo tapes for the first time and airing a number left off the LP (from *The Eternal Road*), the CD includes also Lenya's four songs from *Cabaret*, her solos from *Brecht On Brecht* (in which we hear her in music by those Threepenny Weills Hanns Eisler and Paul Dessau), and two different pop readings of the Moritat. One, with Louis Armstrong, is paired with a lengthy session take in which Lenya has considerable trouble coming in properly on "Now that Mackie's back in town." It was always an article of faith between Weill and Lenya that she had excellent instincts in song without being a musician in the "lettered" sense. Now, suddenly, she can't get a simple line in $\frac{4}{4}$ time—and it is not in the least "syncopated," as the liner notes claim. She and Armstrong work it out against the sounds of a professional taping with all the trimmings—musicians riffing at odd moments, techies calling out warnings, and so on. It's delightful backstage atmosphere. Those with a taste for *echt* presentation should reverse the

CD booklet to make the artwork reflect the original LP design of Lenya daydreaming against a leafy background.

Capriccio, a German firm that specializes in recording Weill, from classics to forget-me-nots, has gathered historical documents in transcriptions of 78s from 1928 to 1943. One of the two discs, devoted to *Threepenny*, offers eight minutes of the original Macheath, Harald Paulsen, and twelve of the original Polly (till she quit before the premiere), Carola Neher, along with two sides of the Ultraphone cast album. The style overall is racier and talkier than we're used to today; Paulsen's parlando in what Marc Blitzstein called "The Ballad of the Easy Life" completely obscures the melody. Neher was by all reports a charmer. *"Eine Sumpfblüte,"* Ernst Josef Aufricht called her, *"unter dem Mond von Soho"* (a swamp blossom under the Soho moon). Yet she clearly was more actress than singer. Capriccio provides also half of *Kleine Dreigroschenmusik*, an eight-movement suite for winds. Otto Klemperer conducted the premiere and recorded the four movements here presented: not merely a "playing" of *Threepenny* tunes but a recasting, with interesting music not heard in the stage work. There's more: three cuts of French interpreters veer wildly from the Berlin *Threepenny* style, in slower tempos with very emotional delivery and, at times, lots of vocal tone. An amusing dance-band arrangement of the Moritat offers two-and-a-half minutes of irresistible music-making using Weill only as a point of departure. It's the essence of crazy jazz.

The second Capriccio disc, called *O Moon of Alabama*, collects the original "Tango Angèle" recording used in the first performances of *Der Tsar Lässt Sich Photographieren*; Lenya in *Mahagonny* and *Happy End*; two cuts from *The Silver Lake*; and then, from across the Atlantic, the six sides of the Weill-Lenya BOST album as well as the last song Weill wrote with Brecht, *"Und Was Bekam des Soldaten Weib?."* The *"Alabama-Song"* crops up three times on the disc, reflecting its popularity, which made the very word *Alabama* into a Berlinwide fetish. It was a nickname, a brand name, a dance. The Berlin staging of *What Price Glory?*, retitled *Rivalen* (Rivals, 1929), interpolated "Oh, Susanna" just so Hans Albers could sing it, in German, as *"Ich Kam aus Alabama."*

Kurt Weill: Berlin im Licht, on the Largo label, is a most unusual item featuring an elaborate booklet in three languages and offering, mostly, pieces not otherwise recorded. This includes the important early song cycle *Frauentanz* and suites drawn from Weill's incidental score for Strindberg's *Gustav III*; from his one work with Erwin Piscator, *Konjunktur*; and from *Marie Galante*. Two bits of *Johnny Johnson* confront the German entries, sounding very much as if Weill had written them back in Berlin. Not because of the music: because of H. K. Gruber's rough, word-oriented delivery. As with some of the aforementioned *Threepenny* 78s, the aim is to *present* the songs, almost without expression, even without singing. Gruber, a Weill specialist, is not only the disc's male vocalist (opposite Rosemary Hardy) but its conductor.

There is singing galore on Deutsche Grammophon's two-disc set with David Atherton conducting the London Sinfonietta in the shorter *Mahagonny*, *Happy End*, the *Berlin Requiem*, the *Threepenny* Suite (now we hear it complete), the Violin Concerto, and a few odds and ends. In superb sound and furbished with notes, texts, and English translations, it's pure Weimar Weill, with an especially brilliant reading of the Requiem. Atherton gives us a fey *Mahagonny*, however: the women, Meriel Dickinson and Mary Thomas, croon their way through an opera version of lounge singing. *Happy End*, though missing the "Bilbao-Song" on some silly technicality, is much more spirited, with Benjamin Luxon almost wild in the "Song of Mandelay."

The American equivalent of DG's German Weill is EMI's *Kurt Weill on Broadway* from 1996, a sampler of five Broadway titles, including that stupendous nineteen-minute first scene of *The Firebrand of Florence*. With twenty more minutes of this score, the disc offered our first substantial experience of what had been Weill's least-known American musical. A product of the contract EMI made with the conductor and musicologist John McGlinn during the crossover vogue, the disc favors opera singers. Led by an extremely rich-voiced Thomas Hampson, McGlinn's crew gave Weill one of his best discs; yet a further twenty minutes is devoted to what was at the time Weill's other mystery score, *Love Life*. Elisabeth Futral, Jerry Hadley, and Jeanne

Lehman assist Hampson, and McGlinn made certain that even the smallest bits were sung to the nth. Such dependable opera names as Donald Maxwell and Richard Van Allan take part, the West End regular Simon Green sings *Firebrand*'s souvenir seller, and Simon Keenlyside, who has lately become one of Britain's greatest baritones, appears as *Firebrand*'s villain. Interestingly, McGlinn had tenor Stuart Kale shrivel down his tone as *Firebrand*'s lead comic, the Duke, perhaps because it was originated by a non-singer. McGlinn himself takes part in the *Love Life* sequence, which includes the first version of "I Remember It Well," popularized in the rewrite that Alan Jay Lerner set into *Gigi*. Generally, to complete the historical re-creation, McGlinn consulted with Weill's house conductor, Maurice Abravanel, "in matters of both style and tempo."

A real curiosity is DRG's *Tryout*: Weill and a very game Ira Gershwin singing excerpts from their *Where Do We Go From Here?* and Weill soloing on songs from *One Touch of Venus*, all to Weill's very efficient keyboarding. Then H. K. Gruber rejoins us for *Kurt Weill: Life, Love and Laughter* (BMG), seventy minutes of dance-band arrangements of the kind often made of pop music in Weill's lifetime. Max Raabe's endearing tenorino fills in with a vocal chorus now and again, but the focus is on *Schnauze* und *Schwing*. Note *Marie Galante*'s "*Le Roi d'Aquitaine*," an exceptional waltz amid the stamping fox trots, and one unique item, not recorded elsewhere, "Mile After Mile," from *Railroads On Parade*. The final cut, "*Kanonen-Song*," tears the house up.

Now to the classical Weill. Some may enjoy looking into the source, Ferruccio Busoni, though it seems likely that, however much Busoni taught Weill, Weill was always Weill. Nobody was his source. Again, to quote Lenya: "There is only one Weill." There are several Busonis, but his central work is the Piano Concerto. John Ogden played the classic first-ever reading (EMI), followed by Garrick Ohlsson (Telarc) and Peter Donohoe (EMI). They're all great.

For a long time, Weill's Violin Concerto was *the* Weill concert piece. Then, in 1968, EMI released Gary Bertini's reading of the two symphonies in a "Weimar special" album with unusually elaborate insert notes by Ian Kemp (with fourteen musical examples) as well as back liner notes by David Drew and a George Grosz on the cover. Simply the raw power of the First and the inveigling melody of the Second were revelation. *The Gramophone*'s Jerrold Moore called these "pioneer performances rather than great ones," but I still recall the excitement at realizing at the time how much more there must be to Weill than his famous stage works. The following decade saw Edo de Waart offer the same coupling (Philips), but more recent performances may be getting more out of this pair, particularly in balancing—or emphasizing—their acerbic and wistful sides. The CD couplings leave room for bonus tracks, too. Antony Beaumont, on Chandos, adds the Quodlibet, Weill's suite from *Die Zaubernacht*; on Naxos, Marin Alsop and her Bournemouth Symphony play an oddity not recorded elsewhere, Robert Russell Bennett's eighteen-minute *Lady in the Dark* suite. These orchestral medleys were popular in the 1940s and 1950s. Decca was thrilled to follow the first (of two) *Oklahoma!* cast albums with a Bennett *Selections From Oklahoma!*, conducted by Alfred Wallenstein on two ten-inch 78s, complete with Dr. Bruno David Ussher's concert-program melody guide. ("Then, under the animated violins, the violincellos intone the charming 'Oh, What a Beautiful Mornin',' giving, however, only a hint of this infectious love song . . .") Bennett rescores *Lady in the Dark* from Weill's original, creating in "Girl of the Moment" exuberant clashes between woods and brass till the strings soar in the release. Without slipping in anything of his own, Bennett does employ the seldom-heard verse to "This Is New" and some of the "Dance of the Tumblers."

For the cantata Weill, Capriccio offers its house conductor, Jan Latham-König, in a double bill of *Der Lindberghflug* and *The Ballad of Magna Carta*, so Brecht faces Maxwell Anderson for the first time since that disastrous party in New City. Both readings are fine, with soloists both German and American (including the King John, Noel Tyl, who in a wonderful touch of bio surprise has lately become an astrologer). The disc includes a performance of the *Lindberghflug* from 1930, conducted by Hermann Scherchen—the original version, partly composed by Hindemith. Capriccio identifies which sections are his and which are Weill's, giving the listener a chance to compare the styles of the two reigning enfants terribles of Weimar music. A heavy mist of W.A.Y.B.A.C. sonics of course covers everything, but one can hear the singers very clearly.

Now to Weill's first operas, the three one-acts. Capriccio supplies the only recordings, though Latham-König, on hand for *Die Zar Lässt Sich Photographieren*, is spelled by John Mauceri (for *Der Protagonist*) and Andrew Davis (for *Royal Palace* paired with the other Weill-Goll piece, *Der Neue Orpheus*, in BBC performances). Each of the trio, on a single disc, comes off quite well. Still, cabaret was in the air, as we know, and this is when Weill learned to tango. The Edel label has preserved two CDs' worth of original-casts in Berlin's twenties variety shows in *Bei Uns Um Die Gedächtniskirche Rum*, taking in such stars of the form as Claire Waldoff and Max Hansen. Some of Weill's people turn up— Trude Hesterberg, Kurt Gerron, Ernst Busch . . . and Lenya sings "Seeräuber-Jenny," perhaps Weill's purest cabaret turn. Edel prints texts in German only, but Jody Karin Applebaum's Helicon disc, *Songs of the Berlin Cabaret 1920–1929*, provides English translations as well, along with reproductions of the very chromatic sheet-music covers. Applebaum's voice lacks variety of color, but she really gets into the spirit of the songs, an appealing group in the first place. Note the wicked little quotation of Wagner's *Tannhäuser* at the start of the second verse of *"Ich Träume Jede Nacht von Elisabeth!."* Is this in the published piano part, or a jest by the very adroit pianist, Marc-André Hamelin? Ute Lemper solved the translation problem by issuing *Berlin Cabaret Songs* (Decca) in both German and English editions. Lemper offers the best selection of these three cabaret tours, though the crypto-lesbian romp "Wenn die Beste Freundin" is of course more authentically saucy on Edel with the original trio of Marlene Dietrich, Margo Lion, and Oskar Karlweis.

Enter Bertolt Brecht. Though it appeared after *Die Dreigroschenoper*, *Aufstieg und Fall Der Stadt Mahagonny* was the first Weill-Brecht collaboration. Strangely, this essential piece claims only two studio recordings. Columbia made the first, in 1954, right after Lenya's *Berlin Theatre Songs* had proved a huge hit, giving the Weill Renaissance its most effective start-up infrastructure after the De Lys *Threepenny*.

This *Mahagonny* also introduced Columbia's House Weill Team, with Hamburg tapings under conductor Wilhelm Brückner-Rüggeberg and casts hand-picked by Lenya. Columbia didn't simply issue *Mahagonny* but flourished it, with a libretto booklet of essays by H. H. Stuckenschmidt and Lenya, reproductions of Caspar Neher's projections for the Baden-Baden *Songspiel*, session photographs, and other souvenirs. Stuckenschmidt catches the very Life and Work of my two subjects when he starts off with "Nothing is so characteristic of the intellectual state of Europe between two world wars as the dichotomy between anarchy and order." The former demands a "Pirate Jenny," the latter a "September Song." Lenya had to sing her *Mahagonny* Jenny with accommodations in pitch, just as she had in Aufricht's Berlin "theatre" version. Otherwise, this is a superb and historical performance, the first crucial release in the repositioning of Kurt Weill among musicians.

Capriccio's *Mahagonny* is not competitive, and among DVDs even Catherine Malfitano and Gwyneth Jones cannot save an idiotic Salzburg Festival production (Kultur). Euroarts has a better one, from Los Angeles, with Audra McDonald and Patti LuPone; that makes it sound like another "theatre" version, but it's strictly in style. The best DVD is the much maligned but actually quite thrilling Met staging, by John Dexter, with Teresa Stratas, Astrid Varnay, and Richard Cassilly, culminating in Brechtian bravado as the supers march right into the auditorium bearing their picket signs. Issued in a twenty-one-disc set for James Levine's fortieth anniversary at the house, it has been promised for separate sale in the future.

With *Die Dreigroschenoper* we come to another exhibition piece, the needs-no-introduction original cast of the 1954 Theatre De Lys revival (MGM; Decca). Aside from its historic importance, the performance is unique among *Threepennys* for its merrily characterful ensemble, clustered around Lenya's comeback, in what Germans call her *Paraderolle* (signature part). She appropriated "Pirate Jenny" from Polly, as in the Pabst movie (in its place, Jo Sullivan sang the "Bilbao Song," not on the disc), interpreting more freely than in any of her several other readings of the number. For instance, on the repeated "Asking me, 'Kill 'em now, or later?,' " she rejoices on the first utterance, with a casual little twirl on "or later." Then, on the second, she appears awed at her own power. Scott Merrill is the only Macheath who truly sounds like a devastating hunk; most of them sound like Hans Albers. A censorious MGM officer forced Blitzstein to tame his translation at the last minute, creating havoc at the mikes and a false impression of his work. But the cast—which is not entirely "original," as Martin Wolfson had replaced the premiere's Leon Lishner as Peachum—pulls it together with a kind of crafty delight.

No other *Threepenny* compares to that one, not even Lenya's Columbia-Hamburg set, of course in German and the first to include "Lucy's Aria," cut in 1928 and now a regular feature. Spoken introductions create that good old Brechtian *Verfremdung*—and note, too, that Lenya gets an extra solo in the second-act finale. In 1928, Mrs. Peachum sang this with Macheath (and the chorus), and Charlotte Rae duly takes stage in the De Lys reading. But Brecht's 1931 revision reassigned those lines to Jenny, and Lenya sings them for Columbia. Still, the crucial point in this performance is its generally light atmosphere, epitomized in Lenya's carefree little laugh in the *"Zuhälter-Ballade."*

Certainly, there's nothing to laugh about in Vanguard's old Vienna recording, with opera singers (and the cabaret maharani Liane) groaning along with F. Charles Adler's turtle-slow tempos. Producers seem unsure whether the work is an opera (for at least a few real singers) or a beggar's opera (for actors ham-and-egging through the music). Worse, the piece has been getting darker over the years; it's supposed to be a comedy. In 1976 at Lincoln Center (Columbia), Raul Julia and Ellen Greene led a zombie jamboree that appalled Lenya with its lack of fun. The Ralph Manheim–John Willett translation sounds more shocking than faithful, but the conductor, Stanley Silverman, reinstated Weill's original instrumentation (which was by then getting fudged here and there), even unto building an acoustic Hawaiian guitar of the kind available in Berlin in 1928.

The cast of the 1994 Donmar Warehouse (Jay) snorts and shrieks in those in-your-face regional working-class accents without which today's English stagings would feel politically incomplete. Judging from the performance and the booklet's photos, the director, Phyllida Lloyd, wanted a raving ugly *Threepenny*, but the work should charm the public while revealing society's crimes: to show how easily fame and power fool us. Among modern versions, I vastly prefer Decca's mixture of opera and cabaret, reaching from the Wagnerian depths of Helga Dernesch's Mrs. Peachum to the Jenny of the pop singer Milva. Ute Lemper sings Polly: but who will get "Pirate Jenny"? Decca amusingly declares a tie. The two women share the number, each in her own cut. With bits of linking dialogue, this is a very theatrical *Threepenny*, as the opera folks get dramatic on us and the cabaret gang go arty. "Lucy's Aria," orchestrated by the conductor, John Mauceri, is included.

Happy End was introduced to disc by another Lenya-in-Hamburg LP, a concert version with just Lenya and a chorus. (David Drew's notes in the libretto insert took the listener through the narrative scene by scene.) Besides the Atherton reading and a Capriccio disc, there is a cast recording in English (Ghostlight), using the excellent Michael Feingold translation heard on Broadway in 1977, when Meryl Streep played a gala Hallelujah Lil. This performance is from San Francisco in 2006, by far the most theatrical of the *Happy End*s.

In the wake of the flash success of the De Lys *Threepenny*, MGM recorded more Weill, including the better of two versions of *Der Jasager* (the other is on Capriccio). But it was EMI that issued the only performance of *Die Bürgschaft*, with Julius Rudel leading the 1999 American Spoleto Festival cast, a solid version of a confusing piece. Note that Weill's amanuensis Lys Symonette did the English translation in the libretto booklet.

Der Silbersee brings us to the most controversial of the Weill discs, that of the City Opera's *Silverlake*. This was no mere translation, but a very adapted rendering. Frau von Luber (Elaine Bonazzi) appropriated "The Ballad of Caesar's Death" from Fennimore (Elizabeth Hynes), presumably because the director, Hal Prince, couldn't place the aggressive music in Fennimore's sweet nature; and *Konjunktur*'s "Muschel von Margate" turns up in a Friendship Duet for the two leads, Joel Grey and William Neill. Even Kaiser's lovely line, "Whoever must go onward, the silver lake will carry," never got translated in any form. Still, I don't find all this as irritating as I do this latest in Joel Grey's gallery of wistfully courageous Little People; he sounds like a four-year-old teaching an elocution class. That isn't the Olim that Kaiser had in mind. Olim has a sweet side—but, remember, at the start of the narrative he's a by-the-numbers cop who shoots lawbreakers.

Oddly, Capriccio's *Silbersee* has also been fiddled with—not the music, but the dialogue. This includes Olim's important scene with the offstage chorus in which Kaiser starts to guide him out of the real world into storybookland; Capriccio's version fudges this. Nor does Frederic Mayer's Lottery Agent, whose solo (with the refrain "Interest and compound interest") caps that scene, aid in the character transition. Over at BMG, Markus Stenz conducts a *Silbersee* not only more faithful to Kaiser (Olim's transition scene is what Kaiser wrote) but to Weill (as when Graham Clark's Lottery Agent goes marvellously over the top in his "interest" solo, veritably freaking on capitalism). Our old friend H. K. Gruber plays Olim, and Helga Dernesch, our redoubtable Mrs. Peachum on Decca, makes Frau von Luber her own.

With Germany behind him, Weill comes to Paris and reunites with Brecht for *The Seven Deadly Sins*. This was the second stage work in Lenya's Columbia suite, right after *Mahagonny*, and Lenya again reprises her old part unforgettably. She needs downward transpositions in what is basically a soprano role, though Brigitte Fassbaender (Harmonia Mundi), a mezzo, sounds fine in the original keys. Elise Ross (EMI) is not as intense, but her conductor (and then husband), Simon Rattle, gets more out of the music than most. A DVD (Kultur) cuts the dancing in a production so cheap and stupid that one finally knows what a threepenny opera really is. However, the audio is available on CD (Erato), and Teresa Stratas' superb reading of the music is worth a detour. Kent Nagano conducts, and the coupling is Weill's Second Symphony in possibly its best performance, more dramatic and incisive than those mentioned earlier.

A curious CD on Koch Schwann gives us *Marie Galante* and *Davy Crockett*, with soprano Joy Bogen as the only soloist. It is handy to have the *Marie Galante* songs and orchestral pieces together in one place (the *Berlin im Licht* suite of the work is limited to the non-vocal items), and conductor Victor Symonette, Lys' son, has a good feeling for the music. So does Bogen, albeit in chansons that possibly need a true French *fantaisiste* like Odette Florelle, who originated Marie. It's not a question of range, for while Bogen is a soprano, Florelle alternated her head voice with cabaret chest tones, sometimes shifting line by line. French singing in the 1930s was extremely playful but also extremely dramatic. Bogen doesn't play, and not till the final *"J'Attends un Navire"*—the work's one lasting favorite—does Bogen really cut loose. Her *Davy Crockett* songs, on piano only, reveal what a terrible lyricist H. R. Hays was; perhaps this is the real reason Weill dropped the project.

There is no recording of *A Kingdom For a Cow*, but Capriccio supplies a single CD of its German matrix, *Der Kuhhandel*. Phoenix offers the show on a DVD—shockingly, I'd say, as we lack videos of *Threepenny*, *The Silver Lake*, and all the American titles save *Street Scene*. In the event, the production, from the Vienna Volksoper, is more overdirected Eurotrash, with the action cartooned beyond meaning. The piece is better served on the CD, without distractions; it is also better sung. In fact, *Der Kuhhandel* is one of Capriccio's best Weill issues, Latham-König as solid as ever and Eberhard Büchner and Lucy Peacock quite winning as the lovers. Similarly, the libretto booklet is better than Capriccio's usual in this line, with a fine essay by Jürgen Schebera and, for once, large print and roomy letting. Lionel Salter's English translation is tip-top.

Weill is now in America, and we listen as the artist remixes his colors. For Broadway? No: for America. Just as he changed the pronunciation of his surname, he changed the way he wanted to be heard, re-inventing himself with a revised options menu. And, to quote the last line of *Knickerbocker Holiday*, "That's an American!"

There are, nevertheless, recollections of Weill's German style in *Johnny Johnson*, even if the parlor waltz of "Oh, Heart of Love," the open, trusting swing of "Johnny's Song," and of course "Oh the Rio Grande" are painted in national hues. This was one of the Weill works that MGM recorded because of the De Lys *Threepenny* album's success, and we're in luck, for the disc is a delight. As on *Threepenny*, Samuel

Matlowsky conducts, and his Macheath and Jenny each get a number. But it's an all-star cast in general, for besides Merrill and Lenya there are Evelyn Lear and Thomas Stewart, Jane Connell, Hiram Sherman, and, as Johnny, Burgess Meredith. Even the Cowboy, Bob Shaver, though not as well established as the others, will be known to oldtime recordings buffs for his rousing "Come With Me" on Columbia's *The Boys From Syracuse*. This is a wonderful performance, though the show's off-kilter structures, which lock almost all the action into the script, leave the songs in the corner like a wallflower at a mixer. It's especially frustrating after the opening sequence, as the chorus moves from "Peace, peace, peace" to "War, war, war" to the same music: a genuine plot number. Then one gets nothing but what sounds like unrelated vaudeville specialties up to the finale, "Johnny's Song." Paul Green described his hero, by that number, as "defeated," But doesn't Weill compose music to limn instead his invincible optimism?

The *Johnny Johnson* CD (Erato) runs about thirty-five minutes longer than its predecessor, for it is the entire 1936 score plus cut numbers. Extensive notes by Larry L. Lash and the conductor, Joel Cohen, set the work onstage for us, but the leads' readings are unfortunately little more than functional, with neither vocal tang nor dramatic grip. Naxos did a far better job retrieving *The Eternal Road*, in a single disc of highlights with particularly vivid chorus work.

Knickerbocker Holiday finally made it to disc, more or less complete, thanks to the Collegiate Chorale, which gave it a concert in 2011 under James Bagwell (Ghostlight). Including chunks of lead-in dialogue in a seventy-seven-minute rendering meant leaving out the dance music—not only "The Algonquins From Harlem" (Weill's first essay in full scale blue-note jazz) and the minuet in the middle of "The Scars" but the "Dutch Dance" illustrated in the present book's insert. But the performance is generally splendid. Ben Davis, Kelli O'Hara, and Bryce Pinkham are the singing leads, all in great voice, and if Victor Garber's Stuyvesant is more businesslike than mischievous, he hits all his marks with expertise. The orchestra and chorus couldn't be bettered. But note that Maxwell Anderson's quirky rhyme scheme in "We

Are Cut in Twain"—setting "vivisection" and "perfection" between "separations" and "alterations"—confuses Davis and O'Hara, who change the endings more than once.

Lady in the Dark claims five recordings—six if one counts AEI's transcription of a radio version with Gertrude Lawrence and her original Charley Johnson, MacDonald Carey. It's a chance to hear what Lawrence was like in this greatest of star parts, but it's almost all talking. The first *Lady*s were three-disc 78 sets, one from Hildegarde (Decca) and the second from Lawrence (Victor). Stalling and alibiing as always, Lawrence was nonetheless furious when Hildegarde scooped her. However, this nightclub sophisticate's set was the extraneous release, not least in her soft-shell crooning. Spacing "The Saga of Jenny" over two sides, Hildegarde presents less of the score than does Lawrence, and she even flubs the "One Life To Live" rhyme on "*Noth*ing! *The* thing . . . ," which she delivers as "The *thing*." As with Decca's *Oklahoma!* symphony, the liner notes wax rhapsodic all the same: "The high-sustained violins and subtle use of clarinet passing tones sets [*sic*] the theme . . . ," and so on. And just to show how novel the show was in every respect, the writer thought it necessary to explain what psychiatry is: "Mental medical treatment of the diseases of the mind." Vocalion relays the set on CD, with Hildegarde's *By Jupiter*, Noël Coward, and Vernon Duke albums.

Lawrence's album is theatrical by comparison, and the studio arrangements follow Weill's scoring somewhat, as in the "motoring" music before "One Life To Live" and all of "The Princess Of Pure Delight." Further, snippets of dialogue give one a sense of story—and, in the songs, Lawrence sounds terrific. A tiny bit unsteady in "This Is New," she nevertheless shows why her thin soprano was a crucial factor in her charm, and, unlike Hildegarde, she brings a lot of oomph and variety to everything she does.

Ann Sothern's 1954 television *Lady* (Victor), with Carleton Carpenter (and no one else) of the broadcast leads, is heavily cut in fifties arrangements, but it was a first attempt to get the whole show onto disc. The entire "Huxley" sequence is missing (Lawrence included it), as is "The Princess Of Pure Delight," and there is a waltzy ballet based on "My Ship" that is utterly wrong for Weill. Television Broadway favored these romantic curlicues in the 1950s; Weill's own ballet for *Lady*, "Dance Of the Tumblers," is a nervous, jagged thing. Still, the disc is fun and Sothern quite good. The CD release pairs *Lady* with Victor's old *Down in the Valley* featuring *Brigadoon*'s original lead Marion Bell.

Nine years later came the first stereo *Lady* reading (Columbia), much more complete and in what sounds like Weill's arrangements, though odd touches—piano glissandos, snazzy woodwind toots—are missing. The Met mezzo Risë Stevens is the Lady, utterly unable to speak dialogue naturally but a warm and expressive singer. Adolph Green takes Danny Kaye's part, and he and Stephanie Augustine present the first complete "Huxley" on disc. Best of all, the too infrequently recorded John Reardon gives us the vocals that Victor Mature, on Broadway in 1941, could not, especially one of Weill's most haunting ballads, "This Is New." Lizas tend to sing it, but, according to the score, it is the hunk's solo. Reardon oversings it shamelessly, pouring out tone till the piece rings like church bells when peace is declared. Lehman Engel conducts, as always, superbly, and Sony's CD release adds in the six 78 sides Danny Kaye made after the show's opening, including—most unusually—a number that had been cut in Boston, "It's Never Too Late To Mendelssohn." Employing his trademark infantile gurgles and wheezes, Kaye is uneasy listening for some, but he does revive for the modern the inflections of swing vocalism, a lost art. Note a bizarre lyric error in "Jenny," on "If you don't keep sitting on the fence": Kaye leaves out the "don't," reversing the song's meaning.

Jay issued the most authentic *Lady*, a cast recording from Britain's National Theatre. A clumsy chamber staging and cut-down orchestra sabotaged the piece, but Jay's John Yap observed a historic moment and expanded the pit to take down the first note-complete *Lady* in the original instrumentation. We get the entire "Dance Of the Tumblers," and "This Is New" is larger here than elsewhere, with what appears to be a dance break. Maria Friedman makes an excellent Lady, though she sings the entire role in chest voice. (Lawrence sang it in head voice.) If James Dreyfus in Danny Kaye's role is a trial, everyone else is fine, especially the full-throated chorus. Maybe the habit of casting eccentrics in Kaye's part should be retired. Many years ago, I saw a *Lady* at Westbury Music Fair. Jane Morgan was the star and a cute chorus boy took the Kaye role; everyone was happy. Jay's conductor, Mark W. Dorrell, leads a stupendous reading, one of the best I've ever heard of a Broadway musical; it seems to build inexorably to a climax at "The Saga Of Jenny," which really sounds like a showstopper here.

One Touch Of Venus gave Weill his first taste of that classic element of Broadway infrastructure, the Decca Original Cast Album. Unfortunately, the label hired only Mary Martin and Kenny Baker (and the show's chorus and orchestra) for five ten-inch discs. As two of the sides are given to the Big Ballets and one to the finale reprise of "Speak Low," much of the score is missing—and, at this writing, there is no other *Venus* on disc. It's unfortunate that Decca didn't bring in Paula Laurence for her two numbers, the breezy title song and the sarcastic "Very, Very, Very," which would have lightened an otherwise entirely romantic view of what really was a crazy musical comedy. Laurence always maintained that Martin didn't want her on the album; she finally recorded her songs on *Kurt Weill Revisited* (Painted Smiles).

To catch up on Weill's movie work, try *Kurt Weill in Hollywood* (Ariel), which seems not to have made it to CD yet. The few Weill songs that survived *Knickerbocker Holiday*'s and *Venus*' film adaptations are here, along with the two numbers that made it into the *You and Me* release print. *Where Do We Go From Here?* is of course the *pièce de résistance*, with its vast Columbus sequence. It's extreme Weill—but playing another cut from the score, "Morale," you wouldn't place it as Weillian for a million dollars.

This brings us to *The Firebrand of Florence*, Capriccio's "unidentified flying object" (as the French put it) because it's unlike all other Capriccio releases. The cover art is in a wholly different style from Capriccio's usual languorous line drawings: a colorized photo of the original production with all the leading players in view. Capriccio doesn't identify them, so I will: Beverly Tyler (at far left), Earl Wrightson (in brown, looking right), Lenya, Melville Cooper, and, being restrained, Boyd Heathen as Maffio, Cellini's sworn enemy. Nor is this a Capriccio studio reading. It was taken down at a BBC concert conducted by Andrew Davis. Rodney Gilfry sings a virile, passionate Cellini, centering the action as Wrightson apparently didn't. Lori Ann Fuller plays Angela, Felicity Palmer a sultry Duchess, and George Dvorsky reclaims the Duke from the role's non-singing original with a suave musicality. In all, this is—finally—the comic opera Weill envisioned from the start and one of the best Weill recordings ever. One bitty little flaw is a rhymed narration to link the numbers, spoken by Simon Russell Beale. This was useful in the concert itself but it becomes tiresome in repeated listening on disc.

Street Scene gave Weill his second original Broadway cast (Columbia), and, recently, Naxos released seventy-five minutes of a 1949 Hollywood Bowl concert. The latter is in fairly good sound, though at first one microphone fails to do its job. The Broadway disc, at fifty minutes, was one of the longest show albums of its day, ingenious in abridging the score. For instance, "Moon-Faced, Starry-Eyed" was left off the album because the prelude includes it in a non-vocal setting (as radio play) just as the curtain rises. In the score, the radio offers only two As of the refrain; the recording expands this to a full AABA chorus, so that the song be heard, if only by the orchestra. Further, that original cast is utterly right, the wonderful singing actors that Weill sought all his life: Polyna Stoska, Norman Cordon, Anne Jeffreys, and Brian Sullivan. Naxos has Stoska and Sullivan with Norman Atkins and Dorothy Sarnoff, the latter two capable, though Atkins lacks the voice that Cordon brings to a complicated part: a villain with feelings. Naxos does contain much more of his role than Columbia does, taking in one of the work's central numbers, the second-act trio for the senior Maurrants, billed as "There'll Be Trouble." The Ice-Cream Sextet is here as well—Columbia omitted it, to Weill's regret because ice cream was one of his favorite American things—along with the last airing of the "Heat" trio that gives *Street Scene* its ironic final curtain, capping extraordinary events with a shrug. (The Hollywood Bowl concert brings the entire chorus in on it.)

In the early 1990s, *Street Scene* got its first complete recordings, both from Britain. As one preserved an English National Opera production

(TER), critics simply assumed that it was more theatrical and heart-felt. They weren't listening. The other performance (Decca), a studio creation using Scottish Opera forces, is not only much better sung and played but dramatically more vivid—especially important because Decca, like TER, includes the dialogue scenes. Josephine Barstow, Samuel Ramey, Angelina Reaux, and Jerry Hadley lead a cast filled with such star drop-ins as Kurt Ollmann as Harry Easter and Arleen Auger and Della Jones as the Nursemaids. (Barbara Bonney sings yet another Weillian Jenny, this one a sweet young girl who has just been graduated from high school the day before her family is to be thrown out of their apartment.) John Mauceri conducts a superb reading, rising to a tremendous climax in "The Woman Who Lived Up There," one of Weill's greatest numbers and, in its use of the main strain of "Somehow I Never Could Believe," the culmination of Weill's use of *Leitmotiven* to catch, at once, the strangled anxiety of city life and the indomitable spirit of its people.

John McGlinn was to have recorded *Love Life* with Thomas Hampson and Judy Kaye when he was directing EMI's crossover output, but the project never materialized, and *Love Life* is now the only one of Weill's Broadway musicals to lack even a basic recording. *Lost in the Stars*, like *Johnny Johnson*, has an LP abridgment and the complete score on a later CD. As before, the LP is preferable: Decca's original-cast reading, Weill's third and last, is excellent, with lashings of the script to miniaturize the entire show. Maurice Levine conducts the LP; his CD counterpart, Julius Rudel, leads a performance (Musicmasters) so muffled in its recording tech that it seems to be occurring in a galaxy far, far away. Still, this is one of Weill's best scores; it's worth hearing not only complete statements of each number but the powerful second-act opening, "The Wild Justice" (not on Decca), and a cut number, "Little Tin God."

There are countless single-disc Weill vocal recitals of all kinds. Steven Kimbrough favors the unusual, with piano (Arabesque), including all four Walt Whitman Songs; and with orchestra (Koch Schwann), on the American shows, and taking in some cut numbers.

Helen Schneider (Rhino) overinterprets in screwy arrangements that tear the numbers apart. A squad of pop names from Marianne Faithful to Todd Rundgren and even the grating bluesman Tom Waits combines on one of those trendy rock cover compilations, *Lost in the Stars* (A&M). Lou Reed gets through "September Song" hitting scarcely a note of Weill's vocal line.

Somewhat peripherally, Robyn Archer recorded twin LPs of Brecht songs in the 1980s for EMI, preserved on one seventy-three-minute CD containing most of the programs, with excellent liner notes by John Willett. Archer performs in English, with such crisp diction that EMI didn't need to include texts, and Willett helpfully points out all one needs to know—for instance the quotation of the four-note back half of the *ur*-theme of Wagner's *Tristan und Isolde* in Hanns Eisler's "Madam's Song." In Dominic Muldowney's arrangements (he also conducts, and composed the last selection), the music is handsomely set off, and the listener can establish perspective on just how influential Weill was in creating music fit for Brecht. That "Madam's Song" sounds like *The Threepenny Opera*, right down to the gladhanding banjo. Brecht himself is one of the composers collected herein, stealing again: from "There Is a Tavern in the Town" and "Un Bel Dì" for his own setting of the "*Benares-Song.*"

Two discs from this crowded field are outstanding, Teresa Stratas' *The Unknown Kurt Weill* and *Stratas Sings Weill*, both on Nonesuch, with Richard Woitach accompanying at the keyboard on the first and Gerard Schwarz conducting the Y Chamber Symphony on the second. As Lenya's officially designated successor, Stratas—grand, intimate, and ferocious in Weill—was entrusted with the first recorded performances of some of Weill's rarest songs, mainly on the first disc, where the lyricists include Jean Cocteau, Oscar Hammerstein, Weill himself (on "Berlin im Licht"), and Anonymous (in a traditional Berlin ditty about meatballs). This was a release of historical importance, and Nonesuch treated it lovingly, with not just texts and translations but elaborate notes by Kim Kowalke and rare photographs. One shows Weill and Maxwell Anderson in their plane-spotting watchtower during the war. Anderson seems to be joking with two comrades but Weill, who took his American citizenship seriously, scans the skies for signs of hostile visitation.

Stratas' second disc gathers up some familiar titles, and her performances are even more intense than on the first disc, including a few smash-and-grab high notes thrust into Stratas' lazily insinuating "I'm a Stranger Here Myself" and the direst "*Surabaya-Johnny*" ever heard. It's literally a far cry from what Lenya does in these songs, singing Weill back to his classical roots in Stratas' Big Lady soprano. Yet one sees why Lenya wanted Stratas to take over this repertory. It was a question of commitment, of how fully one identifies with the music, even of what the music means in twentieth-century history. The difference in their respective performing styles didn't bother Lenya, it seems; she must have expected it, for the two women were very different personalities. In an essay on the back of the *Stratas Sings Weill* LP, Stratas told of caring for Lenya in her last time on earth. It was a rainy day, and Stratas told Lenya how much she disliked the cold half of the year. "Lenya," she then said, "what seasons do you like?," and Lenya replied, "I love them all."

Index